Beyond Short Street

A ceramic artist, author and teacher, Owen Rye is a member of the International Academy of Ceramics and is at the forefront of the contemporary woodfiring movement. His book *The Art of Woodfire* was published in 2011 and he has inspired many ceramic artists to follow the woodfirer's path. His work has been widely exhibited in Australia and internationally and is to be found in public collections in the USA, China, Korea, Germany and France, as well as in many Australian collections, including that of the Australian National Gallery.

Beyond Short Street

OWEN RYE

With Drawings by Tony Hanning

ARCADIA

First published 2021 by Arcadia
the international general books' imprint of
Australian Scholarly Publishing Pty Ltd
7 Lt Lothian St Nth, North Melbourne, Vic 3051
Tel: 03 9329 6963 / Fax: 03 9329 5452
enquiry@scholarly.info / www.scholarly.info

ISBN 978-1-922454-92-8

Cover Design: Amelia Walker
Drawings by Tony Hanning

For Barbara, Tom and Mike

CONTENTS

To misquote Blaise Pascal: *I am sorry this book is so long.
I have not had the time to make it shorter.*

PREFACE

A deep motive for making literature or art of any sort is the desire to defeat the formlessness of the world and cheer oneself up by constructing forms out of what might otherwise seem a mass of senseless rubble.

— Iris Murdoch

At an age where the candles no longer fit on the birthday cake, an autobiography may be looked at as pure nostalgia. I prefer to regard it as review. How did I get here? Let me think about that for the next few hundred pages.

Memory is the source here, with all the dangers that implies. I have not ever kept a personal style of diary. What you see is an assembly of disconnected fragments, part remembered, part missing, some of it probably better than the original reality. Past pleasures and adventures have been revived and relived.

Some of this book is about people; but it is not an exposé. There are no intimacies or shocking revelations; well, maybe just a few that were unavoidable. To former and present colleagues and friends who expect this book to include them, and find it has not, I apologise. Think of it this way: your reputations stand intact.

My professional life has one way or another involved ceramics from the age of about 17. I have worked with archaeologists and people interested in the ceramic arts. I have also worked and lived among students, scientists and historians, tribesmen and nomads, farmers and academics, rulers and peasants. This is not a book specifically about ceramics. It's about how life brings changes and diversions, large and small, planned or entirely unimagined, and how one person dealt with all of that.

Who to thank? So many have helped so much. Above all Barbara, whose love and support over many years allowed me often to stretch where I had thought I could not reach. Alan Peascod, mate and mentor, master of ceramics, who talked me out of making many mistakes and into some sense when that was needed. Jack Troy, poet, writer and woodfire potter. Jack's writing is an inspiration for me. Chester Nealie who shared whatever he had with generosity. Janet Mansfield for her friendship and patronage. My sons Tom and Mike, partners in endless discussions.

I am extremely grateful to people who read the first draft of this book and told me about its many deficiencies: Jack Troy, David Angel, Morag Fraser, Tony Hanning, John Bowen, Rowley Drysdale, Thomas Rye and Michael Rye. Tom read through the revised version and suggested some more useful changes. For any flaws in this final version I am responsible.

Deeply felt thanks to Tony Hanning for his drawings and maps that add so much. I enjoyed our collaboration. It's a great pleasure to have such a multi-talented man as a mate.

And for the final book you hold in your hand now, I am grateful to Nick Walker and the team at Australian Scholarly. It has been a pleasure to work with them and the result is better than I could have imagined.

Special thanks to Maureen Swanage for her help. Many more have helped me along the way, some mentioned in this book and some not. So much help and support and friendship. I am grateful to them all.

A few names have been changed where it seemed appropriate. The reader will not notice the difference.

1
BEGINNINGS

No delusions are more familiar than those inspired in the elderly by nostalgia.

— Philip Roth, in *American Pastoral*

It was a Sunday, in 1944. There was activity in many parts of the world, but having just emerged into it I was unaware; one of those rare people born during wartime, when most men were 'away' and women were not inclined to bring children into an uncertain world.

I was taken home to Berridale, a village in the Snowy Mountains of NSW. Our house is still there, on its triangular island surrounded on each side by a street: Myack Street, starting not far away and heading south into some remote places; Boundary Street, beginning right there and ultimately heading up past Jindabyne into the Snowy Mountains; and the third, Short Street, starting and ending as the third side of our triangle. It's a short street indeed, not even the length of a football field. That small triangle still occupies a large space in my consciousness.

Now about 900 people live in Berridale in a nondescript jumble of house styles, mostly without aesthetic merit. It's a stretch to call the town attractive. Only someone who lived there could love it. From the softening perspective of time and distance though, it was attractive when I was a boy. In a child's way of thinking the whole world was like that. If a replica existed now it might seem like a tree-changer's idea of paradise; but those simpler times have gone leaving only memories, some facts and some warm imaginings.

* * *

In the 1950s parents trusted their kids, leaving them free to explore and socialise. In my town there was so much space for a boy to roam. With only 150 people, houses were spread out on large blocks, sometimes 100 metres apart. Nobody was concerned about a child wandering alone. Everyone knew them; they were not just children of a family, but children of the town, almost everywhere offering a friendly reception. The blacksmith shop was special. Charlie Robinson would point to a conveniently placed stump in the shop and say *'Sit there and don't move'*. A piece of iron he was shaping would come out of the forge glowing orange. As he bashed it against the anvil with a hammer sparks would fly and my ears ring. I wonder if watching him work has any connection to my later love of working with fire?

One advantage of being a child of the whole town was to go almost anywhere and receive a friendly word. Nobody thought much about dangers for children. There were some: being bitten by a snake, chased by a bull or accosted by the few local child bullies. Children now are taught to fear 'strangers' but that danger feared by modern parents, child molesters, is a more recent concern. Such people would not have survived then; a few of the bigger men would have had a word with them.

Everyone in the district knew all the comings and goings of everyone else. This was commonly known then in the polite version as who was doing what and who they were doing it with; less politely but often, described as who was up who and who was paying the rent. All small communities are like this.

If you could see them you might consider the people conservative. The reality was more subtle than that. They were survivors, of cold winters, hot summers and hard work, none of which promoted fancy notions. Nobody was wealthy. Most had enough, some just enough. They had no counsellors or financial advisors and no need for them. Whatever you faced you sorted it out. The education level was not high, promoting a close focus on what was at hand rather than restlessness about what might be out there.

The party line helped everyone with tracking everyone else. This had nothing to do with balloons and fizzy drinks, and no connection to elections or opposing ideologies. The party line was a telephone system where everyone was literally connected—by a wire running along poles, from house to house and across the countryside. Everyone could listen in on, and sometimes even comment on, any ongoing conversation simply by picking up their handset. It was the primitive version of a conference call, like a forerunner of phone tapping. In country towns now the news is spread by the person in the local post office.

It meant nobody had any secrets. The gossips always had an appreciative audience for their latest bit of scandal. Anyone who missed the direct dispersal caught up rapidly when later phoned by someone else bursting to pass on the news. There were some benefits apart from the gossip. As an example, knowledge of a bushfire anywhere in the district was transmitted instantly to everyone and the local men went off to fight it. There was no formal organisation to do so.

The primary school in town was small enough that classes were combined in two groups. That wins respect for the juggling the teachers would have had to do. Each morning we marched to the Colonel Bogie March, saluted the flag, honoured our God (there was only one in those days) and pledged loyalty to the King (who in 1953 became the Queen). Thinking back on all that helps explain why I am now a hermit, atheist and republican.

We children knew what was normal and what was unusual. Inside our house, without looking outside, I knew who was driving past partly by the time of day and partly by the sound of individual vehicles. I could tell when a stranger drove past our house. That is not possible now; at my place in the country they all sound the same as they go past.

When the Cooma airport was built, I knew if the evening DC6B flight to Sydney was on time, in the winter at least. Although it was 16 kilometres away, on a frosty clear night you could hear the engines revving up and then hear the take-off. Not much else broke the night silence. Maybe the howling of a fox sometimes, warning us that the chooks were in danger.

For entertainment as a child I could watch a dog chase its tail, or climb a tree, lay back and watch the clouds and the shapes formed in them, imagining what those shapes represented long before I heard of Hermann Rorschach. For drama though, nothing in my childhood matched the excitement on the day Mrs Bradbury's goat got out. So many people running about, such dust and flurry.

For adult entertainment there was of course the pub, but that was restricted almost exclusively to adult males. The Oddfellows Hall was the real centre of secular social life. There were no movies then; we went to the hall to see the pictures, classics like *Swamp Thing* and the *Creature from the Black Lagoon*. We watched Audie Murphy, the Bruce Willis of the 1950s, win World War 2 single handed.

The hall often hosted concerts and dances, or more exciting for a small child sometimes even magic shows or puppet shows or hypnotists, at all of which I sat entirely enthralled. For music we were not exposed to Mozart or Beethoven. We had Pinky Harris and Sid White on stage, and music that originated with Hank Williams was played on guitars in the plinka plinka plunka plunka style of country music of the day. So 'Mansion on the Hill' may have been the first live music I heard, and 'The Blackboard of my Heart' was a solid favorite of the crowd. That style of music still appeals to me, although no longer exclusively.

Musicians work with sounds and silences, and that other essential element, time. It's enlightening to listen to contemporary popular music, and then go back one decade at a time listening to a random sampling from each. Getting back to the 1950s reveals a distinct slowing of tempo, an easier pace, a stroll rather than a run, reflecting the pace of life in general in my small town. The words busy, and hurry, were not in common usage; and it's a satisfying part of my life now that they rarely intrude. I've been told I look puzzled when someone asks if I have been busy lately.

* * *

During the 1950s the cockies of the district were making good money from selling wool and some of their affluence helped the town along. On Fridays the farmers from surrounding areas went to Cooma, the local big town, to buy their week's supplies and visit the Australian Hotel, to discuss the weather and the latest local happenings. Their wives shopped, had tea in the Bluebird Café and discussed their version of happenings. The weekends, at least Saturdays, were given over to sports; cricket, tennis and rugby league. For players and spectators alike, this was as much about the social gathering as it was about defeating teams from neighbouring towns. The small population meant sometimes there were not enough men to make up a team so us kids had a go as well, in the adult teams.

On Sundays the good folk of the district went to church. This served two functions. One was to publicly display their goodness. The other was, again, to take advantage of an occasion to socialise. My mother, and later in life my father were regular Anglican churchgoers. This led to them volunteering me as an altar boy at the age of around 12 or 13. I did not warm to dressing up in robes and appearing in front of the whole congregation handing items to the parson, Charlie Starr. The only good part of the job was going with him on Sundays when he went to other churches around the district, especially the ones in the mountains in winter. Driving through snow, occasionally being unable to make it, felt like adventure. Now, religious men are often accused of paedophile behaviour, but Starr was a decent and honourable man who was never anything but kind to me. That has not led me to accept his teachings though, a firm atheist I will remain. In fact, the embarrassment associated with the altar boy role probably helped begin my atheism.

When I was five or six, my mother would send me off to the shops. O'Brien's general store offered everything a household might require, rather like a shrunken version of a modern shopping mall: everything from a bag of flour to a rabbit trap, a pound of tea and a needle to sew up wheat bags. All there in a wonderful jumbled profusion of jars and bottles and tins and sacks, with kitchen utensils and gold panning dishes hanging on the wall.

Household needs like flour and sugar were available in cotton sacks that a child could only carry unaided after they were seven or eight years old. Some familiar items we shop for now were not available in O'Brien's. No carton of milk; that came from your cow if you had a bit of land or from the neighbour's cow if they had some extra. No bread; that came from the bakers. Hot bread was placed outside George Daniel's bakery door at 4 am along with a money tin for payment. Nobody considered that the money might be stolen.

O'Briens had no frozen chooks, but ours could get pretty cold in mid-winter. They lived in a pen in our backyard, to protect them from foxes, and were let out through the day to roam and peck. We were close to the origins of our food, unlike people now who associate food with shiny supermarket shelves. We knew exactly what it was. When we ate chicken, we had not only witnessed its death but participated. Our chooks lived a contented cluck of a life until, shall we say in their mature years, their intended role as egg layers was fulfilled. Feathers and dust drifted up as we kids chased them around until we caught one. In the back yard, on a stained wooden block, my father removed their heads with a small axe. While the beheading was taking place, the other chooks clucked their disapproval and strutted away.

Our 'lamb', which was generally much older than that title suggested, came from Jim Suthern, the tallest man I had ever seen. He would come into our house, ducking under the door frame, and dump a half sheep on the kitchen table. My father cut it up with a saw and cleaver into manageable portions. The remnants after butchering went through the hand mincer on their passage to becoming rissoles. The dog got the bones.

Some of our vegetables came from the garden, but the growing season was limited by the cold that started in early autumn and sometimes carried through nearly to Christmas. Glasshouses would not have helped much since their contents could freeze and there was no practical way to heat them. The bulk of vegetables came from Jim Hoskins the greengrocer. A relative of my mother, he always made sure the change he gave me when I did the shopping was a little bit in excess of the calculation. I was then allowed to keep it for my efforts in carrying home the heavy sack, or exchange it for lollies. My missing teeth suggest I did that that more often than current wisdom would dictate. In the local growing season vegetables were also commonly supplied by some of the Chinese market gardeners, like Yens from Adaminaby who travelled around selling their produce. These Chinese were remnant families from the goldfield days in Kiandra in the 1870s, who had never moved on.

Most of the local families including mine had lived through hard times during the 1930s Depression. I recall my mother inviting passing wanderers in for a cup of tea, in the old spirit of bush hospitality. It's not as difficult as it used to be to understand that time when men could not work and women could not feed their families; coronavirus in 2020 brought similar hard times for many.

Hard living created strong attitudes about keeping stuff, not wasting anything that might be useful. My mother kept almost everything that came into the house; old newspapers and magazines, worn clothes, discarded furniture. Each time she filled a shed to overflowing my father built a new shed. The attitude was summed up by Bob Woodhouse, a somewhat eccentric farmer from nearby. In the 1970s he bought the remains of an old Land Rover from my brother. When I asked him what he was going to do with the small pile of junk he said: '*It might be good for something even if it's no use for anything*'.

* * *

Almost everyone my age has seen a cultural transformation, from being surrounded as a child by a large nurturing family to now being a part of a small nuclear family, the rest dispersed widely. In Berridale I had many aunts and uncles on my mother's side who loved me as their own, and many cousins, all these relationships well understood. Walking into any of their houses uninvited, as though I lived there, being fed when necessary and staying as long as I liked was all completely normal.

One woman in the family could substitute for another in times of trouble. When my mother was ill she would be replaced by one of my aunts who would take over looking after me. That family of interchangeable nurturers included the uncles as well as the aunts. A day with any of them was as easy as a day with my father. When I first got married my uncle Tom gave us a blanket as a wedding present. I still have it and still use it on cold winter nights. It is much more than just a blanket. It is a remnant of that warm and nurturing family, still in action. Tom, the eldest of my mother's siblings was the kindly uncle I wanted to be like when I grew up. My mother said years after he died, she wondered about some decision and decided to talk to him about it, or tell him about some little success, before she realised that he was no longer there.

Our extended family was connected through earlier generations unknown to me as a child; but adults knew the connections. Each carried a mental kinship diagram that extended out to include the genealogy of the whole small town. They not only knew about all relationships but understood how to evaluate them in terms of social respectability. They knew that this connection was a 'bad lot' and that one merited a respectful nod or a conversation when passing in the street.

I knew little about relatives on my father's side. They lived 'away'. Travel was limited then because the roads and the cars were not well suited for it, unlike today when it's easy to visit distant places. My father and his brother spoke on the phone rarely. Once after a long call he and my mother sat and calculated how long it had been since they had last talked. As an adult, I was surprised at how close I felt to members of my father's family when I finally met them, and what good people they seemed to be. The immediate bonding was unexpected but extremely pleasing.

An unfortunate fashion has developed for people to circulate an annual family report to anyone who they think might be interested. I suspect that in reality many recipients are completely disinterested. The report documents the phenomenal achievements of each member of the family in the preceding year. I had thought once to invent such a document and circulate it, with mentions of Nobel prizes, Oscars, knighthoods and other inventions. In contrast to this nonsense, before I was born letters that came in carried the best news anyone could receive—that their men 'away' were still alive. Or—the worst news.

When I was young World War 2 was fresh in all minds. At family gatherings that continued late into the night, the men in one room and the women in another, the men would sometimes talk about the war that coloured each of their lives. I was not given instructions to stay away, but instinctively knew that the talk was not for my ears.

War was not the only subject of discussion when the males gathered at night. My father was involved in the Labor Party locally, and eventually in preselection committees. He was the local Labor and union go-to man so we were often visited by politicians, old fashioned ones who were there to help people. We often had a houseful of people discussing the latest political developments loudly, long into the night. My mother told me later that my father had been offered preselection for a safe Labor seat in the NSW state elections but had declined because he was not interested in leading the kind of life that would involve.

During the war my father joined the army but only got as far north as Southport in Queensland. Initially, like most young men from the bush in those days, he could shoot straight and so was assigned to using a machine gun. Then it was discovered that he could drive a truck, qualifying him for the armoured corps, driving a tank transporter. Eventually he was made an instructor. A photo shows him standing beside a giant truck, the wheels considerably taller than he is. It is quite possible I am here because of his driving skills; he never had to leave Australia.

Three of my uncles though, went off to New Guinea as Papua was popularly known then. One of them, Clarrie Butler, was toughened by it, and had been wounded in action; in the male ethos of the time he never spoke of it. Another, Kevin, who had a university degree was initially placed in army intelligence and then became a military newspaper correspondent towards the end of the war, before ending up as part of the occupation forces in Japan.

The other, my most immediate uncle lived across the road in the house my grandfather had owned. His birth name was Herbert, but everyone called him Herb except me. As a small child he had affectionately nicknamed me Tiger Kelly, after a character in the popular comic strip Ginger Meggs. I named him Tiger in response, and that name stayed with him for all members of my immediate family.

He was a big, gentle man. I never saw him in a temper. He was a drunk; and if that sounds harsh it is, but not in the way you perhaps imagine. I have no harsh feelings towards him, only the opposite. He used drinking as a way of treating post-traumatic stress disorder, although nobody had heard of such a thing in those days. He was traumatised by his wartime experiences and never learned to contain them or forget them. Like all his generation he was reluctant to talk about involvement in war, but he told me a few things about his time along the Kokoda.

He showed me an army slouch hat with a neat hole front and back where a machine gun bullet had passed over the top of his head just nicking the skin. In a darker moment he told me that to save the life of a mate and perhaps his own while they were digging a trench, it had been necessary to cut an attacking Japanese soldier's head in half with the edge of a shovel. The horror of that stayed with him.

He was in my thoughts many years later, when I went to the Bomana War Cemetery in the hills above Port Moresby, in Papua, at the southern end of the Kokoda Track. Almost 4000 graves stretch far away from wherever you stand. And as you look at the names you see the ages; 19, 17, 20, 18, 20,19, on and on, only rarely someone in their 30s, and the true horror becomes clear: all those adolescents who never became fully grown men. It has been part of my luck in life to never be involved in war.

Later in life Tiger became the manager of the Gaden Fish Hatchery on the Thredbo River, where trout eggs were hatched into fry, small fish to be released into rivers and dams. It saddens me to say that by then I had lost contact with him. He died relatively young, presumably because his liver no longer had the will to keep going.

My grandfather, Tom Butler, a man of the generation that knew the difference between a sulky, a dray and a buggy, died when I was three or four years old. For many years I had carried unnecessary guilt, believing I had killed him. An old man then, thin and weakened, he was walking in the back yard of our house and, angry with him for some reason, I bumped into his legs with my pedal car. My mother saw it happen and her anger with me remains clearly in my memory. He died the next day.

A momentous adult insight after all those years revealed I had been carrying a painful subconscious error. The reality was that I had not hurt him; he had died of a heart attack. The insight resulted in a surprisingly strong relief from the burden I had carried for many years. This truth helped me to understand how analysts looking into someone's childhood might help them cast out their demons.

Tom Butler kept diaries most of his life. I found them in a cupboard on the veranda at Tiger's house, illustrating how much at home I felt there, going through their cupboards; or maybe it confirms that I really was the 'stickybeak' my mother said I was. The diaries were most interesting when he wrote about his time as a union organiser for the AWU, the first general Australian worker's union formed in 1894 from earlier shearer's unions. He travelled around western NSW in the early 1920s visiting shearing sheds, persuading shearers to join the AWU and collecting membership fees. The diaries mentioned Bourke, the Hay Plain and all points west, and sometimes mentioned walking all day from one place to another in the heat. He must have been a determined man; he was not welcomed by many of the station owners.

Later, in the 1960s I saw Tiger building a fire in the backyard. When I went to have a look, he said he had cleared out the back veranda. There were the diaries, burning; documents that should have gone to the NSW State Library, or to the AWU historic files, somewhere where their value was recognised. Gone. I managed to retrieve two, for 1924 and 1932. I have them now; but the loss of the others still disturbs me. A man's life was in those fragile books; a man who mattered to me.

The 1924 diary shows that his activities had been restricted to a smaller area. The furthest he travelled was to Condobolin but mainly he had worked around the Monaro with some trips as far as Yass and Collector, and around the area that in 1927 became Canberra. Later he became a stock and station agent—ironically, a friend of graziers.

* * *

My mother Kathleen was typical of the times. As she said once, comparing her life with the travels around the world of her sons, *'I never moved more than fifty yards'*. She had crossed the road from her childhood home to her married home. She had no serious involvement with anyone other than my father, but when younger led a normal social life in town. That involved tennis, church, and that most important of all social events, the Saturday night dance, the only circumstance in which a young man and a young woman could respectably merge bodies.

She was a nurturer, not just with her immediate family. There was always at least one visitor, usually more, sitting at the kitchen table in our house. The other room, which never had a name but in other houses might have been called a lounge/dining room, was reserved for more formal visits, from people around the district who were seen as slightly upmarket including Bill Cogan, grazier husband of her sister May. All visitors were offered, and almost always accepted tea. The constant around-the-table discussions often started early in the morning and continued through the day, with a constant shift change of visitors.

She sometimes lamented living in a household of males. She had three sons but to her regret no daughters. I was the first of those sons, followed five years later by Richard (universally as an adult known as Dick) and eight years later by Phillip, who became Phil as an adult.

My mother retained something of her Irish ancestry and had many sayings that I have carelessly forgotten: *'the fog was so thick a dog couldn't bark in it'*. One of the ancestors, also named Thomas Butler, was born in Ireland and buried in 1860 in the Myalla cemetery in Cooma.

* * *

As a child I saw my father Stan, as he was known to everyone, as big and brave and strong, and wanted to emulate those qualities myself. Later it seemed that may have been overestimated; or was I just seeing changes as he aged?

I have warm memories of cold clear nights when he would go outside and stand in the dark with his hands behind his back, looking up at the sky. I would stand with him and adopt the same posture, wondering what he was seeing, not thinking to ask. Sometimes in winter, on the rarest and most precious of occasions we would see the lights of the aurora dancing way up there.

My relationship with him was both close and distant, all mixed up together. He was an old-fashioned disciplinarian when I was a child, which means that what he saw as bad behaviour was rewarded with a smack on the bum, or worse. He had codes of behaviour he expected me to meet; failing meant his discipline was physical. Physical discipline was normal then, before its negative effect on children was understood. He was never verbally or emotionally unkind.

Although he talked with friends and relatives in the most amiable way I for some reason found it difficult to have discussions with him, but later as an adult was surprised and elated to learn that he could actually talk to me, and surprised as a teenager to discover that he was a capable speechmaker, a skill no doubt developed because of his involvement in politics. When he was old, I became the driver on road trips we shared. That was when our most profound discussions happened.

He was a traditional male; he was rarely ill, and made no complaint if he was. He never discussed emotions. In part that was normal then for adult men, but I suspect it had also derived from the most traumatic event of his life, one he never discussed with me, one I suspect that he could not allow himself to remember. He never wanted to recreate the emotions involved. My mother told me about it.

He was born and lived his early childhood in the small town of Tuena, between Goulburn and Bathurst. When he was eight his father took him on a trip to Sydney. While waiting for a tram on Anzac Parade, his father stepped back for some reason, into the path of an oncoming tram, and was killed. There he was, my father, a child from a tiny town, in the middle of a large city alone; his father dead in the most gruesome circumstances. I cannot describe his emotions because I cannot imagine them.

Later, his mother was unable to look after him and his several siblings so he was sent to live with relatives. He left school early, with minimal formal education. As a young adolescent he began to learn bush building, working with a man who practised the art of constructing buildings from whatever was available on rural land. If there were rocks, they would build a stone house; where there were trees, a wooden structure or if clay was available, they would make bricks on site.

By the 1950s Stanley was one of the builders in Berridale, employing several workers. Nobody was unemployed then. The then-stylish double and triple fronted houses they built included ours. All are all still there. He did a variety of other work, remodelling the front of the pub for one, as well as completing many buildings on farms.

One house he built for an older woman, a widow, was his downfall. As builders do, he received a series of payments as the work progressed. The last would be the largest. This last consisted of recovering all the remaining costs of wages for the whole crew, himself included, of recovering the costs of materials, and of providing his business profits.

This last payment was never made. She had run out of money. He had the option of legal action, but then she would have to sell the house and would have nowhere to live. The dilemma caused agonised discussion at home; take legal action or go broke himself? He decided that he could not *'have her sleeping out in the cold'*, a figure of speech of course, because that would not have happened. She would have found something, someone would have helped her, taken her in. He was worried that in a small town where everyone knew everything about everyone he would be viewed as heartless and cruel if he had taken the legal approach. Worse, his fear was that nobody would contract him to build for them anymore, as small-town retribution. That may or may not have happened. Fearing what might happen is not always the best predictor of what will happen.

The agonising result was that he had to let his men go. They were not just workers. They were a mix of friends and relatives, good men all. One was our next-door neighbour, one a relative of my mother. Stanley had to pay back the costs of materials to the supplier in what now seems like a Dickensian scenario. The supplier in Cooma was a wealthy and somewhat heartless man who saw no reason to be generous. Instead he employed my father for a partial wage to work in the building supplies section. The rest of the wage was held back to pay the debt. This humiliating step down from the prestige of an independent life as an employer to being a worker gave little scope for any pride in achievement. It also meant a meagre income. Fortunately for him, he never wanted much in the way of things. He only had things with an immediate practical use. But for the family it was a struggle.

Coming into adolescence, I was painfully aware of the change in status. Looking back, I was only concerned about the material aspects of it; embarrassed because our car was older than most in town, our house was not as elegant as some others, because we did not have things others had. I got a bike for Christmas, to my great excitement until the let-down when I realised that it was second hand. It was probably donated by some kind hearted family member or neighbour rather than bought. That was the ethos in an area where nobody was rich and very few could be considered well off. Help your neighbours.

Stanley finally paid his debt and walked away from that job on the day it was settled, and eventually ended up with better and more prestigious work. In reality of course he had never been ostracised and his personal standing in the town had never been changed in the way my adolescent sensitivities had imagined. It is possible that people knew about his principled decision and he was respected for it.

I had focused on the negatives, but now see it differently. A lesson learned without being aware of that then, was that people can help each other with no concerns about how—or if—that will be paid back. Another lesson was that people can make their own entertainment and create their own pleasure without needing to buy anything. We played cards or other games at night, played music, or just sat at home and talked or read books. The key to entertainment involved people interacting, and caring about each other's well-being and happiness. Entertainment now usually involves looking at screens, or 'going out'. Am I wrong in thinking that has led to less general caring about other people and more antagonism towards some?

I had underestimated my parents, excessively worrying about possessions, not valuing what good and kind and giving people they were. We had sufficient to keep us fed and warm and provide us with all the human needs other than things. My extended family, people who mostly lived close by, provided warmth and love also. That was a critically important lesson about what matters in life and what is less important.

Considering I have just downplayed the value of 'things' I am fully aware that there is some irony in me being a maker of things, things for which people are willing to pay what seems to me high prices. The sale price for one pot sold in my last exhibition would have paid in 1949 for the house that my father built.

* * *

At home we made our own entertainment. We had a gramophone, that played 78 records. That is not how many we had; it is the speed they rotated, 78 times each minute. A later version is known now as vinyls. My brother Phil still has the gramophone. It's the size of a modern refrigerator. My small device that holds hundreds of songs fits in the change pocket of my jeans. With the gramophone you had often to change the needles that ran in grooves on the record (hence 'in the groove') to make the noise, because they gradually lost their sharpness and wore out, and the music became blurred in sympathy. I assumed the musicians were getting tired of playing the same thing over and over.

My family members preferred to play real music. Stanley played a banjo mandolin as a special treat, as well as showing us magic tricks with cards and coins when he was in the mood, and I am still fascinated by magicians. My mother told me that when she was a child the whole family was involved in real music, my grandfather leading playing the fiddle and whoever else was around joining in. My brother Phil learned to play guitar, as have my sons Tom and Mike. I stand out, with no skills at playing any instrument.

We were never short of entertainment when my brother Dick was around. Music had soaked into his organs. He would pick up any musical instrument, frown, have a quick muck around with it and then regardless of its need for blowing or plucking or bowing or fingering, he would play a tune on the thing. He played rhythm guitar in a band for a time, entertaining in the snowfields. He sang rock and roll with the noisiest of them. I pointed out once that he was not being paid much for the time he put in. His reply was that once the music stopped playing other kinds of playing began, the snowfields kind. That was the real reward.

There was no television, no computer games, no screen time. For amusement we sometimes played card games, 500 or crib. Euchre was reserved for the more sophisticated households of the district. As an alternative we played the then popular game Mah Jong.

One entertainment at home was much quieter. I loved reading. Adults had always read to me. A child learns to value reading, hearing the words and imagining the story, feeling the close warm contact with another person. In our house reading was respected. When someone was reading everyone stayed quiet so as not to interrupt. That was regarded as extremely bad behaviour, an attitude influenced by my father. Because he left school when he was young, he had not learned to read properly. He later taught himself and as a result he considered reading a great achievement. On many winter nights we all sat together, facing the fireplace, reading in a warm congenial silence.

* * *

I had been free to wander around the town as a smaller child. Entering adolescence, that became 30-kilometre meanders, usually down to the Snowy River, walking along the ridge of (as we called it) Barney's Range or by following the Ironpot Creek to the river. Digressing, it seems such a shame that bureaucrats now decide to change place names that locals have used for many years. Now it's Varney's Range. I suspect that none of the locals would know who Varney was. That point is somewhat weakened because I doubt anyone knew who Barney was either. But it sounds better.

The worst renaming blighted the little town of Nimmitabel with that unnecessarily harsh version of the original beautifully romantic name Nimity Belle. Another change for the worse is renaming Woolway Creek, near Berridale, as Wulwye. The original made complete historic sense and the new none. It's also easier to spell.

My generation delighted in being in the bush, but needed to do something more in it than just walking about. Fishing was one such thing. I learned about that by going off often for a day with my father, or my uncle Tiger. We fished for trout, a foreign fish that were stocked into the local rivers and streams.

The Snowy River in the days before Jindabyne Dam was completed in 1967 was a perfect place for fishing, where fishing was not just about catching fish, but mainly about being there. A catch was a bonus. Along the Snowy, kingfishers flashed iridescent colours as they passed, and platypus occupied the deeper holes, popping up occasionally in the middle of concentric ripples. Sand banks between ti-tree stands made easy walking.

CANBERRA

QUEANBEYAN

Great Dividing Range

TUMUT RIVER

MURRUMBIDGEE RIVER

Great Dividing Range

YAOUK

CABRAMURRA

KIANDRA

DEEP CREEK DAM

EUCUMBENE RIVER

ADAMINABY

TOOMA DAM

EUCUMBENE DAM

KHANCOBAN

Snowy Plain

COOMA

BERRIDALE

Treeless Plains

MT. KOSCIUSKO

THREDBO

JINDABYNE

MYALLA

NIMMITABEL

DALGETY

JACOBS RIVER

MACLAUGHLIN RIVER

JINCUMBILLY

SNOWY RIVER

BOMBALA

DELEGATE

The possibility of stepping on a brown snake focused the attention. Now thanks to the Jindabyne Dam the remains of the river are a lifeless stagnant frog pond of slime except for the rare occasions when water is released.

At one point known locally as the Gorge, the Snowy narrowed and ran fast between vertical walls of rock rising thirty metres above the water. The ultimate test of bravery, some would say stupidity, for a teenage male was to climb through there. I did it once and experienced true fear greater than any before or since, several times reaching a point where there was no obvious choice of handholds to go forwards, and no way back; the only obvious choice was falling vertically into the racing water.

We did catch some big trout sometimes, four and five pounders, where the Frying Pan Creek flowed into the rising waters of the newly constructed Eucumbene Dam, covering fresh ground as the dam filled. The fish were growing much faster than their normal rate because of the excess of food their new habitat provided so they were that rare and valuable combination: big, but young and stupid. The small size of their heads confirmed that diagnosis.

The Gungarlin River on Snowy Plain was another good alternative for a day's fishing with my father. It was difficult to reach then in the old cars, with steep climbs and muddy bogs. It carried vast numbers of smaller trout. It was isolated, with only a few snow lease holders around through summer and nobody in winter. Four-wheel drives have made it unattractive now. There are people where once there was solitude.

* * *

Much of my experience of the Berridale district later, when I was a student in Sydney, came from my search for local materials to be used in my ceramics; clay, limestone, granite and such. There is clay in the region; good usable deposits on the banks of the Wulwye Creek and on the freezing plains near Adaminaby, and down at the MacLaughlin River. In ancient times fluid molten granite thrust up to the surface and solidified. Now it has worn down, by freezing and thawing, expanding and contracting, and shivering off lenses leaving rounded tors. Slowly these have broken down in some areas over millennia to become clay. Veins of pegmatite run across the countryside, at one point passing under my brother Phil's house so it is possible to walk out in his yard and pick up a lump of potash felspar suitable for making ceramic glazes.

Around Berridale the large rounded rock tors scattered around the countryside are known as the Berridale Boulders. They remind me of a family story that I hope is true, about a distant relative who had come out from England to make his fortune. He had not been successful. Instead of enjoying the comforts of the grand home built from his wealth he was employed breaking rocks with a hammer to be used as fill on the roads. The story goes that he wrote a letter home, hiding embarrassment at his reduced condition by saying he was '... *gainfully employed reducing once mighty granitic batholiths to fragmental proportions for the purposes of macadamising the highways and byways of the grand continent of Australia'.* I admit to having never seen this letter—but often heard the story repeated at family gatherings.

The Treeless Plains, one of my favourite areas in the district, is on the southern side of Berridale away from the mountains. This is a broad meandering stillness of gently rolling low hills, with a grand hemispherical expanse of sky and an eternal susurration of breeze. In winter when the westerlies blow unimpeded from snow laden peaks this breeze becomes deadly, sufficient to freeze any living thing exposed for too long. This has been given as the reason for the absence of trees; the seedlings do not survive the first winter's cold. Summer on the treeless plains brings clarity of light, sharpening the view close up, but the distance, such a distance, across the plains creates a hazy heat shimmer where all becomes vague.

These rolling plains extend from Bombala to Cooma to Berridale and Dalgety. They were formed in the distant past during the Eocene some 50 million years ago, when basalt lavas flowed out over the area forming sheets up to 200 metres thick. Now the surfaces of the basalt rock have weathered down to pebbles. The story goes that some of the post Kiandra gold-rush Chinese were employed picking up the basalt stones to clear the land for grazing, and stacking them into the dry-stone fences that still run for miles and miles across the rolling hills. These fences provide the only protrusion to sit behind when the winter wind bites too hard.

Driving along the gently winding road from Dalgety through the plains I see abandoned houses. On a straight stretch Jincumbilly siding sits in proud isolation on the broad plain closer to Bombala. If people are shaped by the land they live in, then the people near Jincumbilly

Siding must have a strong sense of how vertical they are when standing up. About ten percent of the vista is earth and the other 90 percent sky, a grand dome of blue. The best description would be to say that the sky scape contains a little land at its base.

How little has this landscape been affected by man. The archaeologist Josephine Flood has described how the treeless plains were traversed by aborigines in their annual migration from the East Victorian and Southern NSW coast to the mountains. Sites still exist on the plains where stone tools can be found but the people have long gone. Only the breeze remembers them.

My aunt's grandmother, Mrs Suthern died at 103. Not too long before that she sat me, a young child, on her knee and told me about the aborigines passing through Berridale when she was a girl. The flat land in its protected valley was a meeting place for different tribes in the past before their final walk into the hills.

* * *

The average temperature for Berridale is very pleasant. Unfortunately, this average is a mathematical construct, not a climatic one. It's too hot in summer and too cold in winter, cold enough that house designs need to be different to the rest of Australia, and heating is essential. Unlike in the mountains, snow is rare in this town on their fringe. In my time there the biggest snowfall was in 1949, when the snow almost reached the top of the front fence, so as a five-year-old I could step over it and go out on the side of the road when nobody protective was watching.

Convention has it that the Snowy Mountains area was *first explored by Europeans in 1823'* but local folklore suggests stockmen were in the mountains earlier. I am happy to leave the tangles of various histories for others to unpick, but I must mention Strzelecki, the British/Polish count who spent a few years in Australia around 1840 writing himself into history. Some monuments to, and the confusion surrounding, his exploits are amusing. I like the story of his being the first discoverer of Mt Kosciuszko, which he named after a Polish patriot. A plaque on top of Mt Kosciuszko reminds us that aborigines visited the mountains over many thousands of years. The name of the first to the top is frozen in time. Strzelecki was led there by local graziers. In reality some unknown stockman, probably a Prendergast or a Weston, would have been the first white man who wandered up there for a look. We will never know what name he gave the mountain; he probably just said a curse or two for the cold.

After his Kosciuszko adventure, Strzelecki in 1840 went through Gippsland east to west, on to Port Phillip. His route may have been close to my place in Boolarra South. Who knows, maybe he walked right across what is now my backyard. I feel sorry for poor old Strzelecki when I imagine him in the hills near here, staggering along soaking wet from the undergrowth and the rain, covered in mud, slipping down the steep hillsides at every step or clutching bushes to painfully slowly drag himself up the other side, unable to see where he was for the tall trees and the thick jungle-like scrub. Exactly where he went is unknown because he was lost most of the time. In Mirboo North, a town nearby to where I live, is my favourite memorial cairn in Australia. The plaque reads: *'In 1840 Count Strzelecki passed somewhere near here'*.

* * *

For us in the 1950s the rest of the world seemed far away. The Snowy Mountains area was isolated. There was no electricity supply, no town water supply, no sewerage, none of the amenities now basic. The dirt roads were too slippery and boggy to go anywhere much when the snow got too deep, or even in heavy rain, and four-wheel drive vehicles were extremely uncommon, used only on farms. Without electricity, we had a kerosene fridge and kerosene lamps for light. We used wood for heating; a wood stove for cooking, a wood chip heater for hot water for a bath and an open fireplace with wood for warmth. As a kid coming in from the cold of winter, I associated the feeling that all was well with the world with a wood fire, a powerful personal reason for taking to woodfiring my ceramics later in life. Any other form of heating has always seemed unnatural.

The Snowy Mountains were a day trip from our place. They were named originally by someone with a limited imagination, or at least a poorly developed sense of metaphor. Some men in the town, including one of my uncles, had snow leases—land in the mountains where they could take sheep and cattle through the summer, a practice long since forbidden. They built and lived in small huts. The old mountain men could tell where they were with their eyes shut by the sounds of the breezes on the hills. A sighted man could find his way home while he had his eyes closed in a quiet reverie; double insurance because his horse had the same ability. The weather can change rapidly and dramatically but the constantly changing music of the wind is always there, strong and tormenting in the icy middle of winter and light and refreshing at the height of January summer.

We had family picnics occasionally. Driving to the top of Kosciuszko was allowed in those days. As adolescent adventurers a mate and I tried skiing. There was only one ski lift, just past the old Hotel Kosciuszko. We rarely used it, instead practicing a weird form of the sport that involved an hour or so climbing a hill, using the skis in a herringbone fashion, followed by a minute of fast running. A day of skiing consisted of a few minutes of actually running downhill.

I adapted to the cold climate and still cannot survive anywhere hot; moderate cold is a delight. For some time, by choice and against the sensible advice of well-meaning adults, I slept on the open front veranda of our house, waking in the morning with my hair stiff with ice. Some may suggest that was the point where the mental deterioration set in but I felt healthy. My mother, a veteran of many winters and wise in the vagaries of local climate, told me to always take a jumper or warm jacket when I was going somewhere, even in summer. Getting caught out in an unexpected sleet storm without the right clothes could mean death. She understood the mountains and the unexpected dramatic changes the weather could take.

Myack Creek ran through my uncle's land on the other side of Myack Street. It was often covered by ice in winter. It was tempting to try walking on it, tentatively estimating the thickness. When it was thick enough that gave a sense of achievement as it creaked and moved slightly. When it was too thin it was a shivering cold walk home to parents who questioned the intelligence of anyone who walked on thin ice. For me that is not a cliché, but a useful metaphor for many events later in life.

As a grand entertainment for the whole town, bonfire night in Berridale happened in June, when the nights were cold enough to freeze the walls off a bark humpy. This event, with a roaring fire lighting up one side of everyone, had involved community effort, gathering enough fallen branches to build the grand pyre. As a child I imagined the fire could be seen from the moon. Approaching closer than fifty metres might mean hospitalisation. Pagan influences brought into our town by immigrants from Ireland, Scotland, England and Wales probably came closer to the surface on those nights.

That version of bonfire night was discontinued years ago. Today it would probably be considered an infraction of all health and safety considerations. Fireworks now are professionally set up on auspicious occasions, and viewed from a distance. Then, our fireworks were personal and we carried a variety with us. Every boy was warned what would happen to his masculinity if he carried bungers in his pockets. The range of colours and effects of our fireworks seemed to us spectacular then but now would appear insignificant compared to New Year's Eve in Sydney or Melbourne. Our expectations then matched our circumstances. The fizzing whirls, the pretty colours, the whoosh of rockets and the loud bangs were excitement enough.

2
CHANGES

It's not what you look at that matters, it's what you see.

— Henry David Thoreau

Before the early 1950s people in the towns and villages of Monaro were mostly a monoculture, descended from migrants from Great Britain. In the later 1950s that changed because of the Snowy Scheme. This was a massive engineering project that created an inflow of workers from overseas.

Into Berridale came Lithuanians, Estonians, Latvians and Ukrainians, all collectively known locally as the Balts; as well as a mix of Poles, Germans and Norwegians. Given vivid memories of their recent wartime experiences that made for some interesting exchanges of opinion about each other at times. The Poles and Norwegians especially, had some memorable confrontations with the Germans. Rags (Ragnar) Lovstad the Norwegian and Siegfried Teitz the German, said to be formerly SS faced off one day. Rags, a short but stout and sturdy man, ended a heated discussion by telling Siegfried, who towered over him, that a few years previously he had been *'paid five bob a day to shoot bastards like you'*.

The result of the influx was that a third of our town consisted of the old pre-1950s Australians; a third the mix collectively known to the older inhabitants as wogs (or in more polite company the New Australians) and the rest, roughly a third, Norwegians who were brought in to the Snowy Scheme for their tunnelling skills. I understood why in the 1990s, travelling around Norway with Torbjorn Kvasbo. There were tunnels everywhere through their mountains.

The mixed 'wog' group was allocated an area with small huts to live in, just outside Berridale. They organised a scheme for acquiring permanent houses. As they earned money they contributed to a collective fund. Each time there was enough to build a house a name was drawn and the lucky recipient moved into town into a new house, continuing to contribute to the fund, until all were housed. A considerable percentage of the town originated this way. Later the second generation, children of the migrants, joined with many children of the original population to move away from the district, the fate of most small country towns in Australia.

The farming community was little changed by the Snowy scheme but the towns were, most drastically old Jindabyne and Adaminaby, both of which were ultimately drowned under the waters of the new dams built there. Each was replaced by a new town near where the old had been. Jindabyne, largely because of its proximity to the present snowfields, has grown and prospered, while Adaminaby was moved to a windy hillside and has never amounted to much. I stayed in old Adaminaby with a high school friend when the water slowly filling Eucumbene Dam had reached halfway up the street towards their house near the hilltop. It was a weird sight: a town being consumed by the rising waters, never to re-emerge.

The most dramatic change at the time was in Cooma. Now it's a small town on the way between the city and the snowfields, with many cafes and ski hire shops. Then it was the main shopping town in the district, where farmers and residents of the smaller towns went weekly to do their larger shopping. Before the Snowy scheme Cooma would close down early in the evening and nothing moved in the streets except a few people at one or two pubs and perhaps a stray dog. One doctor at the time who had been there for many years was asked at his retirement party what he thought of Cooma and he said they spelled it with one too many 'o's'.

But after the Snowy Scheme started in the 1950s Cooma became a lively place indeed, the nightlife centre of the district, rivalling the attractions of King's Cross in Sydney. The pubs were revolutionised. A few nightclubs opened and workers from all the construction camps around the mountains flooded into town for the drinking and the entertainment and the chance of contact with a woman, and an occasional continuation of World War 2.

For us adolescents at high school, it provided an education unlike any offered by the Education Department. We would head to town in Lyndon Scarlett's '57 Chevy, resplendent in silver paint with a chromed stripe on the back below the fins. Five or six of us, looking for—well, not much in reality but great excitement in our imaginations. The quieter among us, me included, would head for Teddy's Coffee Lounge. It was the first in town and quite possibly the first in any NSW country town to offer Italian-style coffee. We thought ourselves most sophisticated as we played Bill Haley and Elvis on the jukebox and drank coffee, something our parents had never done.

The more adventurous and larger of us, more able to withstand threats of a punch in the head, went to the pubs. Sometimes I went with them. Dodds was lively but Coffeys, near the railway station, offered facilities that prompted adolescent fantasies about what we might do with females when we finally cornered one. They were readily available in the upstairs rooms in Coffeys, for a price—well beyond our means, I hasten to add. For us, and quite possibly in reality, Cooma then was the most exciting country town in NSW.

* * *

When I went to high school in Cooma, between 1957 and 1961, it was possible to leave at the age of 15 (after the Intermediate Certificate) and many of the country kids from surrounding districts did so. That was sufficient education for a lifetime of hard work. I continued on to the five-year Leaving Certificate, equivalent to the current Higher School Certificate. My classmates in the last few years came from the families of the Cooma elite, and the families of educated leaders of the Snowy scheme. Significantly, the Snowy Mountains Authority had played an active role in setting up the Monaro High School in 1954. The sons and daughters of engineers, geologists, and managers melded with those of the local doctors, teachers and professional classes, along with some from the surrounding district. I can guess that there were more parents with PhDs than at any other school in the state. The percentage of Leaving Certificate graduates from the school who went on to university was among the highest in any school in the state. I did not know it at the time but I was learning in a special school for advanced kids.

Contributing to my widening horizons, more than half the kids in my class were migrants. Over 40 countries were represented among the workers on the Snowy Scheme. In my classes we had Americans, French, Italians, Russians, Maltese, Greek, Scandinavians, Germans, Poles, English, Yugoslavs, Dutch and others I cannot remember. For one of the two final years at school Eligio Solari was my quiet Italian desk mate. Some in our community would have called him a 'dago' but he was my friend. Bill Hadfield from Tennessee always denied being related to the Hatfields of Hatfield and McCoy feuding fame. George Boucher was my French mate. I remember Olga and Tania the Russian sisters, Peter Goed the Dutchman and so many others. Many of them went on to achieve in life, such as two of my classmates, my friend Tony Maiden who became editor of the *Financial Review*, and Steve Leibmann who became a well-known Australian television presenter.

Multiculturalism has long since become a common word in Australia, so perhaps none of this sounds unusual, especially if you throw in some from the Middle East and Asia as you would find in any current school. Everywhere in Australia there is a mix of cultures. But in the 1950s for a small country town it was unique. This produced an attitude in me that has carried through life; of accepting people from other nationalities as just being people, of accepting difference as being interesting rather than threatening. Later, working in other countries with different cultures than mine, what might have been a challenge simply became an adventure.

My country upbringing did not allow me to be comfortable with the middle class culture of many of my classmates, who came from highly educated professional families. I accepted their national differences without much thought but was threatened by their seeming middle class superiority, something I did not understand, feeling like an interloper, an outsider, frustrated at not understanding what was going on around me. My upbringing in Berridale among farmers and tradesmen and general workers, and the expectation around town that I would become a builder like my father, had not prepared me well to enter the middle classes and abide by what seemed to be strange ways of behaviour. My future had been restricted in that small isolated town. I was the child comfortable among my own kind, not knowing that the adult would become entirely comfortable among the professional classes. I could not imagine the changes that were coming. We are all prisoners of our experience.

One consequence of feeling misplaced was, in the early stages of high school, becoming the class clown, misbehaving and disrupting. Trying to be funny, without understanding that humour is an ancient method of getting people to like you when you are unsure that you like yourself. Another mild form of protest was to join the Jindabyne junior rugby league team instead of playing for the high school in the district competition.

A strongly competitive part of my character helped at school to balance any feeling of being an outsider. If you can't join them, beat them. That worked better on the sporting field than in the classroom. A high point of this was at one Berridale Easter tennis tournament when Lewis Brooks and I were the 'Junior Male' finalists. Lewis came from an affluent family and had professional coaching. I was determined. Lewis knew the moves and made them. Not knowing the moves helped me play an unconventional game. That began to confuse him and as his determination slackened mine increased; there was no other choice than to win, to prove that his money and social standing did not make him any better than me. Holding the silver winner's dish was never the point. When I look at it now it has EPNS stamped on the bottom, so it was not silver anyway.

3
WORKING FOR A LIVING

I believe that what we become depends on what our fathers teach us at odd moments, when they aren't trying to teach us.

— Umberto Eco

In my early teens, still at school, I learned some of my most basic approaches to work from my father. He was one of my most important teachers although he would not associate himself with that title. His teaching method was different to any used in school. He worked with rarely a word uttered—unlike his amiable conversational behaviour with friends and family. One of my favourite memories of him is of long periods of silence and exertion as we worked together. Working with anyone else, for me, still feels most comfortable when the least is said. The best work companions are the ones who say nothing.

He expected that I would see what to do next without being told, and be aware of every detail. He was indirectly teaching about being observant. That has been valuable when working with clay which sometimes has its own mind and can be quite uncooperative. He was also teaching me about trust. Trust by me that he knew what he was doing and that we would eventually finish the job. Trust by him in my awareness, requiring just a nod towards whatever came next. This taught me the value of being trusted by your fellow workers—and of expecting them to trust you.

We worked within our limits, doing physical work at a steady pace that could be maintained all day, rather than rushing. That morphed into my casual approach now. What's the hurry? What mistakes will you make by rushing, what important things will you miss? What can go wrong if you do it all at the last minute with someone else waiting impatiently? Start earlier.

My clearest memory of our cooperation is preparing firewood for the wood stove that cooked our meals, and the open fire that warmed us in winter. I learned about preparing firewood, skills that later helped when firing wood-fuelled kilns. We would go out in the bush to find fallen logs, load the heavy logs onto a borrowed truck, and at home dump them in a large pile. It was heavy work but somehow almost relaxing, as a day in the bush often is. We tended to work without stopping, a habit of mine still—no rest breaks.

We then cut the wood into lengths suitable for either the wood stove, or the open fireplace. This involved the typical bush approach—use whatever was available to get the job done. Like the ways of closing a bush gate, no two setups would ever be exactly the same. Our main tool was a saw bench with a big circular saw, running in a wood frame. This device was constructed well before the term Occupational Health and Safety (OHS) was invented. The saw blade was bigger round than the length of a big man's arm. The saw had no safety guards. It spun half exposed above the sliding wooden benchtop, its teeth hissing like some insane malevolent creature plotting to bite you in half. The bench had a sliding top so the wood could be pushed past the saw to cut it to length.

A pulley on the bench, connected to the saw blade, was driven by a twelve centimetre (five inch) wide belt of rubberised canvas. A few metres away, the chassis and straight-eight engine removed from an old Hudson car was bolted down to heavy wooden posts. The jacked up back wheel of the Hudson had the other end of the belt running around it. The middle of the belt had a twist so it spun the saw blade in the right direction. The car engine was started with a crank handle that would kick back and break your arm if you were tentative. To get it all going in second gear you stood on the chassis rails on one foot, the other on the clutch, and tried hard not to fall onto the tail shaft when it started revolving. You didn't need to be a graduate of a nationally recognised university to work out what would happen if your foot slipped. The belt flogged and flapped around as it spun at a furious speed, sometimes breaking and flying off in any unpredictable direction. There was no really safe place to stand. The ability to jump to one side very rapidly was a useful survival skill.

As the unmuffled engine roared and the belt spun, clouds of steam poured from the 44-gallon drum connected to cooling hoses on the engine. Occasionally we had to stop it all when the water boiled too much.

My job was to pick up the large logs—alone when they were within my capacity, with my father's help when too large, and lift them across to the saw bench. Then the log was pushed along so the wood could be moved through the saw. The sawn piece fell off to one side and the log was slid along so the next piece could be cut off. Doing my job involved avoiding the spinning drive pulley with the belt whizzing around it and the saw as I slid the logs across, meanwhile constantly kicking away small pieces of fallen wood to avoid stumbling. My father worked the bench, pushing the logs through the whirling blade and then helping to move the log into position for the next cut. That was wood cutting. Everything had to be done like you meant it; there was no room for caution and absolutely none for inattention. This was not a job for the faint hearted, totally unlike the genteel character of the chainsaw that serves the same purpose today.

We would work for hours in an almost meditative state—not amiable, not with any emotion, with just a prolonged concentration on the work itself. The work day started with a large heap of logs from the bush and ended with a neat conical pile of firewood for the wood stove, or the open fireplace. Each was then ready to split down to a usable size later; work for another day.

Continuing a family tradition, my sons still help me prepare wood brought in for my kilns, or for the wood heater in the house, and it is still a pleasant day working together. We no longer split the wood down with an axe, which was tiring, but use a mechanical log splitter. The work is easier but the risk of removing a hand in the machine is a new consideration.

A memorable episode of working with my father happened at the age of perhaps sixteen, when I had been 'out' the Saturday night before and drank a full bottle of port, a feat I cannot now imagine, one I never repeated. He came in early on the summer Sunday morning, woke me, and asked me to help him. With me in a state of exquisite pain, we went to the worksite where he was building a house. He asked me to dig a hole suitable for a septic tank, about two metres by one and a half metres and about one and a half metres deep. As the summer sun rose in the sky, I suffered the worst day of my life to that point. I still cannot adequately describe the agony of that work. He taught me the perils of drink, without a word of reproach.

Stanley also taught me, indirectly, about patience in work, about how to take a long-term perspective. He built houses, work that takes time; up to 6 months. What I absorbed from this was the attitudes required for long term projects. Do the work a day at a time, completing what you can complete in a day, not worrying about what remained to be done. Persistence gets you there. This attitude later helped me complete a doctorate, the work of years. It even later helped with firing anagama kilns, a six-month project by the time the work was made, stacked in the kiln, fired and then cleaned up for exhibition and sale. It amuses me to compare that approach with the work habits of my mate Alan Peascod who had to have everything immediately.

* * *

The 1950s was increasingly a period of prosperity and developing economic wealth, locally driven by the Snowy Scheme and the employment possibilities it offered. Added to that were more traditional developments. Every farm had several workers who could rely on lifetime jobs. Replacing labour with machinery came later. Increasingly high wool prices made farm life attractive. There was no incentive for males raised on a farm to leave, and females were inclined to consider marrying into other farms.

When I was about to finish high school local businesses around Cooma approached school leavers with offers of jobs. I was offered several: one was as a teller in the Commonwealth Bank; another working at Waugh and Josephson's, the local distributor of earthmoving machinery, with the promise of a rapid rise to a managerial role. I declined all offers. Being the bulldozer king of the Monaro was not compatible with a curiosity about the wide world, and standing behind a counter all day promised punishment for some unspecified crime.

The employer's difficulty finding workers was the result of a low wartime birthrate. For me and other war babies it brought great fortune in life, offering choices that later generations could not imagine, allowing risk taking because other jobs were always there, and letting anyone with no experience begin a new occupation. It set me up for life.

* * *

Near the end of high school I decided that working outside would be preferable to being imprisoned all day in an office or shop. Becoming a surveyor became my ambition. Now, that makes no sense at all, considering my lack of any abilities in any field of mathematics, but what seemed sensible then was the lure of working outside. Harry Granger, a Cooma surveyor, agreed to take me on for the school holiday before my final fifth year at high school (there were only five then, not six as now). I offered to work for no wages and he agreed to cover all the costs. He was working on the Snowy scheme at the time so I had a minute cameo role in that grand development; so minute as to be recorded nowhere but here.

We worked mainly around the Tooma Dam, and at the small Deep Creek Dam site, which had two distinctions. One was that it was in such a narrow valley that the sun in summer only rose about 10 a.m. and was gone again by around 3 p.m. Even at the height of summer the place was damp and cold most of the day. The other was the sole famous episode in that dark valley, the discovery nearby of the wreck of the aircraft Southern Cloud, which had disappeared without trace in March 1931 on a flight from Sydney to Melbourne. Tom Sonter, a worker at the Deep Creek site, went bushwalking nearby in October 1958 and by sheer good luck walked right into remains of the wreck. In the thick scrub it would have not been visible from even a few metres away. He solved the long-standing aviation mystery. A memorial displaying some remains of the aircraft is in the main street of Cooma.

Working on-site through the week, we stayed at the Tooma construction camp, a series of small huts, mostly two-man accommodation with a few administration offices and slightly more salubrious accommodation for the managers. No women at all, only men. The place was all go most of the time. The contractors demanded that work happen at the fastest possible rate. The exception was on Thursday afternoons when the pay came in. Most men were paid in cash. The wages were dramatically large for the times, given site allowances and the highly desired 'danger money'.

About 3 p.m. each Thursday afternoon a car and a van would pull in and stop. A short man in a suit would get out of the car and two very large men would emerge from the front of the van. Flanked on either side by his minders, and carrying a small suitcase full of money, the man who ran the gambling school had arrived in town.

Several women also emerged, from the back of the van. Soon a line of men formed outside each of several huts set aside for the purpose. The isolated camp now boasted two services hard-working men required.

Men died working on the Snowy Scheme. One fell down a shaft right in the middle of Tooma construction camp when I was there. He was cut in half as he fell across a supporting beam some thirty metres down. Work went on while a few workers removed his remains, clearing the site so work could continue. There was no stopping for something like that. The American contractors were in a hurry.

Harry and I came close to annihilation one day. We were estimating: working out how much rock had been removed from a quarry used for the rock and earth fill Tooma Dam. The rock was freed by blowing it up with explosives, so it could be carried on to the dam site by large trucks. As we worked, the men who drilled the rock and placed the gelignite explosive were working nearby. We did not notice when they left, and carried on until a Land Rover came into the quarry at high speed and stopped near us, the driver yelling that we had two minutes to get out of there before it all went up in a grand explosion. It would have been the equivalent of instantly scattering our ashes.

Everyone who worked on the concrete spillway of the Tooma Dam developed excellent reflexes. The spillway, an overflow for water if the level rose too high in the finished dam, was a steeply sloping structure, 45° near the top and 30° nearer the bottom. Standing on concrete at that angle was more difficult than you might guess, and much steeper than anything you would normally encounter.

The method of building the structure was, starting at the bottom and working upwards, to weld together a framework of reinforcing steel rod and then pour concrete into a formwork. The welders constructing the reinforcement used oxy and acetylene gas cylinders, each roughly a metre long and 20 cm round. As a cylinder ran out of gas, they would simply let them go to slide down the concrete. The speeds these cylinders reached near the bottom were high enough to cut a man in two, so stepping aside when you saw one coming required some fancy footwork to avoid being bisected, or slipping and following the cylinder down.

The roads in and out of the construction sites were practical rather than luxurious, steep in places, narrow and always curving, following the meanders of the mountains. Everyone drove at high speeds, partly because there was a challenge, universally accepted, to set the shortest time along the Snow Ridge Road between Cabramurra and the work site. The latest time was chalked up on a blackboard in the camp so everyone knew what time to beat. The mountain sides along the road were littered with the remains of vehicles that had not made it. Men who survived these incidents were not terribly disconcerted. Wages were high enough that they could buy another car in Cooma on the next visit, for only a few months' earnings.

4
TRANSITIONS

I don't know where I'm going but I'm on my way.

— Carl Sagan

In everyone's life there are times of transition. The new begins, and the old is minimised or forever abandoned. Formal changes common to everyone, events such as births, deaths and marriages are called rites of passage. Leaving high school and moving to Sydney was one of my momentous transitions. But there had been an earlier one I remember well—the point where my childhood stopped. This involved an event conducted in private rather than a public ceremony, and now is the first time anyone else will be aware of it.

At the age of ten I dug a hole. Do not ask why I began; I cannot say now and probably could not have explained it then. This was not just any old hole; it was a work of precision. The corners had to be sharp and square and the sides precisely vertical. I must have inherited some standards from my father through genetic osmosis, or some comment overheard.

When the hole was finished to my satisfaction, I climbed down and sat in it. It was maybe a metre deep, a metre long and half a metre wide. I was below ground level, unseen by anyone. It was a perfect place for private thoughts.

Sitting in the hole, I became aware that I was too old to be playing with childish toys any more. This was such a strong vision that I still see it clearly, and remember it as though it is happening now. What I needed to become was not clear, but I was very clear that I was about to move on to another stage of life; it was necessary to stop being a child. I remember an emotional struggle, accompanied by a sense of what now I would identify as incipient grief, like there had been a death in the family. The difficult transition point meant that I would no longer feel the childish pleasure with my toys, but also that I was facing an uncertain future, unaware of what was coming in place of those pleasures.

This was resolved before leaving the hole, which because of its depth

was a more difficult effort then getting into it. Soon after I carefully packed up my toys and put them away permanently, in one of our many sheds. After that day I never got down in the hole again. Its purpose had been realised. Over the years it gradually crumbled and later my father decided it was a hazard, and filled it.

The hole is the grave of my dead childhood, but a visit now cannot have the proper solemnity. In what some people call progress, it has been lost under a shed, a large one that my brother Phil built to house his machinery. Standing on the concrete floor is not like any normal graveside visit; nor is placing flowers on oil dripped from machines. Fortunately, I never mourned for that lost childhood, always being preoccupied with whatever might come next.

The hole was the first awakening of an awareness that grand life changes require acceptance. There is no way back. That hole in the backyard in Berridale was a preparation, unknown then and unconsidered until now, for dealing with major changes in life.

There is a standard cliché question: what advice would you give your 10-year-old self if that was possible? As I emerged from the hole my older self would have said: if you want to do something you can do it. Doubt will eventually be replaced by knowing. Just keep going until its done. That may take your whole life. If you don't want to do something you don't have to do it. Whatever happens, you will adjust.

* * *

Analysts and counsellors will suggest that events in childhood and youth stay with them through life, influencing behaviour, moderating decisions. The source may be remembered well, or have settled into unconscious realms.

My travels have included some wild remote places, but I cannot recall being too worried about what the dangers might be. That may mean the fears in some places were so traumatic they have been sublimated but that explanation does not feel right. A better explanation is naivete; but my early freedom to wander about my town, safe and secure seems to have translated into adult travelling and exploring, confident about finding new pleasures. Mostly, curiosity overcame fear.

That contrasts with lack of confidence in some social situations as an adult. It's a relief that feeling has decreased over the years. Feelings of alienation, not belonging or simply feeling different, can be traced in part to adolescent embarrassment about our family financial situation, imagining that other people would be disdainful. Now I know my childish concern about not having material things was misplaced. The reaction of people around the town at our reduced circumstance was more probably met with empathy than disdain. It's also clear now that being in a loving family was far more important than worrying about money. My parents' concept of poverty was not related to money but more to quality of life. Poverty to them would have been the absence of family and community. Lack of money was simply something you dealt with.

The discomfort in feeling like an outsider in social situations began with feeling out of place in the high school environment. My experience in a working class town created a social mismatch in the mainly middle class high school environment leading to confusion about what experiences to discuss, how to behave, what to think. Fortunately, my adolescent rebellion was expressed as misbehaviour rather than misdemeanour.

Insecurities still emerge sometimes, in social situations, depending on what other people are involved, depending on their social standing. The desire to hide in the corner at my exhibition openings is probably related, and my early terror of speaking in public. To my enormous relief that last one has now been overcome. Clive James in a television interview said that he *always felt like the youngest person in the room*. These feelings of not quite belonging are now only minimal but they are still there deep underneath the skills acquired to counter them, the skills that mask them.

This personal mild insecurity is different to doubt, a sensation felt by, I suspect, almost everyone involved in the arts—doubt felt about artwork in progress can morph into doubt about oneself. I will not embarrass friends by naming them, but some of the best-known artists among my friends have privately confessed to deep doubts and insecurities, totally at odds with their public persona. Robert Nelson the art critic wrote in a review in the *Sydney Morning Herald* in 2019: '*Doubt is integral to artistic method. You don't doubt the artist, because you understand that he doubts himself … All artists ultimately believe in themselves but only after doubting the wisdom of their vision. Doubt is integral to artistic method, which always follows dubious pathways*'.

Grow up in a small country town, then leave and go out into the world. What would have happened had I stayed? We have all asked ourselves—what would have happened if I had made different life decisions?

Obviously, everything would have been different had I stayed instead of leaving at seventeen. It might have been better, who knows? Some imaginary lives are. If I had done what was expected of me as a child and become a carpenter in Berridale, I would probably be wealthier now. But that alternate life would have been constrained, every day seeing the same people, the same hills, the same sky. It's easy to imagine the limits of such a life and forget about the intimacy, the feeling of being enveloped in a protective social hug. It's facile to imagine the lack of stimulation, the lack of cultured lives and rich discussions, and to overlook the positives such as the sensitivity to tiny details of changes, and the warmth of belonging; a reassuring smile, a hand on a shoulder, knowing you are at home. Something that I never found in large cities where people are hurrying, internalised, unaware, uncaring.

The attitude of my parents was the start of my good fortunes. It was: it's your life, do what you wish with it. We don't understand your decisions, but don't let that stop you from following whatever you want to follow. They gave me and my brothers freedom. That of course meant the consequences were mine. If it went wrong that was on me.

The choice between staying and leaving was between a large life in a small town or a small life in a large world. My brothers had the same choice; Dick eventually left. Phil stayed, allowing me to compare his staying with my leaving. His awareness of the local people and the local district is intimately more detailed than mine. People all around know him and know nothing about me. I never got to know how it is to live an adult life with the people who shared my childhood. We have diverged so much over time that when I meet one of them it's quickly apparent that we have nothing in common.

The friends of my youth have become aliens in my adulthood. At rare and usually brief meetings we try to make conversation but it's *in memorium*; we remember each other well enough to say hello but then there are painful silences. We have difficulty in finding some common point to discuss. Our lives have diverged so much they no longer touch anywhere; the vital links that create real conversation have all gone. The past is just that—gone.

I go back to the town occasionally to look around the district and to see Phil. We still own the house that I grew up in, home to my mother and father. For many years it provided warmth and security in times of trial or triumph. It was always a safe place to go, as long as my parents lived. It saddens me that now the old house that used to be filled to overflowing with family, now sits isolated and deteriorating.

I am not a tourist, seeing only the superficial. I see what happened in time past, what has been lost, who is no longer there, what has changed. Perhaps this is where the idea of ghosts originated, with people who can see people who are no longer there.

Most of the people I knew as a child are there permanently, in the cemetery, my mother, father and a brother included. It's a place to think about my inevitable demise, walking around and looking at headstones. I would love to see the long-gone adults of my childhood, not just memories. At the local cemetery I see where they ended up, or more accurately ended down, in the ground. Colm Toibin said it well: '... *home was some graves where my dead lay*' (in *The Empty Family*, Picador 2010). Their names come back: the people of the four winds, the Sutherns, Westons and Eastaways. Strangely the north was not represented. The Olivers, the Aitchesons, the Bents, the O'Briens, the Woodhouses, the Clarks and Brookses, the Reids, the older ones all gone now, remembered by just a few survivors from that time but unknown to most of the people who live there.

Those adults I knew as a child still exist for me although all are now long dead. Their names remind me of long-ago events, helping my mind to wander. Comparing the old days and the new days. Now, having travelled and made friends around the world means most of my friends are far away, not nearby to talk about shared experiences. And the people in the cemetery are inaccessible. Seeing them, all remaining close together, evokes the virtues of lives lived in a small community; the familiarity, the easy knowledge of the local area, the comfort of old friends and intimate personal histories. The virtues of my life of travel and living in distant places are so different; awareness of other cultures, the knowledge of other possible ways to live, the excitement of change.

Silently those old people in the cemetery go with me now wherever I go. They set my basic standards at a young age, about what is right and wrong, how to treat people, about living in general. I have not always met their standards but I have always been aware of them. These were good people in the old traditional sense.

* * *

Something else that lingers on from the 1950s, not just in me but in many who were children then, is the ongoing damage of polio. Before a vaccine became available it was a world-wide epidemic, causing weak breathing and muscle deformities that could cripple. I remember a bout of extreme fever and a long stay in bed but compared to many others my case was relatively mild. The immediate result was the loss of muscles on one leg, making it shorter than the other, meaning I could run faster in a clockwise circle than the other way, but would never become a straight-line sprinter. A slight curvature of the spine remains—a hollow back, if you will.

None of that has been a handicap in any way that mattered. The result though in later life is the condition called post-polio syndrome. It's also relatively mild so far. The polio may have contributed to my breathing problems now, although smoke from kilns inhaled over many years is probably more the culprit. Other symptoms are fatigue unrelated to activity (I prefer that to being described as lazy), intermittent muscle weakness, swallowing or speaking difficulties, and a range of orthopaedic problems. For these late onset problems there is no cure, but sensible management helps. Maintenance is the aim—no improvement is likely.

5
UNIVERSITY

I was surprised, as always, by how easy the act of leaving was, and how good it felt. The world was suddenly rich with possibility.

— Jack Kerouac

My high school antics ended with a reasonably good set of passes in the Leaving Certificate, but it's difficult to remember much about any of that. John Dewey has been quoted as saying *'Education is what you have left when you forget everything you learned at school'*. I have remembered the people but forgotten the formal lessons.

Meanwhile the government offered university scholarships. The one that suited me was a Teacher's College scholarship. I had no interest in being a high school teacher but the attraction of going to university was strong and these scholarships provided access for people from poor financial backgrounds. I enrolled in the Industrial Arts course at the University of New South Wales, in Sydney. This course trained teachers of what had formerly been called manual arts, including metalwork, woodwork and technical drawing. It promised to have some relationship to my father's work as a builder.

Going to university in Sydney was a life changing experience, perhaps the most significant development in my life. Off I went, the second in our family—and the second from Berridale—to do so. My uncle Kevin Butler was the first; he had studied economics. It's easy to conjecture that I went with some strong emotions but it's difficult to remember what they were. What is remembered with vivid clarity is that on that life-changing train ride, a departure from everything familiar, my father went with me. Luckily, an acquaintance of his, a farmer from the district, sat opposite us and provided the conversational solution to what would otherwise have been long painful silences. We had little material in common for conversation.

At the time, wondering why he came along, I was not sure whether to be annoyed that he doubted my ability to deal with a strange new situation; or pleased that he had expressed his caring for me in a way plain to read. I prefer the second explanation. It was an act of great kindness and love from my father to a seventeen-year-old adolescent. I had not yet realised he carried those feelings. That one act speaks for everything that was left unsaid. He was not a man to express such emotions openly and I had probably earlier been misled by his methods of discipline which were hard and uncompromising. I have also been guilty at times of remaining silent instead of speaking about love, assuming that actions would say what words had not.

He had arranged for me to stay in Blacktown, with relatives of relatives. This arrangement had some disadvantages. One was the sheer distance from the University of NSW, involving long trips by bus, train and another bus to get there. Another was the social discomfort of daily discourse at home with people who were older, of an entirely different disposition in most matters. They were kind, well-meaning people who understood my country ways and provided my physical needs for food and sleep; but they could not supply the essential company of peers.

Eventually the impasse was solved when my girlfriend from high school Patricia moved to Sydney. Using the argument that the daily trip was too long, and thanking them for their kindness I moved to Burwood, around the corner from Patricia. The landlady, who had only this one room to rent, had rules. One was—be in by a certain time. No late nights. Another was: no visitors are allowed, although an occasional male calling in was tolerated. What she really meant was there will be no shagging in my establishment. I knew not if this dictum came from some religious dictate, or could be explained by my adolescent interpretation that it was a simple unwillingness to deal with envy: 'If I am getting none then I will make sure you don't either'.

The arrangement came to a sudden end when she was out one day and I had a visit from Patricia and several of her female friends. When the landlady came home unexpectedly, they tried escaping through a window, which was large enough to handle one at a time. The landlady, hearing strange noises, used some innate awareness to catch on to what was happening and raced outside to witness the spectacle of not just one but a stream of females exiting backside first, with considerable flashing of skin caused by the method of exit. That was it. I was out. Expelled.

I moved to more congenial quarters in a boarding house at 25 Burton Street in Concord, close to the intersection of Burwood Road and Parramatta Road. It was a rather grand looking establishment. Originally a sophisticated two-storied mansion with wealthy residents, it had deteriorated to lesser status, with twenty boarders. It was run by a bespectacled thin faced East Londoner and his motherly wife, kind and generous people both. Rent was seven dollars a week, half my scholarship income. That included evening meals. The wife took pity on some of us younger ones and provided a sandwich lunch as well, with the request that we not tell any of the other boarders.

My $14-a-week income compared with the average male wage of around $44, and the minimum wage around $36. The remains of my scholarship after rent paid transport to the university each day, but was not enough to cover much else. It was supplemented by working through the summer vacation at various jobs including truck driving and casual farm labour. Savings from that work combined with the scholarship paid university fees, bought books and left a little for amusement.

Sometimes when turning my pockets inside out, nothing dropped on the ground. At those times travel to the university and back meant hopping on the back step of a bus and off again as the conductor approached to sell tickets; then hopping the next bus and continuing like this until the trip was done. This could require hopping six or seven buses to complete the trip. Sometimes a conductor would have a kind heart and a Gallic shrug on my part when asked for the fare was a signal for him or her to turn away and collect fares from others who could afford them.

I could only afford a shared room in the boarding house. I shared with a Dane, Arne Neilson. The inconvenience of sharing was minimal because Arne worked night shifts as a welder so he was gone before I arrived home and returned after I had left in the morning.

The other boarders were a mixed lot. Old Mr Clark (nobody knew his first name) had polio as a youth and wore a set of metal leg callipers that made walking difficult. They were obviously painful to the point where he was continually ready to upbraid anyone who came by. Anyone who really annoyed him risked a whack with one of his wooden crutches. A healthy boarding house spirit of 'we are all family together here' meant that his ill temper was accepted by all with some understanding and no recriminations. He was often helped with difficult tasks by anyone who happened to be nearby—upon which they were scowled at for their trouble.

My old friend Dick who lived upstairs was in his sixties. He was blind. He had been brought up in the bush, and one day, well away from town, he had been bitten by a snake. The wisdom then was to apply a tourniquet and keep it wound tight using a stick. After the half day it took for him to get to medical help the leg had become septic. The final result of the sepsis was blindness. By the time I knew him he had become adept at living with blindness to the point we tended to forget about it sometimes. His party trick was that you could hold out a banknote and by just lightly feeling one corner between finger and thumb he could unerringly identify its denomination. Nobody short changed Dick.

Dick was good mates with Jock the Scotsman. They were about the same age and had about the same capacity for beer. Not excessive, just enough to make weaving their way from the pub back to the boarding house pleasantly congenial. I often weaved with them.

Jock's particular form of blindness had nothing to do with his eyes which were entirely functional. He had a gambling problem: his horses never seemed to run in the leading three in any race. On Saturday mornings he would shower and dress in his Saturday best and take himself off by bus and train to the races at Randwick or Rosehill, wherever they were that day. Usually around midnight he would walk back in looking dishevelled and tired, having bet everything, not even taking the wise move of leaving his fare home in his other pocket. As result he was fit but usually broke. There was no risk in lending him the fares to get to work the next week, he always squared up on Friday nights at the pub and bought the lender a beer in gratitude.

One weekend he came home with two hundred dollars, a lot of money then. He arrived in a taxi, so that before he said a word we all knew he had finally discovered a horse with four healthy legs. We immediately formed a committee to decide how he should spend his fortune. The consensus was that it was so poignant to see him come in late on most Saturday nights, he should buy a car. The next day, Sunday, a group of us who knew cars (none of us younger ones actually had a car but we had the wisdom of youth) took Jock for a long walk along nearby Parramatta Road, which had many car yards. Jock had become pretty excited about the idea and enthusiastically sat in many vehicles until we decided on a particular Falcon. He had his cash in his pocket and we persuaded him to put it down as a deposit. The proposal was that he would make a payment every Friday until it was paid off. The car needed some minor work so he arranged with the dealer to pick it up the following weekend.

His plan was to go to the races on Saturday and pick up the car on Sunday. At this point there is no prize to you the reader for finishing off this story. He diverted to the dealer on Saturday morning before going to the races, got his deposit back, put it on a sure thing that would bring in enough to pay off the car outright—and lost the lot. Back to long walks home on Saturday nights. He never won any significant amount again.

Two boarders were my age. Barry Roberts worked in the drafting section of the NSW Lands Department in the city, preparing maps, but took no interest in that work. His only interest was in flying. The Government then supported education of all kinds and that included learning to fly. Barry could rent a Cessna for $2 an hour, the rest paid by his flying scholarship. He had nearly enough flying hours to get his commercial pilot's licence. He needed to safely complete a long trip to achieve that aim. He asked me to join him and share the costs, on the basis that he was allowed to take passengers as long as they did not have a pilot licence themselves. He had to do the trip with no coaching.

Off we went, first to Young, where Barry's family lived. Then on to Adelaide, crossing the Hay Plain at five hundred feet, following the road. A Maserati passed us on the road below and disappeared off into the distance, obviously doing some 150 miles an hour. From Adelaide we headed back to Mt Gambier where I had my first flying lesson. Taking off, as the plane left the ground Barry said 'you take over', and climbed into the back to look for his camera. I taught myself to fly in the following few minutes. Making no sudden changes to anything kept us up there. While I pretended to fly, Barry photographed the Blue Lake. We then flew east along the Victorian coast. At Port Campbell he flew in low and dropped the aircraft over the cliff and down to sea level where we flew in and out among the 12 Apostles, a spectacular act that would probably have us jailed now.

In Melbourne we slept in a motel for the first time on the trip. Up to then it had been a sleeping bag in the corner of a hangar, but we had a little money left and were keen to get home the next day. Because of rain and fog it was a marginal day for visual flight, but we left Moorabbin anyway headed for Kilmore Gap north of Melbourne. There the cloud closed in and we were flying blind. We could see nothing outside the aircraft. Our altitude was a thousand feet and surrounding hills were higher. I clung to the seat frame until we were in clear air again. From that day onwards Barry was more circumspect in his decisions about whether to fly or not according to the weather.

Another brief but significant boarding house adventure involved stealing a car. A new bloke from the Northern Territory turned up at the boarding house. One Saturday night when there was nobody else around, he invited me to go out with his mates. We cruised around the back streets of Marrickville and eventually stopped near an old Holden in a back lane. Two of the mates got out, started it and drove off. We had been seen and reported. Soon after a cop car stopped us and we were escorted off to the station. Deeply frightened, I imagined jail, shame, expulsion. One cop took me into a small room to question me. He seemed to work out that I was not quite in the same category as the others, who had been taken off to the cells. He asked about my employment and I told him I was a trainee teacher. He suggested there was not a bright future in teaching kids to steal cars. He told me to bugger off and never do it again. I have not and I still owe him one.

* * *

Personal changes accelerated rapidly. Country values became city values; a protected environment became one of vulnerability and exposure. Concepts of small-town finances, where nobody was wealthy and people helped each other were not useful where everything had a cost. I was known to all in my small town, but a nonentity in the city. The number of people you knew was infinitesimal in the vast crowds of unknowns, like that brief glimpse of a star on a dark windy cloudy night.

For vacations I travelled by train between Central Station and Cooma. Sometimes, to save money on the return trip, the friendly people at the Cooma station would organise a free ride on a freight train. Changing trains one winter night there was a two hour wait on the platform in Goulburn in mid-winter, the waiting room closed. I shivered for hours and from then on was a paying customer.

Each transition from city to country was confusing. Going home, that easy familiarity had faded. There was a surprise when someone passing said hello, with some affection; in the city streets nobody said anything to you. Family and friends asked: *'What have you been up to?'* As a child that question had meant *'in what way have you misbehaved today?'* How to answer that? How could I talk to them of the intricacies of struts and stresses in engineering classes, petrology and thin sections in geology, the metallurgy of lead, the canons of ontology or seeing the corpses in the fifth-floor dissecting room of the medical school? Of walks through suburban streets where nobody was familiar? I had the newly-found language for these things but they did not. My ability to translate was lacking, leading to saying nothing. Some years after my graduation, in a moment of mutual warmth between us my mother asked: *'What was the course you did at the university?'* Someone had asked her and to her embarrassment she was unable to say.

My silences had not been sullen, resentful or angry in the common adolescent manner, but had more in common with the infant who puts his hands over his eyes and thinks nobody can see him because he cannot see them. It was easier to escape than explain. People in the small town, and in the city, knew nothing of life in the other. The gap rendered me stateless, needing some way to fit in by bringing the differences together. It's ironic to conclude that I had been extremely lucky to have attended a high school where the students were high achievers, easing the transition.

With the changes old emotions and attitudes no longer had a use. In those first few years it all flooded in: new foods, new drinks, new clothes, new ways to communicate. All these developments felt positive. Even so I would have to work at it to get there, whatever there was.

The possibilities that would later open up were unknown then. The more immediate problem was struggling with that shift in social strata from working class to the middle somewhere. The shift was never completed of course. Now I have a mixture of both and can move from one to the other depending on who I am talking to at the time, with an adjustment of language and concepts.

* * *

A university education then was not the common experience it is now, when almost thirty percent of Australians have a university degree; in the 1960s about two percent of the population attended university. At the Vice-Chancellor's welcoming address all the new first-year students at the University of NSW were in one hall. The Vice Chancellor, Philip Baxter, explained that only one third would graduate. Our small part of the university, the Department of Industrial Arts, had thirteen students commencing when I did. All finished and graduated.

My attitudes began to change. In this expanding world I felt smaller and smaller, beginning to realise how much knowledge there was to accumulate and disturbingly, how little I had. Some fellow students were from rural backgrounds, some urban, some working class, some from the richer suburbs, but none of that seemed to matter much. We were all smart enough, more or less equals in our capacity to learn. The lecturers were excellent communicators and the lectures enlightening, starting off intriguing flashes of thought.

* * *

The Department of Industrial Arts was situated across Anzac Parade from the main university campus in Kensington; a few kilometres from where my grandfather had been killed by a tram. Among the gaggle of weatherboard structures, the only building that gave a sense of permanence was the brick Psychology building. One can have fun speculating why the psychologists were placed so far away from the rest of the university.

All signs of our humble past existence are long gone. That small wedge of land has for many years been the home of NIDA (National Institute of Dramatic Art), the theatrical institute which has trained many famous actors and other theatre and movie people including Mel Gibson, Cate Blanchett, Sam Worthington and director Baz Lurhmann.

I look back with affection to many leaders I have encountered. Professor Leslie Haynes is one. He was genuinely interested in his students and their achievements, and helped me to begin a life of travel and adventure by arranging the necessary introductions to people who could make it happen. It's easy to remember him as a patron rather than as an administrator. He the first of many to teach me that the caring and helping I had been shown as a child was not limited to family but existed in the wider world. So many others have helped me since then, encouraging me to follow their example by helping others where possible.

The Industrial Arts course Haynes headed up was a new development. Previously NSW high schools had offered Manual Arts, with subjects such as woodwork, metalwork and technical drawing, that could lead on to working in trades. Les Haynes was not satisfied to continue that tradition. He wanted to add academic substance to its practical base by including subjects such as engineering, metallurgy, geology and psychology, delivered in other parts of the university.

In our department we learned, or at least we were taught, how to make quality objects. As teachers Haynes hired leading craftsmen, already high achievers: Ivan McMeekin to teach ceramics, Helge Larsen silversmithing, and Norman Stocks furniture design. In the first year we had a short course with each, sampling what they could offer. From there we were expected to specialise. Initially I assumed Norman's woodworking would appeal, having from an early age made things from wood in my father's shed, well stocked with woodworking tools.

Entirely unanticipated, my involvement in ceramics started in 1961, when we did the introductory course, and became full time in 1962. I had never heard about potters. I had no idea what they did. Given my origins, like many others at school I had no comprehension of any form of art. A few at high school who did art classes came from art-aware families but others were there just to make up the numbers. That was the thinking then; if they are no good at anything else put them in an art class.

Out of nowhere the pivotal moment of my life, the brief moment that would determine my whole working future, arrived when Ivan McMeekin had his first session with us. He introduced us to the potter's wheel and demonstrated throwing.

I was fascinated. A lump of mud rose almost of its own volition, guided gently to become a tall jug. No snake obeying the charmer's flute ever rose so gracefully. From that brief moment of epiphany evolved a lifetime of commitment. It was magic you could see but not explain. There had to be a trick involved somewhere. I was in, knowing about working with my hands, but this was entirely new.

The choice was made there and then, in that few minutes, with no doubts. This was the one. It still astonishes me that a youth with no previous experience of such things could be so captivated by something in such a short time; but that was it. Like some Islamic decree, from that point *It Was Written*. A Christian might call it *Seeing the Light*. Perhaps the decision came from a simple desire to learn how to perform that magic trick. Whatever the truth, here I am, still fascinated by the medium a lifetime later.

* * *

Much later, in my late thirties, I had learned the skills of throwing to my best level ever, able to make a thin—and even—walled pot from 20 or 30 pounds of clay pretty damn quick. But eventually I realised that in making worthwhile objects skill alone is not primary. Many things involving great skill in the making are simply dull and characterless. Blunting the skill to produce a certain character in the work, allowing some humanity to intrude, is mostly my aim now. This allows some naiveté to show through in the form, some wandering off line rather than rigidly clinging to classically beautiful curves. As Alan Peascod said to me once, first learn precisely the classical proportions and then distort them slightly. The variations will be stronger than the formula.

All that came later, much later. Initially throwing, the only way to make ceramic forms allowed by McMeekin, was damnably difficult to master. The great man said it was like learning the violin. It would be at least five years before you were able to knock out a proper tune. He compounded the frustration by supplying us with Leach wheels. That instrument of the devil consisted of a three-legged wooden frame containing a big horizontal wheel down near floor level connected to a smaller one at the top. Clay was placed on the top one, and the large one was spun by kicking on a wooden lever attached to it by a chain. If that sounds confusing try making something on the damned thing. Every part of the body is off balance, wobbling about like a fat man having his first ride on a unicycle. Trying to coordinate both hands and both legs and avoid falling on the floor all at once while manipulating a lump of mud that refused to cooperate in any way was my introduction to the magic.

Years later Ivan took a few tentative steps into the modern world and designed a wheel that was a little more amenable. This one had a big horizontal flywheel low down, and you kicked on the top of it to make it spin. Heavy weights around the rim kept it spinning. This meant the wheel head on which the clay was placed would spin for some time, and you could sit still and concentrate on your hands rather than your body balance. The magic began to happen. I still have my version of that wheel, placed away in storage in a shed forty years ago and untouched since. Ivan even went so far as to design a rather ineffective system using an electric motor to drive the wheel via a belt. That made sense, and I have used properly designed electric wheels ever since.

Some potters, Ian Jones for example, and my good friend Chester Nealie, still prefer the old-style kick wheel because it imparts a looseness of character to the form being made. I wish them well in that endeavour. As the saying goes: '*some swear by them, some swear at them*'.

When first working on the wheel my hands were clumsy, like lumps of dead meat, lacking anything that might be mistaken for aptitude and finesse. My mind was not cooperating either, not providing focused images of what to make. Fragments of form here, fragments of ideas there, contributed little to match the assured togetherness of the works of the Industrial Arts teachers. Helge's work in silver was precise, in contemporary Scandinavian style and Norman Stocks furniture seemed to contain nothing that could be improved. Achieving their levels of craftsmanship seemed highly unlikely.

It took many years to become aware that it takes many years, and to also become aware that there is no need to emulate others seemingly far more skilful. Seeing work made by others who think and act in ways I can never hope to match, I can just admire it, having now gained the confidence to say '*I admire what you do, but I will just carry on and do what I do, and be content with that*'. Along with that, it's now possible to comfortably answer a question with '*I don't know, I don't have a clue*'.

* * *

Most object makers will say that music is an important—or essential—aid to the making process. Ivan McMeekin would often use musical analogies to explain an idea that was difficult to verbalise. Ivan's wife Colleen was teaching cello in that fine old institution the Sydney Conservatorium of

Music, so music was significant in their family. For example, Ivan might be trying to describe a hand movement and he would say it should be a more a 'glissando' than a 'pizzicato'. Wishing to appear worldly I would nod wisely and afterwards consult the dictionary to find out what he was talking about. I wonder what he would have made of the Korean master Lee Kang Hyo using loud heavy metal to help him throw slip at large pots and smear it around—to produce some of the best pots anywhere.

My version years ago was to play the same music over and over until it eventually became hypnotic, creating a state of mind where conscious thought was suppressed and the hands and eyes could function almost independently of the brain. That happens more readily now without the music, a relief because listening to the same music a thousand times had its drawbacks.

* * *

As a child I had no knowledge about art history and practice, but like every child I saw something of the beauty of things, the land and the sky and the animals and birds, and I drew things until I was told that the drawings were not very good, and I sang until I was old enough to feel embarrassed about singing. So those early insights about what could be the content of art were never translated into the practice of it. Everything I was learning at university was fresh and new.

In 1960s and 1970s the idea of a potter was of a man with a beard and an apron living at the end of a rough dirt road in a tumbledown cottage with his 'studio' in a lightly converted chook shed. The description has changed several times, in an attempt to make the work artier and more valuable. What used to be a potter became an 'artist potter', then a 'ceramicist' and now a 'creative', a term which deserves only satire. Which illiterate turned an adjective into a noun? Why not creator, a perfectly acceptable noun? Whatever the word, I am not convinced that these new forms of artperson are doing anything more profound or moving than some of the old potters were doing. It just looks different.

There were few potters around in the early 1960s. In Sydney it was possible to see every ceramics exhibition; there were not many. I was also interested in painting and managed to see most exhibitions. Macquarie Galleries in Macquarie Street and David Jones gallery in the department store were important venues for ceramics, and Kym Bonython's gallery in Paddington for painting.

Abstract expressionist painting inspired me, loving the sloppy freedom of it, the casual approach to sloshing paint around, and the distant connection to aspects of the straggly Australian bush with light and shade. My career as a painter was brief. Trying to do abstract expressionism produced bad results; the apparently unskilled nature of it belied the skills and insights involved. I gave up, thinking perhaps rightly, perhaps wrongly, who knows, that I had no talent, not realising the virtue of long persistence to develop a mature art form; not aware that the more you do something the better you become. Where ability is lacking practice builds it. With that awareness, a serious go at painting in my next life might work out better.

My awareness of collecting and burning wood in Berridale was a point of contact with Ivan McMeekin, helping to make sense of Ivan's lectures about the theory of wood combustion. He had made a deep study of the science and explained it clearly and logically. We learned about the water gas reaction and the effect of temperature on the balance of carbon dioxide and carbon monoxide; science explaining experience.

Ivan had developed the Bourry box kiln, a device praised more among woodfirers now for its efficiency than for its aesthetic consequences. For Ivan it was the perfect tool for producing his beloved Song-dynasty inspired celadons, which he fired in reduction in saggars. Wood burning surrounds them with a juicier form of reduction than oil and is much more pleasant to smell and handle.

There was something deeply satisfying about the concept of firing kilns with wood, a natural material. Nature was something we thought about in those days; nature was something you went out into for wood. Nature was associated with beauty, and places to be with friends and lovers, before it became recast as 'the environment' and became something distantly out there that was in great peril, that we should leave alone.

Firing with wood was not feasible though, on a university campus in the middle of Sydney suburbia, because of the smoke; and the drip-feed oil kiln we used as students was not very satisfactory in any way. It was difficult to fire. The drip plates coked up and choked off the flame. Getting oil on-site and stored was a problem in that clean university setting.

Installing an early version of a gas kiln designed by Werner Gaebler was a revelation; firing became a manageable process.

* * *

Ivan hired a studio assistant, Paul Briggs. Paul was an ex-hippie from California, in his thirties. Before beginning the assistant job, he had made something of a living in Sydney making and selling leather sandals. He lived extremely frugally. I used to visit him in his one-room flat in Woolloomooloo. In it he had a mattress on the floor, a spare pair of jeans, two sets of underpants and t-shirts, some sandals and a radio. The radio was an old valve type that he had carefully disassembled and then remade, joining the components together by soldering long pieces of copper wire between each. The radio was then strung completely across one wall of the flat. When he turned it on the valves lit up and you could almost see the electricity flowing around. I valued Paul's company and his stories about San Francisco and was deeply saddened when his heroin habit developed to the point that he overdosed and died. That taught me to never touch the stuff.

It's probably a little-known part of the life of Peter Travis but Peter was a student with us for a year, from memory 1965. He was older than us other students and his gaiety—in both senses of the word—livened up the place considerably when he was around. Peter and Ivan had absolutely nothing in common apart from a passion for their individual interests but they managed to get along amicably. Peter, then at the beginning of his ceramics career was clearly multi-talented and had an acute sense of design. Notably he designed Speedos, skimpy men's bathing gear. Later he designed and built kites, glorious large multi coloured things that illustrated the sky. Later again he was colour consultant to the new Australian Parliament building.

Ivan and I walked into the ceramics studio one morning and Peter was sitting on the wedging bench with his head held low in his hands. Ivan, somewhat concerned asked if he was all right. Peter looked up after a long pause and said '*I've been trying to work out whether or not I'm a genius*'. Ivan patted him on the shoulder and said '*You don't need to worry about that Peter, other people will decide for you*'. In later years I always welcomed meeting Peter, with his big smile and his extravagant gestures.

Sometimes we had significant visitors, Shoji Hamada for one. His importance on the world stage was clearly indicated to us students by Ivan's anxiety that all should be perfect for him. Hamada demonstrated that a large reputation does not necessitate a large ego. He did not insist on Japanese food; he had hamburgers with us students. He was happy to talk with us with no condescending. I can still see him working, sitting cross legged at his Japanese style potter's wheel Ivan had commissioned especially. He threw pots, twirling the wheel with a stick that fitted a slot on its rim. It bothered me that the wheel was revolving the wrong way until he explained that's how they did it in Japan. His pudgy fingers made pots that appeared casual, far from formal western classical ideas of form—an approach that has informed me ever since. There was so much more to learn from him but as an 18-year-old beginner I was not ready to absorb the depths he demonstrated.

I see him now, a brush in one hand, a pot in the other. The remnants of a smile suggest some past pleasure is warming him again from within; or he may just be pleased that he does what he does. He moves the brush with a practiced and decisive motion, casual and light of touch. The dark iron pigment becomes a flourish on the pot. It may represent a plant or a dancer or some abstraction. No matter which, it is just so, inevitable, assured.

Michael Cardew was another visitor, also with a world-wide reputation in ceramics. Ivan had managed Cardew's pottery in England while Cardew was in Nigeria and they knew each other well. Cardew was in Australia in 1968 primarily to work in the Northern Territory with aborigines involved in establishing a pottery. I do remember one thing Cardew said to me—later relevant with my woodfiring where there were many disasters and few sales in the early days: 'Finances my boy are not a matter of money but a matter of temperament'.

Gwyn Hansen Piggott also worked with us for six months, after returning from France to Australia. She had previously worked with Ivan as an apprentice. She was experimenting with on glaze enamels, and was not amused many years later when we were talking about 'old times' and I associated her time at Industrial Arts with the unpleasant smell of burning volatiles when the enamels were fired. She had thought I would remember her bright bubbly personality.

Ivan enjoyed getting away from the university and as undergraduates we did many field trips with him. We stayed in some fine old country pubs on these fully funded trips, notably in Lithgow and Gulgong. I can still see Ivan and our group sitting on the upper veranda of the Gulgong Commercial Hotel on a balmy spring evening, beers in hand, having a lively discussion. My first impressions from those early 1960s visits contributed to my ongoing love of that little town.

The purpose of these trips was to see ceramic raw materials in situ, and learn what to look for when searching for new ones. Few materials were available from pottery suppliers then. The ethos of the time, and certainly the core of Ivan's practice, was to use materials you had personally located and processed. I liked this idea more as a concept than a reality. Letting others do the hard work of digging and processing seemed to me like getting to the point, which was making things, more quickly. Strange that now in my seventies I have returned to winning some clay from a local quarry and welcoming the process of preparing and using it.

We also did one trip to Mittagong, where Ivan had started up Sturt Pottery, part of the Sturt Workshops initiated by Winifred West. The pottery had a rocky financial start and there was tension between West and McMeekin which eventually led to Ivan leaving and becoming a lecturer at UNSW. I have since done workshops and exhibited at Sturt, a valuable establishment with workshops for various media, good working facilities and a well-run shop and gallery.

* * *

Sometimes random pure luck determines our whole future. Conscription of young men to become soldiers in the Vietnam war had been introduced in 1964. The method of selection was to draw marbles from a barrel, each with a birth date on it. I missed out by being born before the starting date. Otherwise life could have been much shorter—and would definitely have been different. Dick Ferrers-Guy, one of my good mates at school, was destined to be one of Australia's wildest rock and rollers. Instead he was shredded by a grenade in Saigon. Two of my classmates at university were also called up; my best mate at the time, Terry Kirk, had good luck and missed out after an unsatisfactory medical exam. Ian Thomas was conscripted and later ended up working for ASIO for many years.

* * *

In the four-year undergraduate course (three plus an honours year) I studied subjects including engineering, geology, English, chemistry and physics. In the third year for my two major subjects I chose ceramics and psychology, and specialised in abnormal psychology. It was necessary to do an internship; mine was at Callan Park Asylum, in Rozelle. I was interested to work in the area where the criminally insane were housed for life but was not allowed anywhere near the inmates who were considered too dangerous for any contact. Instead I worked with what we would now term the intellectually disabled, people with no capacity to care for themselves who had been placed there by carers who could no longer care for them.

I had no idea what to do with them so mostly we just walked around, me leading, they shuffling along behind. Then we sat, nobody speaking. If I did speak their answer would usually be a smile rather than an attempt to speak. They were gentle people far removed from their profoundly dangerous neighbours. The criminal inmates also had poor communication skills which instead of words usually involved violence. One researcher had attempted to establish some form of exchange by giving them canvases, oils and brushes. Some of the paintings I was shown were chillingly threatening. It's ironic and amusing to me that the Callan Park buildings later in 2008 were repurposed and became the Sydney College of the Arts. I hope their paintings were more appealing.

* * *

The parts of the Industrial Arts course designed to produce school teachers taught me that I was not going to be a school teacher. Our teacher training, an obligatory aspect of the scholarship, was carried on separately to the university at Sydney Teacher's College in Missenden Road, Camperdown, opposite Royal Prince Alfred Hospital. There the theories of education were passed on to us by Mr Stimson, who seemed to be totally devoid of a first name. He was a stern deliverer of the duller aspects of epistemology. That did not endear him to me. Nor did my occasional outbursts of criticism aimed at what seemed to me his stodgy ideas endear me to him.

For our practical teaching experience, and presumably a satisfying revenge, he organised for me to be sent off to Cleveland Street Boy's High School, by reputation one of the worst in Sydney. The expression 'a tough school' probably originated there. The reputation proved well deserved. I still feel grateful to Mr Stimson for final proof that I was not suited to a life involving pimply adolescents.

On my first entry to the woodwork room where I was assigned to teach, one young thug held another down over a desk, with a chisel to his throat. The whole mob looked at me expectantly as I entered to see how I would pass this test. '*Kill him*', I said, and went back out the door I came in. On re-entering a few minutes later they were all waiting expectantly, obviously highly impressed by my ethics and willing to go along with anything I said.

* * *

Near the end of the undergraduate course Haynes encouraged me to enter a competition sponsored by Ampol, a well-known Australian owned petrol and oil company. The award was for 'Australia's most promising Industrial Designer'. I submitted photos of my latest ceramics along with whatever else they asked for. With the help of some no doubt glowing references from Les Haynes, and I guess a word here and there from his influential designer mates, I won it. It was 1965, I was 21.

Patricia and I went off to Adelaide, to accommodation in a fancier motel than I had seen before, with a thick carpet, and expensive drapes and furniture. The award was presented by Frank Walsh, the South Australian premier. The event was held in a large room filled with illustrious men in suits. I was well out of my element. So, it appeared, was Walsh who had an obviously well-earned reputation for using complex words in the wrong context, and for being uncomfortable with the media spotlight. The amount was $5000—which at the time I write this would be the equivalent of more than $60,000, a stunning sum for someone so young and impressionable accustomed to living on a scholarship of $14 per week.

Hal Missingham, then director of the NSW Art Gallery and one of the competition judges, played to my impressionable nature. At the celebration dinner after the award ceremony, he told stories about what some artists did with their winnings from awards, such as in one case putting the cash on a bar and drinking till there was none left. His stories were valuable. They inspired me to use part of my winnings to buy a sports car, an Austin Healey 100.

These were badly made in England, and quite unsuitable for rough Australian roads. Mine was well past its best when I bought it, but it was low and sleek and red and could be driven with the top down. Something usually fell off within 100 metres of starting. Having a wheel fall off on a freeway was a highlight. Another highlight of a different kind was being stopped by a traffic cop, in Randwick. When I protested that I had done nothing wrong, hoping that I had not, he agreed and said he had just wanted to have a look at my nice car. Eventually high speeds, wet roads and over-confidence began to challenge the law of averages, and having the car catch fire each time I started it helped the decision to sell and buy a VW beetle.

In a more sensible move, I used some of the money to pay off a bond over the Teachers College scholarship. I had no intention to go teaching. Paying the $1000 was a relief for one my uncles who had been guarantor. I was free, no longer bound to anyone or any place.

* * *

Patricia and I were married in 1965, following our feelings, ignoring what eventually proved wise advice from my parents. We did the full church version, in Cooma, accompanied by several uniformly dressed females and a few males in suits they had obviously hired for the occasion. My best man, fellow student and good mate Terry Kirk drove from Sydney in his Mini, and many people from around the district looked out their Sunday best for that most formal and respectable occasion. It was the last time I ever wore a suit.

After a time living in a small flat in Croydon, in the Sydney western suburbs we moved to a flat in Bronte, 16 Pacific Street, on the rise overlooking Bronte Beach. Buying that property now, with its wonderful outlook, would be beyond the reach of most people but in the late 1960s Bronte was a slightly run-down suburb with many ordinary, or at least not wealthy, people. When we first moved there Patricia was working so we could just afford it, although that became easier later.

I loved living in Bronte. Returning from the university on a hot afternoon there was always a cool breeze running up McPherson Street as you topped the rise near the Hotel Charles with your first view of the sea, leading down to the beach. A summer delight was sitting out on the second-floor balcony, luxuriating in the cooling onshore breeze. At night the sound of the waves lulled you to sleep better than any device with a screen today ever could.

From the balcony we could watch the beach fill up at weekends with endless colours of beach umbrella, towels and people wearing almost non-existent beach apparel; it was after all the age of the mini skirt. Watching the constant flow of people in and out of the water and up and down to the kiosks and takeaway shops was free entertainment. On weekdays when few people except locals were about it was possible to enjoy an unobstructed walk. At rare and delightful times dolphins surfed the waves off the beach. In winter the big waves crashed onto the beach and over the rocks and the rock pool, popular with the ice water winter swimmers.

Five or six times over the four years we lived there, early on a Sunday morning, a body could be seen floating in the water off the rocks at the southern end of the beach. The current running from South Head and the Gap had brought us the suicide jumpers who had taken advantage of the popular cliffs at the Gap for ending their woes. The police patrol boat hauled them in and took them away.

6
INTERVALS

It is hard work and great art to make life not so serious.
— John Irving, in *The Hotel New Hampshire*

From the beginning, my university scholarship did not provide enough income so I needed to work during the three-month summer break, earning enough money to last through the year, to buy books and other necessities. It could also buy entertainment and escape from the pressures of study.

My main vacation job around Berridale was driving a truck. Tom Scarlett had one of the two local general delivery businesses in town, picking up freight from the railway station in Cooma, or from suppliers in the town, and delivering by truck to local businesses or farmers. Tom taught me that hard physical work can done in a light-hearted way. He was always joking, telling stories, diverting my attention away from straining muscles and tired back and legs.

Like my father, Tom did nothing to teach me. He just assumed in the country way of thinking that I was old enough to work it out for myself. That lesson was useful later in life when I started working with archaeologists. Lacking any experience or knowledge of that discipline meant just working it out as I went along. The same applied later to teaching in art school, starting the teaching job at the Canberra School of Art with no previous experience. The little remembered from Teacher's College was no help.

Driving licences in those days were provided by local police. I drove the truck to the Berridale police station one day, and told the cop I wanted to get a truck licence. He said that was a good idea because I had been driving it for a year without a licence. Country cops in those days exercised a degree of common-sense and differentiated between anyone who was doing something wrong by any standards, and someone who was not doing anyone harm. For them, not taking much notice of unnecessary rules and regulations was not a crime. I got the licence. The test consisted of driving him to someone's house to deliver a court summons, and back to the police station.

Tom was a hardworking man and I became one also, often loading and unloading heavy items. Bags of cement were nasty, the cement got into your clothes and itched and irritated all day. Superphosphate was worse, it burned your skin. Diesel was the best. It involved fitting a large tank on the back of the truck and turning up at the supply depot where a man would pump the tank full while you stood and watched. Arriving at the farm brought out the farmer who pumped the fuel out into his tanks while you stood and watched.

The hardest work Tom did was carrying bags of wheat each of which weighed slightly more than 80 kilos; something I never managed to do, never quite getting the knack of bending down, grabbing the bag over my shoulder with a bag hook and standing up with it on my back. Many years of doing things like that meant Tom ended up later in life hobbling around with all his shoulder and leg joints ruined.

Second to wheat for difficulty was hay carting, going out into paddocks where the hay had been cut and baled. The standard size bale was about 50 centimetres square and about a metre long. Some were shorter, with more grass and less lucerne. These were nice and light and could be thrown around easily. Some had been pressed longer than usual. With the denser bales of green lucerne, bending over to pick one up by the twine binding resulted in the bale staying put and your feet lifting off the ground. It was agonising. Their weight was not the only problem; there were thousands of the bloody things. A day working with hay bales, especially those big ones guaranteed a good night's sleep. One lesson from hay carting that I apply now is to have four or five trolleys spaced around my place to move anything heavy, along with half a dozen wheelbarrows so there is always one nearby. Another lesson is to do physical work at a steady pace, never rushing.

A frightening lesson involved fire. In the 1950s and 1960s there was no organised firefighting group in the district around Berridale. If there was a bushfire anyone who could went to help deal with it. My role was to take an empty truck to the council yard and load up a large water tank and pump, fill the tank with water and go to the fire. Someone would ride on the back of the truck, working the pump and hose. After one stint I returned to the fire with a newly filled tank, but could not find anyone. Driving around looking for them, I ended up surrounded by the fast-moving fire. Faced with a choice of certain death by sitting still, or possible death by driving through the flames, the sensible option was to drive through the fire. The image of those flames still frightens me.

Among other jobs, a short period working in the baker's shop did not work out well. It involved driving the truck through the day, from 7 a.m. in the morning till 5 p.m. in the afternoon; then having a meal and a short sleep before going to the bakery at 10 p.m. and working through till 5 a.m. or 6 a.m. After a week at the bakery I was supposed to be catching bread thrown to me by the baker from the oven and stacking it on shelves but I went to sleep standing up and woke up with the loaves bouncing off my chest onto the floor.

One day not long after, I woke from a wonderfully deep sleep, sitting in the truck, in the middle of the day, in the middle of a paddock about 50 metres off the road. The roadside fence was torn down where the truck had driven through. I retired from the baking industry that day.

A local grazier, Bruce Haslingden, asked me to work on his farm any day I was not truck driving. Bruce was a good natured, interesting man. One day we started talking about the Olympics for some reason. Bruce said he had been in the 1952 Winter Olympics—and his story turned out to be absolutely true. He said that because the snowfields were close and easily accessible, he was not too bad a skier and when the winter Olympics were coming up, he entered in two cross country events, coming 74th in one. He had the distinction of being one of the first two Australians to be involved in the winter Olympics, a good effort for someone self-taught and self-motivated. And a good lesson for me—that with the right motivation surprising achievements were possible; just go ahead and do it and see where it leads.

As a man to work for Bruce was, shall we say, fairly relaxed. It was not uncommon for me to turn up and ask him what he would like done that day and for him to answer 'Well, you are a pretty smart bloke. You must be able to think of something.' I painted part of his house, repaired the old outside timber-structure laundry that was falling down, and kept him company as he visited his various properties. Once he asked how I got to his place and I said I hitch-hiked. He offered to give me a Jeep he had just had restored. Bruce was a kind, generous and likable man, one of the several good bosses I have been lucky to have through the years. He let me decide how do what he asked, or to decide what to do if he did not ask. That was an extremely useful introduction into later working in my studio alone, developing personal ways to do everything. Bruce was one of several people that I now think of as patrons, in the old-fashioned sense; people who offered support with no expectations of return, people without whom any worthwhile career cannot exist.

7
THE FOUNDATION

There is a tide in the affairs of men, which, taken at the flood, leads on to fortune.

— Shakespeare, in *Julius Caesar*

Finishing the undergraduate degree brought new confidence, dispelling doubts about the new world I had entered. I received the delightfully named A. W. Wonders Prize, 'For General Proficiency', as the highest graded graduate in my year.

But confidence, even when combined with proficiency, was little help in thinking about what to do next. Only twenty-two years old, I was like a dog chasing a butterfly, not knowing what to do if it caught it. The future was not at all clear. I wanted to go off and be the bearded potter at the end of the lane. Perhaps in the Snowy Mountains, selling souvenirs to tourists? The souvenirs idea had shocked Ivan and I never really thought it was practical. Living on a poor income was a frightening concept, after experiencing my father's struggle.

Soon the answer was presented. Les Haynes showed me the next level, industrial design; and provided the ladder. He was friendly with some of the better-known Sydney industrial designers. Carl Neilsen was an academic and teacher with an active design practice, and one of the first consulting industrial designers in Sydney. Alistair Morrison had wide interests. Writing under the pseudonym of Professor Afferbeck Lauder he invented Strine, a phonetic and satiric version of Australian English. Stuart Devlin won a competition in 1964 to design the new Australian decimal coins to be introduced in 1966. Colin Barrie was the first director of the Industrial Design Council of Australia, and Gordon Andrews, probably the most versatile of all, had a go at everything including the first decimal banknotes for Australia. They were all high achievers, men to be respected.

With contacts like that, Haynes set me up for a life in industrial design. First the Ampol Award, then if I wanted it after finishing my basic degree, a place in the design school at the Royal College of Art in London. How that was arranged is still a mystery to me, but it was probably helped along by Stuart Devlin who was then in London. The move was made financially possible by the Ampol award funds, or at least what remained after buying a car and paying a bond. The RCA, as those in the know called it, was one of the most prestigious design schools in the world, and entry was extremely competitive. Haynes' support was guided by his enthusiasm, but he was unaware that the enthusiasm of one can be the downfall of another. I was offered the place; I said no thanks. If Haynes was disappointed, he never said so; instead he organised an alternative that I accepted.

I have never had the slightest regret about that RCA decision. Regrets would have come from accepting the offer, rather than from rejecting it. I had very little interest in industrial design. Accepting would have involved working with other people with a totally different mindset, revolving around business and industry. I knew nothing about either. Design work in that setting would have involved working to specifications set by somebody else for things which I imagined as consumer trivia. Worst of all it would have involved working in a city office and to a country boy accustomed to wandering about in the bush this was close to a life sentence, albeit in a comfortable jail.

Another alternative was offered, a scholarship to do a PhD at UNSW. This was a new and innovative concept at the time. Not the PhD itself; that was long established as the pinnacle of academic awards. People who did a PhD in those days often began later in life, confirming a successful career in their field. Only in rare cases of genius was it commenced by anyone young. But I was simply a guinea pig, not a genius.

The university decided to experiment and see what happened if people just completing an honours degree were offered PhD scholarships. Three of us from Industrial Arts were selected. My first reaction was to gaze skyward and wonder if I was ready. That tinge of doubt remained all the way through; would it ever be finished successfully? Many years later, supervising postgraduates myself it was obvious that each of them had those feelings to some extent. It's part of the process.

At the beginning, stressed, I had no plans about where to go with it, consequently none about how to get there. Haynes as supervisor recommended research into industrial design as the focus, but I did not know where to start or where it might lead. In that discipline I am no wiser now than I was then. A year of floundering about, increasingly agitated and lost, led me nowhere.

Starting off I had decided, grateful to Haynes for his good intentions and support, to give it a tentative go. He set me up with part-time work with Carl Neilsen. Carl had a ground floor office, one of three in a building a short walk uphill from George Street. His was the first door on the right off a corridor. The last was occupied by Alistair Morrison. I was the first to arrive in the mornings, letting myself in with two keys, one for the street door and one for the inner. A few minutes later I would hear a key in the outer lock and hear the door open slightly. This was Alistair Morrison. He would peer into the corridor and, reassured that nobody was there, would hasten though the outer door, slam it, run down the corridor, open his door as fast as possible, go through and slam it behind him. Every morning he followed the same routine. I talked to him a few times but never did ask the reason, whether he was being chased by creditors, frightened of spiders of just plain eccentric.

The first job with Carl was designing a case for an AWA television set. Perplexed, I bumbled around, disinterested, going nowhere, painfully aware of my lack of drawing skills, making sketches were just clumsy compared to Carl's. My 'rendering' was awful. Carl was a good man, and with the right enthusiastic ambitious pupil he would have been a good teacher. But I was not enthusiastic and had no ambitions. My design career had reached its end.

I moved on in other ways that felt much more positive and were, in retrospect, wise. I sat down with Haynes to discuss my PhD. Nervous, feeling ungrateful, worried that he might be difficult, but determined to have my way regardless of anything he said, I told him of my total disinterest in industrial design. There were only two alternatives. One was to pack up and leave the department with thanks but no regrets and blunder off into the unknown. The other was to totally change the focus of my postgraduate work to ceramics, and start all over again. Having discussed it with Ivan, the plan was to investigate using Australian materials in porcelain bodies and glazes. Little was known about that at the time.

Haynes to my great surprise simply said if that's what you want to do then that is what you should do. Just the kind of thing my mother and father would have said—it's your life. Many years later, I am still in debt to him for that act of kindness combined with common-sense. If he was disappointed at the failure of any ambitions he had for me—or for promoting his department—he never mentioned it.

Given Haynes knew little about ceramics Ivan was the obvious choice of supervisor. The arrangement was never formalised. Universities then were not unduly burdened by rules and regulations. There was none of the obsessively examined committee approvals, accountability, key performance indicators, annual reviews and all the idiocy that makes academic life intolerable now. If you needed help you asked someone, and they helped you.

Ivan was entirely supportive. Over four years the poor man must have been driven to the point of screaming with my endless questions, theories, discussions. He probably survived because of his technical obsessions about ceramics. Obsessiveness was and still is a prerequisite for anyone going anywhere in the arts. Ivan said so himself in an interview with Lorna Grover.

Ivan's research had mostly concentrated on stoneware. He was interested in but not well informed about porcelain materials. Col Levy had worked with him as an apprentice earlier at Sturt, so Ivan suggested contacting Col who had been developing porcelain. I visited him at Bowen Mountain frequently over several years. Later I realised that Col had been remarkably generous, spending a day with a student who had virtually nothing to offer him, each time losing a day's work. Yet one more person who gave unselfish support.

My research again bogged down, for new reasons. Ivan's experimenting with materials was empirical, as was Col's. They depended mainly on experience and observation, a kind of try one thing and see what happens approach, one small step at a time. They had not been trained in scientific method and the art of experimental design for larger projects. I needed the ability to design broad experiments, seeking the most information for the least time and effort. Ivan's approach to me was unselfishly helpful and I have always felt grateful for it; but he did not have the strategy for such a complex project.

When my need for another supervisor or advisor was explained to Les Haynes, he was pragmatic: *'find someone and if it's necessary and they are somewhere else, I will give you money for plane trips'*. Off I went to Melbourne, to the ceramics research section of the CSIRO in Moorabbin, to meet Elijah Tauber. Elijah had studied at the ceramics school in Sèvres, the ancient French porcelain manufactory. He had worked for many years as a ceramics research scientist of high repute. Precisely the man for the job.

He welcomed me in his gentlemanly Polish style, offering me a seat and a cup of coffee. When we were settled, he asked me what he could do for me. I explained my project, my difficulties and my need for assistance. He thought for a while and then asked me if the main aim of my work was to achieve the award of a PhD. I supposed it was. He then suggested that he knew of a PhD thesis in Hebrew University in Jerusalem. If it was translated, it would be possible to hand in a direct copy with little chance of anyone finding out; and since it had already passed it would guarantee my PhD with no problems.

Accurately reading the bewildered expression on my face, he then said that he could tell that I might have some ethical reservations about that approach, and that perhaps we could look at other ways of proceeding. He had been testing me, and had a quiet chuckle.

For the rest of that day and most of the next, he taught me the rudiments of experimental design. We worked out a plan to complete useful research in the time available, which after all is the guts of any postgraduate project. From that day on I knew what I was doing and it was just a matter of doing it. Everyone at the start of their career should meet an Elijah. Without him it's doubtful the PhD would ever have been finished.

I still have the now-browned photocopies of the notes he gave me on that visit, from his student days at the Sèvres Porcelain Factory. They traced, in detail, the technical history of Sèvres porcelain from the beginning to the mid-1900s. These notes were extremely valuable, and would have been absolutely unobtainable had it not been for Elijah's generosity—and his entreaty to keep them secret, which I have respected to this day.

We followed up every now and then by exchanging letters and phone calls, ironically presaging the external postgraduate courses I later ran in Gippsland, working at a distance. We met in person occasionally, at his place or mine, becoming friends in the process, to the extent of keeping in contact after I left UNSW. I had a letter from him years later when I was in Washington saying that he was coming through and that he hoped we could meet up. I sent him my phone number along with the wish that he would call. Eventually he did. He told me he had heard that there were many muggings in Washington, and that there were remnants from the racial riots of 1969, and he was afraid to leave his hotel room in Connecticut Avenue. I went to meet him and, almost needing to take his hand and lead him, took him for a walk around some safe streets. Our roles reversed. In the realm of street crime, I became the mentor to that whimsical, gentle and kind man.

* * *

Finally beginning to feel fully at home in the university, the stresses of postgraduate study lessened, partly because of a carryover from Berridale, where sport was almost compulsory. One of its benefits there was the social life involved, another more relevant for me was keeping healthy and fit. At the university where sitting down time predominated, sport helped fitness, and lowered stress levels. Socially people from different faculties mingled, promoting a feeling of belonging to the general university.

I played squash and took it seriously, training for up to fifteen hours a week, and playing for the UNSW club, in the Sydney competition; pleased with playing A grade, thinking that was a grand achievement. Until one day I had a practice match with one of the university club State grade players. I may as well have worn a blindfold and spun around on the spot for twenty minutes. When we finished, I had no idea what had just happened. And he pointed out that the next step up was international competition, at which he had no hope. His coaching advice at the end of that session was: 'The point of competition in sport is not just to beat them; it's to humiliate them'.

Being fit and healthy eased the stresses of postgraduate study, and social life at the university was also developing well. The postgraduate students of Industrial Arts and some of the lecturers had formed a lunch club. Once a week one of us had to find a place for lunch, and off we would all go. One such was Beppis, the Italian restaurant not long opened at the time, and now priced well out of my range. Another was an Indonesian restaurant, the Java, an old weatherboard structure long gone now, that teetered on the edge of collapse into the ocean from the cliff at the southern end of Bondi Beach. For all I know it may have finally fallen in. We went back there regularly, ignoring the sloping floor and the tendency of things to slide off the edge of the table. Of all Asian food I liked the mildness and subtle flavours of Indonesian food best.

Helge Larsen, Ivan and Keith Lodge were regulars and we got to know them as people. I particularly liked Helge the silversmith and his warm-hearted Danish sense of humour. One day his face wore an expression of obvious pleasure about something. When I asked him what he was grinning about, he said that he had just sold a large silver platter for a big price, and had '*finally reached the point where he could not afford to buy his own work*'.

* * *

Eventually I approached the end of the PhD. Thanks to Elijah's help the experiments were all done, with useful results. The big job then was writing it all up. That was done in a kind of frenzy, staying awake about 22 hours a day for two or three weeks, aided by some pills that I guess now are illegal and probably were then. No editing, no changes, just get it down and that was that.

Jock Marcks, my friend from Berridale school days, was living in Sydney and working as a programmer at IBM. As the end of my PhD approached, he told me that IBM had just received a new device from the USA, a typewriter with a memory. It looked like an IBM electric typewriter, the business standard of the day, but it had a computer-driven tape machine attached that could memorise a page of type. It was connected into the mainframe, a series of large refrigerator-sized electronic things that filled one floor of the IBM building. It could all by itself, with no human intervention, print out copies of the memorised page. The boss had asked Jock to play around with the thing and see what uses it might have, and he in return asked me if I would like my handwritten thesis typed up on it.

In those pre-computer days you wrote something out with a pen and a skilled typist converted it into typing. Photocopiers were in their infancy, and their copies faded away soon after they were made. Previously typewriters could only make copies by having carbon paper inserted between the original and the copy. The copies made that way tended to be smeared and not particularly legible. This thing could print originals, as many as you wanted.

The offer was welcomed, and the opportunity to have the whole thesis typed without having to pay a typist was even more welcome. I remember sitting with the typist in the IBM building overlooking Circular Quay as she worked, checking for typos, and being astonished that they could be corrected on the tape without having to re-do the whole page. Whiteout was not allowed in a thesis. The end result was the first thesis in Australia to be completed by computer, on a word processor.

* * *

After five years of work, the first wasted, the PhD was finished early in 1970. The PhD had been another grand life change, so different from being an undergraduate. What seemed like a grand prize was on offer; not achieving it would have been humiliating, never to be forgotten. Achieving it was no easy feat. In those days the PhD was remote and prestigious, and I had doubted my credentials for membership of the club. Some of the necessary incentive came from a sense of competition, 'proving I am as good as you'. Any financial stress had been removed by the scholarship which was generous. As well, taking on some teaching hours in Industrial Arts, a common form of assistance at the time, gave the bonus of learning something about teaching.

Working through the doctorate taught the value of persistence, when giving up had sometimes—often, probably—seemed the most attractive option. Those lessons about persistence have themselves persisted and have often been useful; helping me, for one example, much later in Canberra with trying to develop attractive ash glazes. For two years everything was a failure, the work from every firing was discarded. Then it eventually came good. Later firing an anagama kiln was a similar challenge, with more failures than successes. That gradually turned around. Failures are positive in that they teach you what not to do, but only if you persist until the lessons turn it all around.

With the thesis finished and bound in the traditional style, I carried the three copies up to the hole in the wall at UNSW where they were to be submitted. There was nobody home. I rang the bell several times and finally a bloke wandered out and asked what I wanted. *'To submit my doctoral thesis'*, I replied, handing him the form and reverently placing my hand on the three copies on the counter. *'Right'* he said, picking up the three copies and literally tossing them at least a metre into a box which by the sound they made already contained others. And he turned and walked back into his sanctum behind the wall. For a while I just stood there, empty. What a miserable little end to perhaps the most intense period of my life.

An examiner in the USA (Herbert Sanders) and one in Melbourne (Dr Cole from the CSIRO) each asked some questions. Sanders said I had gone on too much with irrelevant detail in one section, Cole said I had not provided enough at the same point. My oral exam responding to these questions was not too difficult; a Gallic shrug would have sufficed. The doctorate was awarded in 1970. It was the first PhD in Australia relevant to art ceramics. I have no idea whose was next but guess it was not until sometime in the 1980s or even 1990s.

Completing the PhD gave me another confidence boost, especially because some others had dropped out along the way. It taught me the value of overcoming doubts, not by fighting them but by keeping on working despite them. It taught me that discipline is necessary for long term projects, discipline to keep going regardless of getting tired and bored and frustrated with the long march.

The PhD got me started in the two major strands of employment, archaeology and art school teaching, and set me up for a fascinating life of travel, of international experience and outlook, of jobs that were sometimes frustrating but ultimately rewarding, and finally for the superannuation that allows me to indulge any whim in my current life of so-called 'retirement'.

The whole experience gave me a valuable lesson in the role of patronage and how it could change lives for the better. Les Haynes' support was fundamental to the rest of my working life. Ivan, Elijah,

Col and others most generously demonstrated how valuable help and encouragement can be. And lest that sound like it was all handed to me, they opened the door—but I had to walk through it and deal with what was on the other side.

* * *

In Sydney at a function late in 1969, not long before finishing my PhD, by chance I met Frank Harvey, the Plant Manager at Diana Pottery. In the 1960s Diana was one of the 'Marrickville trio' of small industrial potteries, along with Fowlers and Studio Anna, all three now long gone.

In conversation Frank asked me the *'what do you do for a crust'* question. Not knowing then what he represented, I told him about my enthusiasm for ceramics, and for some reason mentioned the brief time working as a volunteer with Carl Neilsen, the industrial designer. It must have all sounded convincing because Harvey, having explained what he did for a living, said that Diana could use a designer. He asked me to phone him later. I did soon after, explaining that it was only possible to work part time. His response was to say OK, start at 7.30am the following Wednesday morning. There was no interview, no request for further information, no paperwork. That was typical of such transactions then.

I worked there for the first half of 1970, while completing my PhD. On the first day, I politely knocked on the door of his office a little before 7.30. No reply. I looked around the corner and there he was at his desk, sitting head in his hands, obviously deep in thought. Unsure, I waited. Eventually he looked up, slowly, and said: *'Do you realise that soon there will be nowhere on earth you can walk where someone else has not walked before?'* My reply is forgotten but I do recall we discussed the occupation of earth by humans for some time. Eventually I asked him what he wanted me to do in the factory and he said, verbatim: *'You are here as a designer; so design, I suppose'.* That was the only instruction he ever gave me. That freedom was inspiration to do the best possible job I could. I suspect such freedom is rare in the world of work generally but is essential in any creative role. Do what you do as well as you can. From the start it was a satisfying job, where using your initiative was the task, providing useful training for later work with the same freedoms. Perhaps in the background somewhere it was also an example of unselfish support of a young bloke by a generous man able to offer that support.

The Diana factory started in the 1940s and closed in the 1970s, when the equipment was sold to Bendigo Pottery which was then undergoing a revival. In Marrickville Road, Marrickville, a then somewhat downtrodden part of Sydney, Diana was a relatively small factory. Inside, time had shifted back fifty years or more. All the facilities were well used and much of the equipment probably had historical value.

Diana produced a variety of what you would call knick-knacks, the kind of thing my mother knew as ornaments, vases and such. Some collectors now value them and they are relatively easy to find in op-shops. Diana also produced more functional items—the ceramic part of electric kettles, and water jugs to sit on the bar in pubs, complete with whisky brand logos. Almost everything was slip-cast in plaster moulds. Some was decorated with decals, but a few women were still employed hand-painting on the knick-knacks. I am not intending to sound negative by saying none of the output was conceived as high-end art. It satisfied an existing market and gave pleasure for many.

Everything was fired to around 1100°C in the 40 metre (120 feet) long tunnel kiln, using 24 cars. The process was never ending, with cars continuously loaded with fresh wares at one end, moving through the kiln and continuously unloaded at the other end.

In the beginning I decided to do each job in the factory for a short while, to understand how it all worked. Most of the workers decided otherwise. They were not about to allow a stranger to mess up their skilled work, but they did allow me to watch and learn. I liked the banter between workers, the kind that goes on in every organisation with multiple employees. At Diana it was invariably good natured, with no signs of conflict. Most of the workers were long term, and Frank Harvey, encouraging everyone to do whatever they did best, had established a good working environment.

Fred the slip caster was an extreme example of job satisfaction. He was a small taciturn man, who as far as I know had no last name, or if he did nobody knew what it was. Fred had a couple of week's holiday due once. I asked him what he was planning. He said he didn't have much else to do so he would probably just come in to work. His family tradition was slip casting going way back, in Stoke on Trent.

I had the most fun working with Aldo de Martino the Italian model maker and John, the Lancashire-born mould maker. This pair had worked together long enough that in their banter they had developed a kind of Italian Lancashire accent all their own. Pug clay (clay from the pug mill, a kind of clay mixer) became known as *poog cly*. It took a while to unravel their dialect. Between them they taught me that making moulds for production was a complex skill requiring considerable subtlety in the forms of the wares so they would release easily from the mould when cast, and would be suitable for later processes like glazing, where it was important that they could be held easily while being dipped in the glaze. I learned that slip casting done properly was most definitely not an easy way of creating ceramic forms. They taught me about precision. Their work was razor sharp, accurate and entirely professional. Their attention to detail was a lesson that has stayed. There is a vast difference between amateurish work and professional work, no matter what it's style or character.

My designs for a series of modernistic table wares never quite made it into production although a few other designs did, such as a candle holder; candles were all the go in the 1960s, but at Diana, modernism was not.

* * *

Another major diversion from studies occurred near the end of my postgraduate years, one I remember well having always been a secret car nut. Only once in my life would I have a cop help me to my car, help me into the seat because I was too drunk to do it myself, tighten my seatbelt and tell me to drive. The occasion? The trials to see what level of blood alcohol should be adopted as the limit for driving in NSW. I loved being one of the guinea pigs. The project was organised by Professor Syd Lovibond, of the UNSW Psychology Department, in which I was a student. My bright red Austin Healey sports car was well known around that part of the university so I assume I was invited to participate because of my interest in cars. It's surprising now to look back and realise that most of the lecturers knew most of the students, in those days when universities were about educating people, rather than about numbers and money.

Sixteen racing drivers and twenty-six 'ordinary' drivers were selected for the trials. We assembled at Warwick Farm racetrack, where motor races including Formula 1 were held in those days. Our instructions were that over the four days of the experiments, we were to be each given four different amounts of alcohol corresponding to zero, .05, .08 and .1 percent blood alcohol. Then each day, after drinking a mix of orange juice and an amount of pure alcohol unknown to us, we were to do driving tests. These involved things like driving down a lane marked by traffic cones facing two traffic lights, one on each side of the road in lanes also defined by cones. As we approached doing 80 kilometres/hour the lights would come on at the last instant, one red, one green and we had to veer into the green lane. Other tests involved rapid reversing into 'garages' marked out by cones, and following convoluted paths through marked lanes; also braking as fast as possible when hearing a particular sound.

My favourite was the one where you had to do some elaborate manoeuvring in and out of spaces, followed by a fast drive around the hairpin corner on the racetrack known as Creek Corner, followed by more manoeuvring, all to be completed in minimum time. One day it was quite obvious to me, as well as everyone else that I was well sozzled, requiring help to get into the car and set off. I can still recreate driving into the hairpin corner and seeing the trees and scenery revolving around the car at a rapid rate, several times. I had spun out onto the grass and was totally disoriented. That night I got up to head to the toilet and crashed into a doorframe; and next morning I was still pretty unsteady and had a bad headache.

We all enjoyed spectating and cheered loudly each time one of our colleagues crashed into a line of cones, spraying them around the countryside. Holden had generously donated four brand new cars for the experiments and they were returned at the end looking drastically second-hand, with dents from one end to another.

The main result was that at zero blood alcohol and up to .05, driving skill was a factor in how well the tests were completed. A history as a drinker or non-drinker made a slight difference. At .08 and above skill, or previous drinking habits, made no difference to the results. Clearly .05 was going to be legislated as the legal limit for driving. In 1968 it was in NSW, and has been in Australia ever since.

* * *

After several years it became clear that the marriage between Patricia and I was the youthful mistake we had been warned about. We had little in common. There was nothing wrong with either of us as people but the combination did not promise a long and contented life together. The prospect of moving apart was difficult because we had a daughter Lisa, and I was besotted by her, a feeling quite obviously mutual. I could not imagine being separated from her.

When we married my interest in ceramics was deepening to some kind of certainty that it was my path in life. I was also developing an interest in sculpture. That did not sit well with Ivan McMeekin who was narrowly focused, insistently and stubbornly so on ceramics made on the wheel. He believed we must make pots for daily use. Other forms of art were the province of other artists. Not wanting to annoy him meant my need to explore welded steel sculpture became a weekend thing. Working at the school all weekend, and hiding the work away until the next weekend, I was away from home seven days a week. Later during the postgraduate years this did not improve much. Fifteen hours a week training for squash took up weekend time, and playing in the competition some evenings through the week. With the continuous focus on my PhD research there was little left over for contributing to home life.

Meanwhile my lonely wife was visited often by my boyhood friend Jock Marcks—the same Jock who helped get my thesis printed at IBM. These visits brought them closer together and the friendship flourished. After they had a night out together that ended in her coming in at 4 am, flushed and not knowing where to look, clothes slightly but noticeably disarranged, I decided that was it. I invited my now former friend to a session at the pub to discuss matters and we did a formal handover. Lest this deeply offend anyone with a feminist bent I should say we were not considering it a deep ethical issue that might be compared to slave trading, but as an attempt to make and maintain peace between two males, allowing me to continue seeing my daughter. I agreed in turn to not interfere in their lives. At the same time, it offered Patricia some chance of a more satisfying life. So it proved; they are still together more than fifty years later.

Eventually, after I had finished at the university, we divorced. At that time divorce was considered shameful, something socially unacceptable, and the three parent families involved suffered. I also suffered for many years, from the extreme pain of parting from Lisa when she was a small child. It was alleviated in some small way by leaving Sydney soon after the split, never to return except for short visits. Working in other countries for years meant it was not possible anyway. As adults Lisa and I have travelled separate paths but remain friendly enough. I have always understood that her main allegiance is to her 'adopted' family.

I left Sydney in 1970; just twenty-six years old, and at the end of a marriage, with a PhD; but no conception of its value, or what the future might bring. My time in Sydney ultimately shaped my entire life. First, I saw Ivan throwing pots and began a lifetime involvement in ceramics. Later the PhD led into a role in research in Pakistan, followed by international involvement in archaeology. Later again it got me the teaching job in Gippsland—where I have been since 1984.

* * *

The research project in Pakistan was scheduled to begin in early 1971. That left a time gap. On the way to divorce, and unemployed with half a year to fill in—I needed a paying job. One eventuated, assisting to set up a pottery in the aboriginal town Cherbourg, in south-eastern Queensland near Kingaroy. Cherbourg was established in 1900 by the Salvation Army and known then as Barambah Aboriginal reserve. It was one of the so-called settlements, where aborigines from many tribes were concentrated into a few small areas in Queensland, eventually losing their cultural connections to land. It was controlled by the Queensland Government from 1905 and renamed Cherbourg in 1931. Outwardly Cherbourg when I arrived there looked like any small town.

The Queensland State Government, which managed Cherbourg, and the Commonwealth Government both provided money to build a pottery. I was 'The Potter', tasked to set up one of the industries in the town. Others included a cattle farm, a sawmill and a factory producing pre-fabricated houses, as well as a woodworking factory producing mainly souvenir items such as painted boomerangs. When I arrived the pottery workshop was a large, empty tin shed. Carl McConnell had been the previous potter. He had designed an extremely large *noborigama,* a multi-chambered woodfired climbing kiln. This was built during my time there by a professional German kiln-builder. We never got to fire it; later it was only ever fired once, when Kevin Grealy was the resident potter. The pottery operated from 1969 to 1987, and a reincarnation commenced in 2017.

My job was planning the pottery, supervising building and installing equipment including kilns, selecting suitable clays and other materials around the district, and training aborigines to manage the pottery themselves. We built a small gas kiln, intended mainly for testing local clays, many of which were not very well suited to making pottery. Jack O'Chin, the foreman, and several young apprentices and I enjoyed our trips around the district looking for clay though, and we eventually found a few promising deposits. The younger workers tended to spend less time looking for clay and more time looking for lizards; I decided they were good tucker.

8
PAKISTAN

In the beginning chaos, and in the end Chaos; and the vast wonder come between.

— Conrad Aiken in *Preludes*

Everyone has a best year of their life, and a worst year. As the good year 1971 is my contender; the year of my first grand adventure. What is offered here is just a small slice of one large year—and its follow-up a few years later (1977). Taken together they amounted to 12 months travelling the length and width of Pakistan from Karachi to Hunza, from Bannu to Lahore. Those travels could fill a book in themselves—in fact they did. My book *Traditional Pottery Techniques of Pakistan* was published by the Smithsonian in 1973.

The Pakistan experience was my first time out of Australia; coincidentally when many Australians were having their first world travel experiences. Air travel was just beginning to be open to anyone because of better aircraft and lower prices.

Pakistan was a different country in the 1970s than it is now. The northern part of the country was exotic enough that there are many books written about it, including Eric Newby's *A Short Walk in the Hindu Kush*. There was danger in some areas where I travelled. Understanding the intricacies of local culture was essential in risky areas of the North West Frontier, and knowing how to behave as a local helped create some safety. Even in the most dangerous areas, the when-in-Rome wisdom applied. Not carrying anything worth stealing removed the risk of being robbed. Not behaving in ways that were forbidden to locals helped the process of fitting in.

Now the situation is more extreme. Some areas have been opened up to tourism and may be safer. Elsewhere political developments have created a new level of unpredictability. Extreme Islamists attack unwary foreigners in remote areas. Although I would love to revisit some areas caution prevents me; living seems a better option.

My Pakistan story begins with Hitler. In the 1930s the Fuhrer's intentions were clear to intelligent Germans. Many were leaving for safer places. Hans Wulff, an engineer, chose to work in what was then Persia, now known as Iran, where for five years he was Principal of the Technical College in Shiraz. In the preface of his book *The Traditional Crafts of Persia* he describes how the Shah of Persia requested that the college should teach traditional Persian crafts such as silversmithing and woodcarving alongside modern skills.[1] Wulff had to learn about these crafts, studying them in the maker's workshops. Eventually this *'led me to the recording of most of the crafts which were still alive at that time'*. He documented craftsmen and women working with techniques and tools having very ancient origins. Sometimes it appeared that the methods had not changed for millennia. Wulff photographed these people at work and made notes about their methods.

World War 2 then intervened. In 1941 Germans in Persia were interned by the British as enemy aliens. Wulff left his crafts documents and photos in what he considered a safe place before he was sent to Australia, to a prison camp outside Melbourne, along with other Germans thought to not pose any real risk.

The internees were given considerable freedoms in their confinement. Apart from Wulff I knew another of these men well. Willi Kramer was a technician in the Department of Industrial Arts when I was a student. He had also been interned during the war. Willi told me the internees were not considered threatening, and were treated reasonably well; most were there because they had objected to the Nazi regime in the beginning and had left because of it. To counter the monotony of confinement they started a camp university, where each internee taught the others what they knew. The result was a group of extremely well educated and well-rounded individuals, almost all of whom chose to stay in Australia at war's end.

Wulff though, after the war, returned to Persia only to discover his notes and films were lost. It was fifteen years before he rediscovered them and 1966 before he published his classic *The Traditional Crafts of Persia*. Returning to Australia, he was employed as a Senior Lecturer in the

Faculty of Engineering at University of NSW.

Following on from Wulff's work in Persia, the Smithsonian Institution in Washington D.C. established a joint research program, 'Ancient Technology in South Asia', with the University of NSW, with Les Haynes as director. Wulff and Haynes decided to begin the research in Pakistan, in 1969. Wulff asked me to join the team he would lead, but I was completing a PhD and contemplating a divorce, and had to say no. Don Godden, a good mate of mine then accepted the role. Wulff died in Pakistan during the 1969 trip, and Don became the leader. He invited me to join the 10-month 1971 trip. Free from other commitments I could then say yes.

The aim was simple. In Pakistan many things were still made by hand, but as the country began to industrialise the craftsmen and women: blacksmiths, jewellery makers, weavers, copper-smiths, leatherworkers, potters, wood turners and carvers, rug makers and others would be replaced by modern factories. Knowledge of their traditional hand working methods would be lost. Our job was to document them at work, with interviews and photographs. My role was mainly to study the work of potters. In addition to traditional crafts we would also study ancient but still-used agricultural methods such as ploughing with ox-drawn ploughs and irrigation by canals before these were replaced by tractors and pumps.

No salary was offered, just expenses. I did not care. As a kid I had read many adventure books, stories about explorers and mountain climbers and travellers in exotic and dangerous places. This was my chance to live those stories. The risk was not having a proper job, not having a regular income and not living a structured life. Les Haynes offered me a senior lectureship in the Industrial Arts Department, so it was not hypothetical, it was a real choice. But it was an easy one. The imagined rewards far outweighed missing out on a predictable formal career. The lecturer job went to someone else, and I never had any regrets.

This was the big one, the grand adventure, almost a full year followed up by a round the world ticket with many stopovers. Why would you not go? I was young and life was all about opportunities. It's only later in life we reach the transition and start worrying about consequences. That is why adventure is easier for the young. They think about what they have to gain. The older and perhaps wiser think about what they have to lose.

In Sydney, Don and I went to meet Hans Wulff's family, including his daughters Hildegard and Roswitha, the latter a well-known Australian potter. We then went to meet Charles Walton. Charles was a wealthy man, the owner of businesses connected to the cotton industries in Bradford, in England. Charles's hobby—or rather more than that, his serious sideline interest, was photography, and he was centrally involved in photography clubs. Wulff had recruited him as an expedition photographer in the first trip, and Charles was enthusiastic about the second one planned for 1971.

Charles was married to Nancy Bird Walton, the pioneer Australian aviator. She was made a Living National Treasure in 1997. She had learned to fly with Charles Kingsford Smith. I had some experience of flying, and wish I could boast here that she and I became good mates, or that we had long discussions about flying. But the reality was that on my one visit to their house she came in, said hello and went out again. That was it, my ten second exposure to this famous Australian. Enough to see that she looked like her pictures in the media.

My first impression of Charles was of a tall man dressed in a loosely fitting dark suit, at which I was puzzled. Why would anyone wear a suit and tie while relaxing at home? Charles, an Englishman by birth, wore glasses and what dark hair he had left was combed straight back over what was no longer there. He showed us some of his photography from his previous trip to Pakistan. It was inspiring, particularly the black and white images. Each carried a superb sense of atmosphere. He understood lighting. I went away impressed, pleased at the prospect of working with him.

I did not know then that later, at its best, our working relationship would be cool and distant. At its worst we would quietly and grimly dislike each other to the point of subdued conflict, the kind that involves actions rather than words. Like many wealthy people he had a sense of entitlement, and like many country boys from poor backgrounds I had little respect for that, so conflict in Pakistan later was inevitable. In the end we were certainly not mates.

Don and I were though, before the trip. We had visited many pubs and gone to many parties together, and shared many a story, most of them exaggerated. Don came from Bathurst originally and so we were both country boys. He drove around Sydney in a large old straight eight Buick that he manhandled around winding streets with great aplomb and much swirling of elbows. The prospect of travelling in Pakistan with Don was one of the attractions of the trip. That was also to change.

* * *

The 1971 team consisted of Don as leader, his wife Deanie, Charles Walton as photographer and me as specialist in glass and pottery studies. We worked well together in the beginning, but constant travelling under difficult conditions with the same people eventually led to some differences of approach and opinion.

A second expedition was conducted in 1977. We had a larger group then, intended to form two teams: Don and Deanie, John Barlow, my then wife Brenda and I, with Valli Moffatt on part of the trip. Having two teams caused complications. The logistics often conflicted. The more chaotic level of organisation was not helped by some interpersonal aggravation. After the 1971 trip I had published a book about the potters, and had definite plans for 1977. Those plans sometimes conflicted with Don's, leading to disagreements. Not with out and out shouting behaviour, but from me increasing disrespect for what seemed like unnecessary attempts at authority on his part. And from his viewpoint what appeared to be rebellion on mine.

* * *

My first memory of Pakistan is the taxi ride from Jinnah International Airport in Karachi into the city, seeing a man walking down the footpath in pajamas and considering this very odd. Anyone who has been there will laugh at this blunder. The man was wearing *shalwar qamiz*, the baggy cotton trousers and shirt universally worn by women and men alike.

Rather than profound ignorance on my part, which I admit, this resulted from my travel policy then and ever since; arrive having read nothing about the destination and consider the whole thing a personal adventure of exploration and discovery. Even something that is common knowledge can become an exciting personal discovery. The result is missing some wonderful historic sites in countries I have visited; but delighting in experiences such as the sounds and sights of kids playing in back streets, where their mothers hang washing from cords strung across balconies and gossip across the space between.

My mate Alan Peascod, another traveller in Islamic lands, felt the same way. In an email to me he said: *'From my point of view the most rewarding trips have been those where I was (initially) not directly interested in the culture I was visiting. Egypt was a very good case in point. Without any agenda, my guard was down and I was completely overwhelmed by what I saw.'*

In retrospect it might have been useful to read something in advance about Pakistani food. The first night in the Karachi Hotel Intercontinental where Don, Deanie, Charles and I met up, we celebrated with a grand spread of the best of local food. The green beans which I tucked into with gusto turned out to be chilis. Violent ones. The meal was not helped by the local wine. The font used for the printed menu made the word 'wine' read like 'urine' and the subsequent tasting confirmed that reading. Not an auspicious start.

* * *

Ultimately my experiences in Pakistan were at most overwhelming and at the least exotic. Looking back now and reminiscing, I still feel the excitement of meeting people with such outlandish names—the Mir of Hunza, the Wali of Swat, the Rajah of Gupis and the former Mehtar of Chitral were all men that I met; all rulers of what had previously been princely states.

The names of places were also exotic; such as my favourite city Peshawar, in the distant past the capital of ancient Gandhara. So odd, being in these places rather than reading about them in the pages of some adventure book. Never having travelled in another country before this one, it was all so different. The sheer esoteric strangeness of everything was magnified; camel caravans of migrating Povindahs in the desert, or some of the highest mountains in the world, close up. I travelled in mountain valleys where the languages were unique, like Khowar and Burushaski; and was amazed in the remote valley of Yasin to have someone walking behind me ask *'I say, old chap, you haven't heard the latest test scores, by any chance?'*—a local, dressed in *shalwar-chamis* and a woolly Chitrali hat, aware that England and Pakistan were playing test cricket. He had lived and worked in England for twenty years and came back to retire in his home village as a rich man.

One new skill was working with interpreters. It's much easier if the speaker is dominant and the interpreter submissive. Not in any unpleasant way; both people can be good friends on equal terms elsewhere. It works best if the speaker runs the show and decides on the questions. The interpreter's job is to present both question and answer as exactly as possible, although a skilled interpreter will clarify where necessary. Using an interpreter involves knowing just how much to ask at one time so the question is clear and easily understood, and that is not quite as simple as it sounds.

After working for some time with interpreters, I found to my astonishment and delight I could follow conversations in a local language. Especially in the north where Pashto was the common language, after months of hearing English and the Pashto translation, then the reverse, I could follow conversations. In the tea shops, in the street; not completely but well enough to get the general idea. The same happened later when working with Palestinians. I began to understand conversations in Arabic. In either situation I could not speak the language but could understand enough of it to follow what was being discussed.

As the journey continued a different kind of novelty developed. The exotic became the everyday, the extraordinary became commonplace. Everything so startling in its difference had now become ordinary, comprehensible, and manageable with a matter-of-fact approach. That was character building. Learning to deal easily with the totally different culture created lasting confidence about travel to new places, the kind of confidence that converts fearful premonitions into healthy anticipation. After some time there, in a strange reversal the streets, deserts, mountains and the many variations of culture in Pakistan became familiar, and home in Australia seemed remotely exotic and unreal and unattainable.

* * *

The first visit to Saddar Bazaar in Karachi at night was special, all glitter and whirls of colour and contrasts between dark and light, the chiaroscuro of market life. The unending movement, the constant push of people, the gold and silver, the throbbing colours of fabrics and spices and lacquer reminded me of sideshow alley at Australian agricultural shows, with the same hubbub of voices and music, and constant invitations to enter and buy, but on a much grander scale. The mirrors on fabric in the Sindhi style reminded me of the mirrors on sideshow rides. The element of chance in the sideshow was that you might win some prize, in the bazaar the toss-up was that your purchase might be the highest quality, or the lowest. The onus was on you to learn the difference. The price you paid might be way too high through ignorance, or might be a bargain; trying to read the expressions of the stall holder was no help, they were masters of the poker face.

These markets provided a broad education, helping me to learn some of the Urdu language, enough to make purchases from someone who spoke no English, and to learn the cadences and rhythms of the language, making it easier to understand. Every stop at a market stall involved drinking green tea with the keeper, sitting in a back corner surrounded by their offerings. Learning to drink this universal Pakistani beverage, served with cardamom and excessive sugar in Duralex glasses *(would the sahib like a little tea in his sugar?)*, I began to enjoy it and look forward to it. The same cannot be said for the delights of Tibetan style tea in the northern mountains. I never did appreciate this concoction of melted butter and other unspecified liquids, smelling of sweaty yak.

Bazaars served the same purpose as our shopping malls in that everything anyone needed was available, along with a great variety of things nobody needed in every colour shape and size, like our two-dollar shops, full of trinkets and knick-knacks of no intrinsic value except amusement. Walking through the market, weaving in and out between people, feeling the quality of fabric, smelling the spices gave a constant buzz of excitement. Narrow lanes of open-fronted shops and noise and colour and smells unlike anything anywhere else, throbbed with life.

Traditional markets in Islamic countries used to have a standardised layout allowing any type of shop to be located easily by the traveller. The larger bazaars in Pakistan followed this to some extent. Qissa Khawani bazaar in Peshawar was the most traditional in layout. Clothes and fabrics here, gold and silver and jewellery there, pots and pans down another lane, the spice market in another corner. Getting lost was almost inevitable, and navigation by the type of goods on sale was the simplest solution. If I am in the middle of the pots and pans then the spices must be this way; perhaps.

In 1971 these bazaars were the main shopping centres, and modern malls were not yet in fashion in Pakistan, as they have become. Every large city had major bazaar areas: in Karachi the Bohri and Saddar Bazaars; in Lahore the Anarkali, the oldest in Lahore and the largest. I read somewhere that the population density in Anarkali was one person per square metre, which explained why there was never a time in there that you were not actually touching another person. Old Rawalpindi had the Raja and Sarafa Bazaars. Best of all was the Qissa Khawani Bazaar in Peshawar. *'The Story Tellers Bazaar'* was in the oldest part of the city. It supplied all the basic needs for food, clothing and ornament. Over many centuries trading caravans travelling from Afghanistan and countries further west via the Khyber Pass into India paused here to refresh men and camels, and to trade. It was a classic old-style Islamic bazaar, fascinating in its smells sounds and sights. Now it is a prime location for suicide bombings.

Tribesmen carried rifles slung over their shoulder, some wearing turbans indicating by colour or wrapping style their tribal affiliations. Glittering eyes in strong sharp indomitable faces, formed by hardship, looked straight into you with an expression that said they feared nobody. It was easy to believe you had travelled in time to the fourteenth century. Almost everything was as it might have been then.

I gradually found my favourite parts of Qissa Khawani. The street of the gold beaters was one. Here they made gold leaf, by placing thin sheets of gold between sheets of parchment, building up a stack like the pages of a book. Then, seating the stack on a firm base, they would beat it with a special hammer so the gold sheets became finer and finer. The obvious boredom of this endlessly repetitive work was relieved by turning the street into a percussion symphony, each beater matching his time to an ever-changing rhythm that ran up and down the street. Broad grins accompanied the most creative improvisations.

After a time, I developed that sense of fair prices so central to haggling. This is a specialised skill. Pay too much and you are a stupid foreigner. Offer far too little and you are not a person to be taken seriously. Offer a reasonable amount too little and you are haggling. When both people involved know what fair price will eventually be agreed upon, the haggle becomes an enjoyable ritual, and buyer and seller can both pass the time amicably. For veterans it is about entertainment, not money. The process invariably occupies considerable time and involves consuming several cups of green tea, brought on a tray by a boy from the local tea shop, the *chai khana*. The haggling process is pretty much standard in all markets. It has worked for me in the Great Covered Bazaar of Istanbul, in Insa-dong market in Seoul and in the Saturday Salamanca market of Hobart and the Victoria Market in Melbourne.

Another important transaction in Pakistan is *baksheesh,* a fine old Islamic custom. It involves persuading or facilitating, generally with a donation of cash. It may be seen as an act of friendship, as well as an oiling of the wheels. A small donation of *baksheesh* to a traffic policeman, given with a friendly smile, might cause them to forget about a traffic infringement. A friendly gentle pat on the back could complete the process. This is distinct from the concept of a tip in America, which comes after the event. Besides, tip is a much lesser word, harsh on the tongue, lacking the beautiful flow and melody of the word: *baksheesh*. The western outsider is prone to see *baksheesh* as a bribe. That is also a lesser word, crude-sounding, suggesting something illicit, with no friendliness involved. The word gratuity comes closer to the concept of *baksheesh*. Perhaps *baksheesh* is best understood as a combination of all three: a tip, a bribe and a gratuity, all offered in the spirit of friendly progress.

* * *

While we explored Karachi and got some feel for the local life, we were also preparing for the real work of the trip. Our base was the USA Consulate in Karachi, because the funding was sourced from the USA. It came in the form of PL480. This acronym meant that the USA helped poorer countries settle debt in part by allowing trade purchases from the US to be paid for in local currency, which the US would then spend in that country as a form of aid.

The aid was generous and the pile of rupees was very high. For one year the four of us had around a quarter of a million US dollars; the 2020 equivalent would be roughly one and a half million dollars. For one year. In a poor country. We lived well. In Karachi we stayed in modern hotels, giving easy access to the US Consulate. We lived in style in the Intercontinental, probably then the fanciest hotel in the country and the most expensive, or in the slightly down-market Hotel Jabees. Both were designed to be familiar to western tastes, although the chilies were just as hot in the expensive one as they were anywhere else.

We organised how to source funds when travelling. We rescued our vehicle from storage, a Jeep Wagoneer that had been purchased for and used by the 1969 Wulff expedition. As far as possible we established our travel arrangements. In a country that still retained English bureaucratic methods, left over from the Raj, we got together the paperwork that would show local officials around the country we were travelling with semi-diplomatic privileges. A little baksheesh would compensate any missing part of our credentials. Organisation completed, we could get on with the real job we were there for: moving around the entire country observing and recording the work of craftsmen as we went.

* * *

From Karachi we travelled up-country in our trusty machine, the green Wagoneer, heading north along the nation's longest highway (more than 1800 kilometres) from Karachi in the south to Peshawar, via Hyderabad, Multan, Lahore, Gujranwala, Gujrat, Islamabad and Rawalpindi and many places in between. From Lahore to Peshawar the road follows India's old Grand Trunk Road, known to all as GT Road, one of Asia's oldest routes from South-Eastern India to Kabul in Afghanistan, via the border crossing into Afghanistan at Torkham, in the Khyber Pass.

By the end of the year-long expedition the Wagoneer proved itself worthy. All the gear required by four people fitted in somewhere; if not inside, then piled high on the roof racks. Tyres might burst but we had room for plenty of spares. When pieces of the vehicle fell off and were lost, we continued without them. In the remote mountains when we broke a universal joint on the tail shaft, a local craftsman cast a brass replica which with the help of a talented local mechanic, got us back to civilisation. We busted the gear linkage off the gearbox, and got underneath with a spanner and locked it in second gear to get to somewhere where the problem could be fixed. It never really let us down. It is probably still going somewhere, just falling apart a little more rapidly.

We soon learned that the legal Pakistani traffic rules were not acknowledged by anyone. The actual process of driving required a strong sense of life and death and constant awareness of everything around—what fighter pilots call situational awareness. Theoretically traffic drove on the left side of the road, although it was not quite that simple. The Jeep had left hand drive which made it difficult to see oncoming traffic when considering overtaking. We were probably the only ones on the road to think about overtaking—nobody else thought about it, they just did it, anywhere.

Some traffic conventions were obvious; smaller gave away to larger. Headlights were not used at night—to save electricity. Cattle on the road should be avoided. Any gap between other vehicles 30 centimetres narrower than the width of your vehicle was wide enough to fit through. A multitude of long scars along the sides of buses demonstrated the consequences. Pedestrians generally conveyed a sense of total obliviousness to anything around them. Remembering the Muslim belief in '*it is written*', that our fates are predetermined by Allah, a Canadian diplomat once told me he only started believing in God when he watched a man crossing the road in Karachi.

Finding your way around was not as simple as asking someone for directions even if their English was excellent. Often, the person you asked would decide the place you wanted to go was not really very interesting for a foreigner, so instead would direct you to somewhere far away they thought you would find more interesting. Eventually I worked out how to read road signs by learning the phonetic Urdu script, enabling the word to be sounded out. Finding a destination became easier.

Our Western conception of a road is that it is a place where cars and trucks and buses and other vehicles move from one place to another. Some Westerners also believe roads are a place where bicycles are entitled to travel but this can be subject to some debate. As a matter of consensus, we do not believe pedestrians are entitled to walk down the middle of the road ignoring all else.

In Pakistan any living creature including man would use the road in any way they chose. This included such activities as a barber setting up shop—that is, placing a chair—on any part of the road that seemed suitable for hair cutting, regardless of anything that might be passing. Carpet makers placed their finished carpets on the road in some locations so that vehicles running over them would line up and flatten all the threads to give an even appearance. Tile makers could use part of the road to lay out clay in a metre-wide strip up to fifty metres long, before cutting the strip into tiles.

Driving consisted of a weaving progress, manoeuvring between the unexpected and the unanticipated, the fast and the stationary, between pedestrians wearing colourful clothing in the sunlight and black from head to foot on a dark night in the middle of the road. Buses and trucks hugged the centreline, the drivers believing this to be the fast lane and the smoothest surface. Two of them approaching head on had to make significant decisions. In America it used to be called 'playing chicken'; here it was not a game.

On one early morning trip, driving alone on the GT road I came to a situation never to be forgotten. In the dark, two buses, no doubt with their lights off to save electricity, travelling at high speed on the centreline, had met head on. Each had clearly been full of people. They—the buses, and the people, had each travelled almost completely through the other—only the back end of each bus was still undamaged. The human cost was difficult to determine. Taking a count would have involved a complicated search to reattach limbs to trunks and heads to necks, reassembling individual people. Body parts were strewn about like they might be in a war where there had just been an enormous explosion—which in reality I suppose there had been when the two collided.

* * *

In the north, beginning in Lahore, we stayed in the old British hotels: Faletti's in Lahore, Flashman's in Rawalpindi and my favourite of all, Dean's in Peshawar. Rooms in these old colonial hotels were immense. A room in Dean's actually had (for it is now demolished and replaced by a shopping plaza) four separate rooms: a front room with comfortable chairs, intended for receiving visitors or resting; a private bedroom, a wardrobe and dressing room and a bath and shower room. Each was large. From front to back would have been perhaps 20 metres; quite suitable for a British *sahib*.

AFGHANISTAN

KURDISTAN

CHINA

Hindu Kush Range

Kafiristan

HUNZA

△YASIN

GILGIT

CHITRAL

Karakoram Range

KABUL

KHYBER
PASS

DIR

△ NANGA
PARBAT

SWAT

PESHAWAR

KASHMIR

KOHAT

RAWALPINDI

BANNU

LAHORE

PAKISTAN

MULTAN

BAHAWALPUR

INDUS RIVER

*Cholistan
Desert*

SUKKUR

• DELHI

INDIA

KARACHI

*Arabian
Sea*

I am reminded of Peshawar, and Dean's Hotel in particular every night, walking on the carpet on my bedroom floor. A carpet seller, Rahim Khan, had a small shop near the entrance to the hotel. After an initial look at some woven carpets in 1971 and conversation with Rahim, I liked him. During every stay at Dean's we would sit in his shop, drink green tea, and I could discreetly admire his technique of selling carpets to foreigners. He was not dishonest, just creative with his sales talk. Indirectly and sometimes more directly he taught me about carpet origins and qualities. It was a delight, on returning in 1977, to find he was still there. Over endless cups of green tea we continued to solve the world's problems at each visit to Dean's. Then, before finally leaving, I went reluctantly to say goodbye, knowing we would not see each other again. He knew by then my attraction to the carpets but also knew that good quality ones were beyond my capacity to buy. Inviting me to come to his house and see some of his best carpets, he closed the shop and off we went.

I will never see carpets like these again; old and rare, all the finest quality. As we were about to leave, he insisted I choose one; after me saying I could not afford to buy any of them. After I chose one—or perhaps it chose me—he told me I could buy it for the price he paid: a hundred US dollars. After some reverse haggling, me saying I could not rob him and he saying he would be delighted if I did, I took it. It has since then been my favourite possession, treasured every day. If it was sold now it would bring a handsome pile of cash but it's not for sale. Rahim knew intuitively that would be so, that it would always have value beyond money.

The carpet was woven in Bokhara, perhaps in the late 1800s. It is worn overall, and frayed at one end; it has been used and loved for well over a hundred years. First impression is its overall deep red colour, and concentric rectangles of pattern. The central area has *guls* (flowers) in dark grey, and surrounding rectangles contain patterns in a slightly redder red and an olivey colour. What I like most is the changes in colour at one end. About a quarter of it has entirely different colours. Did the original materials run out before it was finished? Was the maker following an old Islamic craft tradition that said Allah is perfect, man is not—so the products of man must contain imperfections? The questions intrigue me; the answers are irrelevant.

* * *

The name of the famous old hotel in Lahore, Faletti's, always seemed to me suggestive of something slightly naughty. I stayed there alone once. The Shalimar Room belly dancing show prompted imagining that, after not having had any female company for months, there might be some. The poster was suggestive. Alas, the dancing itself was subdued and there was not a belly to be seen. There were many veils, all rigidly fixed in place. Adding to the disappointment I was the only person in the room apart from a somewhat tuneless band. The best alternative was to go back to my room and read.

Then, like a gift from the heavens, in came some fifty or sixty boisterous young Australian females. A busload of nurses doing the overland from England to Australia. They were all looking for a good time too, and set about having it. They danced, and drank more booze than the Shalimar had sold in six months. My eyes worked overtime but my feet were overwhelmed—where to start? The young ladies seemed entirely unaware of my desirability and happy in their own company. The party subsided, and I finished the night trudging off alone to my room, thinking maybe tomorrow. Next morning their bus had left before I woke up. The feeling of lost opportunity still resonates. Fifty of them.

Living well in the best hotels exaggerated the difference between our riches and the desperate poverty of most people around us. Inevitably that created feelings of guilt, of the sheer unfairness and injustice of it all. It soon became obvious that we could not really do anything about the poverty; the scale was just so enormous. All we could do was to help some individuals. Some of our funds were used for the original purpose—aid. We could employ people and help out some individuals. Only when we got to the far north were we living on the same terms as everyone else. Accommodation was usually minimalist, a small bare room with just a *chapoy,* the woven-mattressed bed, and a few blankets. We did not eat well; money could not buy food where there was none to sell.

* * *

My work soon became routine. Working with an interpreter, I made enough time with each potter to discover how they worked, and photograph them at work, and their surroundings. Their main piece of equipment was usually a simple potter's wheel, built into a pit in the ground. The most common types of pottery were unglazed red earthenware water pots, and cooking pots. Kilns were simple, made of stone or clay, rarely brick. They were fired with grass, straw, wood or cow-dung for fuel. Potters were poor, earning a few dollars a week. A large water pot sixty centimetres (two feet) tall might sell for a few cents and take up to two hours to make.

This varied. Potters in Multan and Hala, in the south of Pakistan, made more sophisticated glazed and decorated ware, and the methods they used were far more complicated. Ultimately all this was recorded in my book *Traditional Pottery Techniques of Pakistan.*

* * *

The two most intriguing and involving cities I have ever lived in are Peshawar in Pakistan, and Jerusalem—at least the old city of Jerusalem, not the modern monstrosity that is being built by Israel, covering all the surrounding hillsides and destroying the wonderful character of the whole area in the process.

Peshawar has long been a trading centre, multi-ethnic and multi-lingual, where Tajiks, Uzbeks, Afridis, Waziris, Ghilzais, Chitralis, Hunzacotes and others mingled. It is the oldest city in Pakistan and one of the oldest in South Asia. It provides access to the northern regions of Pakistan and to Afghanistan via the nearby Khyber Pass. It was an important centre on the old Silk Road from China to Europe. I loved this city, its dusty streets, its fierce looking tribesmen and old-style markets.

Unfortunately, Peshawar has changed, and it pains me to think that my romantic experience of it is no longer available. The Russian invasion of neighbouring Afghanistan over a decade from 1979, followed by America's ongoing invasion from 1999, has resulted in a large intake of Afghan refugees. The unrest this has caused combines with ongoing local regional disputes. Regularly the news reports bombings and other terminal kinds of unpleasantness not suitable for tourism.

We had freedom to move around without fears of bombing. When in Peshawar we had to see the nearby Khyber Pass. The road from Peshawar to the Pass is for me one of the world's iconic drives, not to be missed. Don, Deanie and I drove through the rounded hills, up the sinuously winding road to the border with Afghanistan. People who knew the area well warned us to not stop anywhere except at the border itself. A few days earlier a Canadian couple coming in from Afghanistan had stopped. They climbed a low rise to take a tourist photo looking down the winding road to the plains below. They were found with their throats cut, possessions and money gone.

Moving from the mediaeval to the modern, I saw U2 aircraft taking off from Peshawar's military airbase, not far out of the city. This was the take off point for the type of spy plane used by the Americans to fly over Russia at heights approaching 70,000 feet, well over 21,000 metres. The best known of these was the one flown by Francis Gary Powers in 1960, shot down over Russia followed by his capture, with wide publicity. The U2 looked more like a glider than a regular aircraft, with its extremely wide wingspan and drooping wings supported at their end by small wheels on thin struts. Like many a jet of the period it's take off was noisy and smoky. The gear supporting the wings dropped away as it gained speed. It flew away with a deep rumble, aimed over Russia to the north. Some sources suggest that these U2 flights finished at an earlier date but I saw this in 1971.

* * *

Every man in the region was armed with a rifle of some description, some ancient in design—matchlocks and flintlocks in the remotest areas, more modern weapons in towns. In Peshawar city most males carried a rifle strapped over a shoulder, or an automatic handgun. Tribesmen of the North West Frontier have always been known for their war-like nature. It has been said that if they do not have a common enemy to fight against (recently including the British, Russians and Americans) they will quite happily set upon each other. To do so they need weapons. A traditional source of weaponry is the village of Darra Adam Khel, about a 40-minute drive from Peshawar, in tribal territory outside the control of central government.

A single street runs through a narrow defile between steep hillsides. Along this street men manufactured weapons of all kinds, whatever they could make from basic materials. It was possible to purchase a revolver, a rifle, a machine gun, even modern weapons such as a grenade launcher.

Each was made with traditional techniques passed on through generations of craftsmen, using simple old-fashioned hand tools such as hand driven lathes, and hand-held files. They salvaged mostly high-quality metal to produce sophisticated accurate copies of modern weapons from around the world. What was formerly the axle from a truck became the barrel of a Kalashnikov. The customer could test any weapon they chose by firing at targets placed high up the hillsides, indicated by small puffs of dust. The valley echoed to the constant sounds of the guns.

Given that we would be travelling in some remote areas where guns were universal the question arose as to whether we should be armed with at least a pistol. My decision was simple. No guns, and don't carry any money when out in villages, or at least an absolute minimum. That money decision also made sense because in the most remote areas there was nothing to buy; and no money meant nothing to steal.

* * *

One of the major industries around Peshawar was smuggling, bringing in goods from China, Japan and Europe via Afghanistan. The Karkhano Market near Peshawar was the main receiving centre. It was in the tribal area so the central government could do little to prevent the smuggling. Tribesmen such as the Afridis involved in the trade were not averse to shooting anyone who attempted to intervene, and national agencies such as police and customs had no jurisdiction in the tribal areas.

Almost anything available in a Western shopping mall could be acquired in this small centre, for a reasonable price. Local production, including opium, hashish and guns was also freely available. A small donation of baksheesh to the Pakistan Customs people eased the passage of any illegal goods back into Peshawar. Once we stopped at the customs post between tribal territory and Pakistan proper. The officer in charge came out from his box, putting on his cap, and asked us if we had anything to declare. We said we had just bought a few items including some cartons of Western cigarettes as gifts for friends. '*And am I not one of your friends?*' he asked. We agreed that he was, and made him a gift of a carton of American cigarettes, upon which he waved us through with a smile. Returning to Peshawar after another visit to Karkhano the customs man of the day said: '*It is illegal to import foreign currency at this post.*

It is illegal to import drugs such as hashish. Are you carrying any foreign currency, or drugs?' We said no. He went back to his post, removed his cap, came back and asked: *'You want to change money? Would you like to buy hashish?'*

* * *

Waziristan is the barren southernmost part of the North West frontier. If that is the extent of your knowledge then you know nothing about Waziristan. It is the land of the most fearsome, and most feared, warriors of the Frontier. Where a Waziri or a Mahsud walks, others step aside. One Waziri we saw sometimes in the north was always alone. A tall man, he was made taller by his distinctive green turban. He was a jewellery buyer, travelling widely, purchasing old gold and silver jewellery as he went. He walked from village to village with the easy loping stride of a strong confident man. The bag of riches slung on his back normally would have made him a target for robbery, probably accompanied by his death, but he was a Waziri: nobody bothered him.

We had hoped to get into Waziristan, specifically to Miran Shah, but that was not permitted by the authorities. The closest we got was Bannu, originally set up by the British as a military base, a walled city where the gates were closed at dusk each day. Local authorities were most reluctant to allow us into the area. One reason for the reluctance was that some foreigners who had gone in unannounced had been kidnapped and held for ransom, and some had been killed when ransom was not forthcoming. After much negotiation, attempting to subvert intractable bureaucracy by invoking our semi-diplomatic status, we were allowed in.

Accompanied by a military escort, our trusty Wagoneer flanked by a couple of jeeps before and aft carrying soldiers with machine guns, we travelled the Salt Road from Kohat to Bannu. This road, named after salt mines in the area, constantly winds between ridges making it an ideal place for tribal ambushes. Not long before, the central government had set up police posts along the road, within sight of each other, to overcome what they described as banditry. Each post was a small round structure with a roof to keep off the sun as the policeman stood inside. On the morning of the first day of manning the posts, a van travelled the twists and turns and dropped off police at each. When the van returned that afternoon each

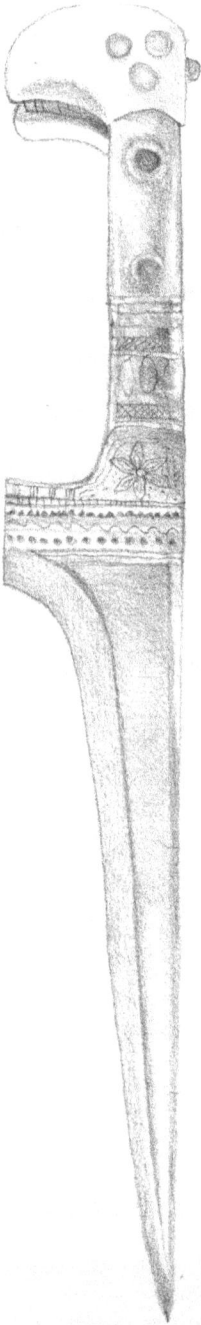

policeman was found dead, their throat cut. The police posts remained as empty memorials to central government impotence at controlling the tribesmen.

Our first appointment in Bannu was with the local administrator. We sat at a table on a nicely trimmed lawn and had tea and were offered hashish, the equivalent of a western bureaucrat offering alcohol. After the niceties he presented us with an automatic pistol, so we could have some practice shooting at a target set up by an assistant. Everyone acted as though this was perfectly normal diplomacy.

I have a knife from Bannu, a beautiful object with a distinctly pointed damascene steel blade and a beautifully engraved metal handle mounted with grips made from bone and antler. One piece of bone has a chip missing, apparently the result of a being hit hard with something. I had noticed that each tribesman carried one of these, and I asked a local assistant we had employed if it would be possible to buy one. He said he would find one for me, and returned later that day with the one I now have; and a request for two hundred rupees. As we were leaving someone else pointed out to me that no tribesman would ever give up their knife, and most definitely none would ever sell this symbol of their identity. There was only one way to obtain one; to remove it from their dead body. Mine had been obtained at more cost than I knew.

* * *

From Karachi almost to Peshawar the Trunk Road travels through the plains of Sindh and Punjab. North of Peshawar, after passing Attock on the Indus River and the city of Nowshera, the road becomes increasingly winding. We travelled upwards into hills that become mountains then finally the extreme heights of the far north, the Hindu Kush and the Karakorum, the western extension of the Himalaya. We worked in many of these mountainous regions including the Swat Valley, Dir and Chitral, Gilgit and Hunza and Yasin.

The Swat Valley has been described as the Switzerland of the north, obviously for its natural beauty rather than its wealth. The main centres, Saidu Sharif and Mingora are some 3 hours by road from Peshawar via the Malakand Pass, made famous by Winston Churchill, then a second lieutenant in the British Army. His first published book was *The Story of the Malakand Field Force: An Episode of Frontier War.* He described the battles in 1897 between the British and the local Mohmands and other hill tribes. Coincidentally 1897 is said to be (various dates have been given) the birth year of the man with that wonderful name, the Faqir of Ipi, who through the early 1900s led the Waziristan resistance against the British, with the ultimately failed aim of establishing Pashtunistan, a new state for the Pashto speaking people, the Pathans.

The British were not the first to fight their way up through the Malakand Pass. Perhaps the most famous attacker was Alexander the Great, who led his soldiers against local tribes in the winter of 327/326 BCE. During these battles Alexander was lightly wounded in the shoulder and later more seriously in the ankle. In the same campaign he later was wounded again by an arrow in the chest that almost caused his death; this time in the city of Multan, much further to the south. Alexander no doubt carried some grim memories of the region that is now Pakistan.

Our passage through the pass was easier than Alexander's and Churchill's. Not a single shot was fired in our direction. We passed through cuttings of a deeply beautiful green rock, and jungle part hidden in mist and fog, winding upwards all the way to where the old Malakand Fort guards the road at the top of the pass. On the other side, at Udegram the remains of Buddhist stupas mark Gandhara, a region that was a centre of Buddhist practice in the past. In valleys along the way vast fields of poppies grew, supplying the opium, and ultimately the Western heroin, trade. Their beauty belied their menace. I was drop-jawed by the unexpected beauty on that first trip into the mountains, not realising how much more there was to come in what must be one of the world's scenically most striking and beautiful regions.

This was reflected in the exquisite beauty of many crafts in Swat such as embroidery and other textiles, jewellery, and pottery, some of the most beautiful objects ever made. *The Arts and Crafts of the Swat Valley*, by Johannes Kalter, provides a fine record.[2] Carved wooden furniture and carved wooden doors and house entrances are the most spectacular in the whole of Pakistan. Western dealers in ethnic crafts and antiques have been aware of this and much of the cultural heritage is being stripped away, exchanged for rupees. When they are spent nothing will be left.

In a small way I contributed to the cultural pilfering. At one place where we walked on our way to a weaving workshop, the banks of the Swat River were eroding away. Floodwaters had exposed new soil on the top of the one bank. The word was that locals were finding ancient artefacts here. Having a good look around led to me finding a piece of pottery part protruding from the soil. Rescued and gently cleaned, it was whole, in the form of a pigeon. It was some years later that I realised it was a child's toy, a rattle—the hollow form contained something that makes it rattle when it is shaken. What child played with it? Like various old things in my home, it's not something I own; it's something I am taking care of until it moves on to the next carer.

* * *

The next stop was the valley of Dir. In the past it was like many of the small states in the north, independent; but it was assimilated into Pakistan in 1969, not long before our visit. Now it is dangerous due to Taliban activity, with bedraggled refugees moving down from nearby Afghanistan and weapons and fierce-faced fighters moving up. When we were there it was not only beautiful but also peaceful. It was spring, the snow had melted in the lower areas and the mulberry and willow trees were in full bloom, and crops were sprouting. Everywhere in the valleys water ran with rippling trebles, in small streams or in man-made channels. All around the valley rich growth contrasted with the mountainsides' dry dusty high desert. Further in the background higher peaks were snow covered.

The first potter I visited was Khan Zada, the blind potter of Dir, a man in his early seventies. Like other potters in the mountains his pot-making was limited to spring and summer; colder weather was not suited to either man or clay. He made pots by first throwing a thick form on

a wheel sunk in a pit, the wheel set in motion by kicking on top of a large flywheel near the bottom of the pit. After some drying this form was thinned to shape by beating with a wooden paddle on the outside, against a rounded terracotta 'anvil' held on the inside. The result was a most elegant and refined finished form. A teapot in my collection is an excellent example of his work. I so admired his pots that my later book on pottery for archaeologists was dedicated to him.

He worked by feel, aided by long experience. This was most impressive when he was stacking his work for firing, in a kind of open pit. The pots were stacked in layers interspersed with the fuel, dried donkey dung, between. Khan Zada managed to achieve this while occasionally standing on pots already set, a feat of skill that few others would ever achieve.

* * *

From Dir we travelled the road over the 3120 metre (10,000 feet plus) Lowari Pass to Chitral. The road was totally closed by snow in winter and only passable to vehicles between June and October. The road had a fearsome reputation for danger. It's narrow, not much wider than a vehicle, terrifyingly narrow for buses and trucks. It has endless hairpin turns, many requiring backing and filling several times to negotiate. Off the sides steep drops disappear into frighteningly deep valleys below. A recently constructed tunnel now replaces some of the worst parts.

Instead of using our Jeep Wagoneer, a wide vehicle for such a narrow road, we hired smaller Jeeps driven by locals who knew the road well. Don, Deanie Charles and I somehow managed to fit ourselves in, cramped between our considerable supplies of equipment and luggage. We crossed as early as possible after the road opened, but some winter snow still lingered. We had many stops and dismounts, to lighten the load over dangerous passages and incidentally to be a spectator rather than a participant if the Jeep did go over the side. We also helped push the Jeeps through wet and muddy passages.

At one point an avalanche had crossed the road during the winter. Seventeen people walking there had been swept away. The snow was thawing as we passed, and their bodies were appearing, partly exposed, partly buried. Further along we passed several groups of Van Gujjars, the Himalayan gypsies moving over the pass to higher country, seeking feed for their cattle and, I suspect, also seeking the exhilarating beauty of the high reaches. Colourfully dressed women with blues, reds, and purples contrasted with more sombrely attired men in browns and greys. Horses carried heavy packs. Women also carried heavy packs as well as small children. Men stayed close with their animals. We exchanged large smiles as we passed.

Chitral valley is located in serious mountain country. The highest in the area, Tirich Mir (7700 metres, about 25,250 feet) is visible from most parts of the valley. It is the highest mountain in the Hindu Kush, and the world's highest mountain outside of the Himalaya, and the Karakorum. Abdul Samad, our guide and interpreter (*Yes sir, I speak nine languages and a little English*) told me he had been a porter on a climbing expedition on Tirich Mir when he was young but got altitude sickness around nineteen or twenty thousand feet and could not continue.

The mountainous nature is stark from the air, as we saw another time when the pass was closed by rockfalls and we had to fly into Chitral. Our aircraft, a Fokker Friendship, was designed to carry around thirty passengers, but because of the altitude of Chitral Airport only about ten or twelve were allowed on board. Flying over the mountains and down onto the airstrip was not possible, the angles were far too steep. The only way in was by flying inside the deep valleys. First, the flight from Peshawar reached the point where the Indus River emerges from the mountains to meet the plains. The pilot would then see if there was any fog in the valley or if it appeared clear. Any sign of fog meant the flight was aborted and returned to Peshawar. Flying by instruments was impossible, lives depended on the pilot seeing where he was going.

If it was clear ahead the aircraft flew into the valley. Then everything, in the best Muslim tradition, was predestined. There was no space to turn around, no way back, and no way to climb over the high mountains to the sides. It was one way only, and in some places that way was very narrow indeed, as the aircraft wings seemingly brushed the mountainsides, especially when we had turned into the narrow valley of the Chitral River, an Indus tributary.

Landing at Chitral was spectacular. The aircraft turned sharply, leaning at an extreme angle, and then seemed to crash onto a narrow and very short runway. At the other end was a cliff face, very close. Full reversed propellers, screaming engines and full brakes accompanied by a mad flurry of dust and small stones allowed a stop just short of the apparent crash into the cliff. The take-off later was equally dramatic. Backed up as close as possible to the cliff, when it moved the aircraft roared at full engine speed along the strip until it dropped off the end into the valley below, turning steeply at the same time.

Chitral is the furthest north-western area of Pakistan. It seemed peaceful when we were there but has a long history of invasions and murderous feuds between tribes. The British invaded in the late 1800s to keep out the Russians, who in turn invaded nearby Afghanistan through the 1980s. Fighters and weapons crossed freely in and out of Chitral. This scenario continued when later the Americans invaded Afghanistan after the Twin Towers event in New York. Mule trains regularly crossed passes into Nuristan, in Afghanistan, carrying weapons from many sources. Despite many invasions nobody has ever defeated the locals; they repulse all comers.

The main town of Chitral is named Chitral. Situated at the base of Tirich Mir, it was until 1969, just before we arrived, the capital of the princely state of Chitral, ruled by the Mehtar, Saif-ul-Mulk Nasir. The Mehtar's fortunes had declined and he was selling off some of his valuables, including beautiful old carpets, priced far beyond my means. My friend Rahim the carpet seller at Dean's Hotel in Peshawar had taught me about quality so I knew these were superb. I heard later some had been purchased by the Victoria and Albert Museum in London. The Mehtar was also selling silver jewellery. I bought two heavy silver arm bracelets, suitable for a princess. She would have to be a young princess; the inside diameter is quite tiny.

In the 1970s what was known as the hippie trail passed though Chitral. It became a significant stopover for the young adventurous travellers with minimal means, and little to carry; unlike travel now by the middle classes on well organised comfortable trips, booked online, to remote places. Adventurers from Europe headed south to India and perhaps Australia; and from Australia headed north into Afghanistan and ultimately Europe and England. They lingered along the way, enjoying the freely available hashish. Most of these travellers I saw seemed in no hurry to go anywhere. Lost in their thoughts, with vacant eyes and distant stares, they sat on verandas, facing the high peaks. And when the hashish munchies hit, the smoker could eat a curry with tomatoes, a regional specialty with potatoes instead of rice, the staple on the plains.

The local opium trade was entirely out in the open. Crops of opium poppies grew over a wide area, and in the main street of Chitral tea-chests full of raw opium sat waiting for European buyers.

The most remote and distinctive tribal group in Pakistan lived in Kafiristan, between Chitral and the Afghan border in Nuristan (*the Land of Light*). *Kafir* means infidel or non-Muslim; the tribe in Chitral Kafiristan is the Kalash Kafir. The Kalash live in 3 valleys: Bomboret, Rumbur and Birir. They are the last survivors of non-Muslim pagan animists with unique culture and languages. In the North West Frontier about 30 languages are spoken; in Bomboret there were 3 different languages used by three different cultural groups in an area of half a square mile.

Don, Deanie and I walked into Bomboret, the larger and then more accessible of the three Kalash valleys. There were two ways in, each of them with difficulties. One was to follow a river all the way. This was described by locals as the easy way. It was, when walking along the riverbanks. Unfortunately, whenever there was some impassable obstacle on the river bank a log had been placed across the river as a bridge. The snows in the high mountains were melting and the river was furious, roaring through narrow passages and throwing large rocks in the air with the strength of its turbulence. The round logs were impossibly slippery, and falling meant certain drowning. We chose the high path, over the mountainsides. It was narrow, at most half a metre, and in places the vertical drop from the side was hundreds but looked like thousands of feet. I photographed my feet, standing on the edge of the path. The background in the photo is the river way below, a long, long way straight down. We used horses to transport our equipment and I had tried riding for a short while but the swaying motion sitting high above that narrow path was terrifying. If I was going to fall it was going to be my doing, not caused by some semi-tame animal.

We were there at the end of an era. Because the valleys were remote, and visitors rare, the ancient culture was still alive. Traditional clothing was dark; grey and black for the women and generally darker greys and browns for the men. The women's headdresses were decorated with small white cowrie shells, formerly a trade item, highly valued in this remote area so far from the sea. Now a road has been built from Chitral town into each valley and public transport by jeeps takes in many tourists. A Pakistan tourism description of the facilities now includes guesthouses, mobile reception and a Disneyland atmosphere. Online images show the women wearing brightly coloured clothes and I assume all the traditional garb has been sold to tourists, the number of which has increased dramatically.

I worked with one potter in Bomboret, recording his methods of making and firing pots. While there, the funeral of a local man was performed. Over several days, the man's body was laid out on an open bed (*chapoy*) in the middle of the village. Constant drumming and dancing was, at intervals, interrupted by speeches about the man's virtues and achievements in life. Our interpreter pointed out that the achievements were in general, as was the custom, somewhat magnified. There was no burial. The man's body was finally laid out in a special area set aside especially for the purpose, to be consumed by local animals (probably wolves) and birds (probably vultures). We were not allowed into that area and I'm not sure I would have gone there if we were.

Our residence was a rest-house, built for government visitors. It was a solid stone and wood building but small and very basic, consisting of several rooms with beds and little else. Standing on the veranda with Don one night, hands behind our backs, listening to the funeral drums and watching the dancing, I was able to fulfil a childhood dream prompted by reading many adventure and travel books. I turned to Don and said: '*The natives are restless tonight, Godden*'.

* * *

In 1977, Abdul Samad had been employed as a guide and interpreter but had become a valued friend. We had shared adventures and in some cases misadventures. A short sturdy man in his fifties, skin the colour of a deeply tanned white man, his hair was beginning to grey. He was barrel chested, with short legs and a steady walking pace that could be maintained all day, like most men of the mountains. At the end of our stay, Brenda and I were extremely happy to accept his invitation to have a few weeks with him at home in Drosh, one of Chitral's significant towns. The dirt main street running between wooden buildings reminded me of

Tony Hanning

the movie version of a wild west town.

Samad went out of his way to entertain, at night bringing in local musicians and singers; I still have recordings on tape. In the glow of soft lantern light, each piece of ritualised music started off slowly and built up to a climax, backed by a simple type of mountain sitar, a hand pumped harmonium and a pair of drums *(tabla),* all played by musicians sitting cross legged on the floor. We were treated with the greatest hospitality. I wondered how hospitable Australians would be to my friend Samad.

By day we went on trips to beautiful places like the village of Madaglasht, further up in the mountains. By a fortunate coincidence there we saw, heard and felt a massive avalanche across the valley a few kilometres away, with large amounts of snow falling thousands of feet down an almost vertical mountainside. Swirls of airborne snow reached us all that distance away. The noise was like muted thunder.

Brenda had been trained as an anthropologist and stayed with the women and girls through the day, learning the Khowar language. One day I was given the rare privilege of meeting the women. In that deeply Muslim household, the women were normally kept well away from any visiting man.

One of my clearest memories of Drosh is waking up one night in our guest room, next to the main road through the town. I looked out the window, an open space with no glass, to see right there almost in touching distance, a pack of wolves. I had been told nobody went out at night because of the danger of attack. My insides went cold as I looked at them. There they were, right there, much larger than German Shepherds, with lean muscled bodies and hungry faces looking all around, leaving no doubt they were vicious predators.

* * *

Baltistan is the region where three mountain ranges meet: the Hindu Kush, the Karakorum and the Himalaya. Nanga Parbat on the western end of the Himalaya is the world's ninth highest mountain. Gilgit, in Baltistan, is on the ancient Silk Road route from Xinjiang in China into India. The modern sealed Karakorum Highway completed in 1978 follows the path of the old Silk Road, at one point through Abbotabad where Osama Bin Laden was killed, to Xinjiang. Near the Chinese border at the Khunjerab

Pass it is one of the world's highest paved roads, at around 4700 metres or 15,500 feet. This must be one of the world's great road trips for anyone serious about driving.

What all that meant in 1971 was that Don, Deanie and I and our 'Pakistani liaison' man, Azizullah Khan Khalil, were getting into some serious mountain country. The way in was serious too. Heading for Gilgit town in Baltistan, we travelled the Karakorum Highway, then a completely new road, only opened a few months before. We were told before leaving that we were the first foreigners to drive along it. Whether this was a privilege or not remained to be seen. We were told that the road, unsealed all the way, was prone to landslides, and to areas of the edge falling away. Of all the trucks that had started the journey in the previous month ten had never been seen again. It was assumed that they had fallen and were lost in the river below.

It was unquestionably the drive of my life. The narrow road was open one way for 24 hours, and then the other way for 24 hours because passing a vehicle heading in the opposite direction was impossible in most areas. If any vehicle had not completed the journey in the allotted time it had to find one of the rare areas where it was possible to stop, overlooking a precipice, and wait there for a day.

Delays along the way took up precious time. One, waiting for a landslide of rocks to be cleared, took hours. This meant that the old Jeep Wagoneer had to be pushed hard to make it in the time we had. Driving after midnight with everyone asleep I slid around corners and took risks that might frighten me now. I clearly remember the look of horror on the face of Khalil, riding with me in the front while the others slept in the back. I glanced at him and saw that he had woken up and was staring wide eyed, his mouth slightly open, at the terrain rushing past.

Before dark we could see small villages and terraced fields high on the mountainsides. At one point, climbing the wet slippery road, we came to a checkpoint. To the east of Gilgit the Line of Control divides Pakistani territory from the area of Kashmir, disputed between India and Pakistan. Military activity was evident as we approached Gilgit. The road was controlled by the Pakistani military. We frequently passed their vehicles, Chinese-made trucks and bulldozers and Russian jeeps.

Although it had been opened for traffic, the Karakorum road was still in parts under construction, and here and there closed for blasting away rock, or by landslides, so we were lucky to get through. Even in the good parts the road was not much wider than our vehicle. In parts where the road climbed high above the Indus River, and later the Gilgit River, there was a drop of 600 metres (2000 feet) almost straight down into the water. Loose rock hung overhead where the road had been blasted out of the vertical mountainside leaving some cuttings 150 metres (500 feet) deep. We were only hit once by a small rock, but we did have several punctures due to the sharp rocks. I have never before or after experienced anything like it.

We did stop sometimes; once to see ancient petroglyphs at the appropriately named Chilas, images of goats pecked into the stone. We stopped for food at several villages; sometimes getting the hottest curry I've ever tasted, or a meal consisting of a spoonful of spinach, a curried potato and a piece of *chapati*, Pakistani bread.

When we finally reached Gilgit we discovered the last obstacle, the Danyore suspension bridge: 155 metres (510 feet) long and less than 2.5 metres (8 feet) wide, crossing the Hunza River. Worse, to get onto it we had to negotiate a tunnel with a bend in the middle, with almost no room for manoeuvre, narrower than the narrowest turn in any parking station.

The bridge used steel cables suspended over the gorge, to hold up wooden slats. The drive across the bridge was the final terrifying stomach-churning prospect. It swung in the slightest breeze. We unloaded everything we could, to be carried across later on small jeeps. I was nominated the driver. If I made it the others would walk across. *If* seemed like a very large word, but I made it. I am not surprised to see that in 2013 this old bridge was replaced by a two-way concrete bridge. Considering the span, and the depths below it, it must be a supremely impressive bridge. A Google search shows various bridges over the Gilgit River; each is described as terrifying.

Gilgit town is a military centre. We woke each morning to the sound of a machine gun close by, hammering away at target practice. There were many soldiers but no potters that I could locate so it was a working break for me. I had a relaxing job as photographer, helping the others looking at different crafts.

It soon became apparent that all the mountain roads in Baltistan were the stuff of epic. They varied from terrifying to near-suicidal, narrow and winding around tight corners, with constant rockfalls and vertical drops into eternity. Arriving anywhere felt like survival. We survived the 120-kilometre drive from Gilgit via Gupis to the valley of Yasin. Many mountain valleys across the Himalaya and Karakorum have been identified as the original Shangri-la but I felt sure as we entered Yasin that they were all wrong. This was it, and we were in it. A village of stone-walled, mud plastered houses at around 2500 metres (8000 feet) sat in the valley among mountains rising over 6000 metres above, with permanent snow over 5000 metres. Everywhere was green. The first impression was beauty and peacefulness among the cultivated fields and mulberry trees.

It was not always so. Throughout these mountains fighting has been a way of life, and every man had a weapon. Don Godden was interested in the ancient matchlock rifles with Damascene steel barrels. He needed to collect some, to study how they were made. We met Mahbat Shah, who made black gunpowder for these rifles using saltpetre, charcoal and sulphur. The simplicity of his methods was perfectly appropriate to this remote valley, and it was easy to see that the same methods had been used hundreds of years ago. Gunpowder was invented not far away, in 9th century China, so its secrets would have travelled back down the Silk Route not long after that. Mahbat Shah showed us how it was done, mixing the ingredients in a stone mortar with a wooden pestle to avoid the danger of sparks, well away from his house just in case.

While we were watched him work, a woman came to us, head down, her head scarf almost covering a very small baby she was carrying. One look and one touch told the story—the child was seriously ill, with a high fever. The woman had heard that foreigners were around and assumed we had medical knowledge, maybe suitable drugs. While she was asking me for help, and her plea was translated, the baby died. Right there. We did have antibiotics but with such a small child a dose of adult drug may have done harm anyway. No matter—all everyone could do was stand in silence as the woman took the baby away. I just stood there, empty, useless.

From Gilgit, we travelled further up the Karakorum highway, to the valleys of Nagar and Hunza, on the Hunza River. Along the way are some of the highest mountains and the best-known glaciers in the Karakorum. In Pakistan there are 108 peaks above 7000 metres (about 23,000 feet) and as many again between 7000 metres and 6000 metres (about 20,000 feet). There are an unknown number of peaks above 5000 metres (about 16,500 feet). Most of the highest in Pakistan are in this Baltistan/Gilgit region.

It's wild country. The tallest mountains reach so far up into the sky that it's hard to believe what you're seeing. They are of the sky, not of the earth. To imagine looking at the top of a high one, look up at contrails where domestic jets fly. Those grand peaks have their own version of contrails, spindrift caused by the high winds blowing snow crystals into the icy heights.

Hunza has been described by the British explorer/adventurer Eric Shipton as 'the ultimate expression of mountain grandeur'. From the lawn of the rest house in Hunza you could see 15 peaks each above 20,000 feet, about 6000 metres; including the Trango Towers, rocks with some of the highest vertical surfaces on Earth. One of them is so steep that snow just falls off it, leaving a giant black needle piercing the sky.

For about sixty kilometres, the road from Gilgit to Hunza passes around the base of Rakaposhi, nearly 8000 metres (26,000 feet) at the peak. There's no way to convey how big that is. On its sides are sheer cliffs over 3000 metres (10,000 feet) high. Glaciers run down the sides to end in the river. The glittering whiteness of snow and ice in them was spoiled, in my eyes, by mud churned in by their passing, leaving them a dirty brown. In the middle of summer with the snow melting the rivers were just boiling torrents of raging mud.

Hunza was a princely state until 1974. We tried to see the ruler, the Mir of Hunza at his palace at Baltit (Karimabad) but he had gone to Europe. His brother entertained, and showed us around his palace, a wonderful structure jutting out over the river, overlooking a magnificent mountain view. He had a collection of Japanese and Chinese porcelain and his Chinese carpets were beautiful. He also had the most elaborate old matchlock rifle possible. The barrel was completely covered with intricate engraving, and both the barrel and stock inlaid everywhere with silver and gold.

* * *

Travelling closely with others can lead to the expedition blues. In 1971 mine revolved around Charles Walton. His important contribution was wonderful photography. But he was a wealthy man, accustomed to privilege. I felt strongly that we were all equal. We often had to share transport or accommodation. Charles saw the best seat in the jeep as his, or the most comfortable bed; the uncomfortable bed out on the veranda was mine. I believed we should take the discomforts in turn. Resentments built up, both ways.

Charles was alcoholic. In Pakistan, where alcohol is *haram* (forbidden) that was a problem for him, especially in the remote areas where it was not available. I still remember Charles each morning at breakfast with his cup of tea, the cup trembling against the saucer held in the other hand, before he had his first drink of the day.

My worst moment, one for which I still feel a slight sense of shame (but only slight), happened in the remote valley of Yasin, in our small 'rest house'. I was feeling seriously annoyed by something Charles had done. He had the misfortune to run out of whisky. I sat the one unopened bottle I had left out on the mantle-piece; and left it there for a day so he would suffer. He could not stop watching it, struggling between behaving like a gentleman towards someone else's property, and getting that whisky into him. When I finally offered him a drink, he took half the bottle in a few minutes. Towards the end of our journey, knowing him better, I felt more sympathy for him than antipathy. His wealth was one source of his constant angst. My lack of wealth felt like a blessing from some wise and benevolent god.

* * *

We tired of the high altitudes, often above 3000 metres, wishing for easier breathing and something to eat other than goat curry and potatoes. I dreamed—literally, while sleeping—of T-bone steak and vegetables with gravy. Relief accompanied our decision that the trip in along the

Karakorum Highway would become our only one ever. We would fly out from Gilgit to Islamabad/Rawalpindi, and hire someone to drive the Wagoneer back to Peshawar.

This is one of the world's spectacular flights, a window seat essential. Soon after takeoff Nanga Parbat was clearly visible. This mountain is regarded by mountaineers as one of the world's most difficult climbs. For them it is distinguished by the Rupal Face, said to be the world's highest exposed mountain face, 4600 metres (15,090 feet) clear of its base below. Almost a quarter of mountaineers who have attempted the summit have died. Looking back towards Hunza you could see high mountains seemingly stretching away forever.

For most of the flight nothing but close-by rock was visible on either side as we flew through narrow valleys. Later, far away on the other side of the aircraft as it climbed above the terrain I saw K2, earth's second highest mountain, standing out like some giant pyramid thousands of metres above the Western Tibetan plateau, with nothing nearby. It is known locally by the much more romantic name of Masherbrum. The exposure of this mountain to vicious weather has made it one of the most difficult for mountaineers. Like Nanga Parbat, for every four who reach the summit one dies. By comparison guided tours up Mount Everest seem almost simple.

* * *

Planning for the trip in Australia before we left, I had considered the medical implications of travelling in these remote areas where self-reliance was critical. I had a doctor prescribe a range of drugs before leaving; antibiotics, anti-diarrhoeal medication and others. In the mountains a broken leg could involve days to get help; urgent surgery at least a week. Few doctors covered vast areas where travel was difficult and dangerous. Dispensers were more common. These were people not necessarily having any formal qualifications, but with some knowledge of drugs and some supplies. They could diagnose the problem and dispense the cure with varying effectiveness.

I began to better understand the origins of the Islamic belief in predestination, in the fates: *'iinaha maktuba', it is written.* It will come to pass. A momentary lapse, a centimetre either way, a burst of gunfire or a contagious disease all determine who lives and who dies in these mountains, and there is little chance of human intervention preventing that fate. Acceptance of the predestination of events would ease the pain of losing someone close, knowing that there was nothing any human could do to change the result. If it is not your time you will survive; if it is you can do nothing. I took in, and still have, some of this belief. This new acceptance came from some kind of Islamic osmosis, absorbing everyday attitudes about death and the nature of existence. If it's your day you will go; if not, no danger or threat matters. Everything can be viewed with the greatest equanimity because you will live for another day.

This has no religious references; atheists like me do not need religious references. It simply helps to take a positive confident approach to the future rather than be hobbled by negative thoughts. It definitely helped while travelling in those mountains. I would sometimes wake in the morning and my first thought was *today might be the day I die; maybe today the roads or the rogues will get me*. Having little control over that allowed the freedom to go ahead and do whatever was intended.

I met a doctor in Peshawar who had worked among tribesmen. He said the most radical medical intervention possible would be to provide every household with soap. This simple hygiene would help prevent many common infections which untreated can mean death. In its absence the smell of the mountain people is something I can recreate with ease: the smell of wood smoke, permeating the walls, the furniture, clothing, even human skin, becoming magnified over many months inside over harsh winters. Heating and cooking fires inside the dimly lit house blended with an underlay of human sweat common to those who cannot wash. The smell is distinctly different from the smell of the average Western homeless street dweller; that is simply an accumulation of human odours, without the woodsmoke.

I had a long discussion with that doctor about drugs—the kind known as recreational drugs. He recommended heroin as one of the 'safe' drugs; not the street variety which could include any impurity used to cut it, but the pure variety. He said he had used it over a period and could take it or leave it, that only those with psychological problems might become addicted. I was not tempted to test his theories, remembering Paul Briggs, Ivan McMeekin's assistant, withering away and dying from his addiction.

I did however try hashish, and opium. I suspect no traveller at that time, the early 1970s, the time of the 'hippy trail', passed through without trying at least one of the available drugs. Hashish was everywhere, especially in the mountains, and in an Islamic country where the ban on alcohol was almost universally observed, it was the traditional drug. Sometimes in the mountains, meeting with local government officials, sipping tea brought by uniformed servants, we were offered hashish. I saw the irony of this, compared to the situation at home where the officials would be arresting me for using it and probably sending me off to jail.

My experience was that I could take it or leave it. The same, oddly enough, applied to opium. It was common, almost universal in some areas. In the Swat valley mile after mile of opium poppy coloured the valleys below the dull earthy hills. In Chitral town, close to the Afghan border, tea chests of raw opium on sale sat in open display in the street. I had no use for this. But I did have a supply given to me by a Canadian diplomat who had been posted home. The Canadian government issued opium as a medicinal grade liquid intended for use as a muscle relaxant when suffering from dysentery. He offered it to me on the basis he could not take it back into Canada. It was, as he said, a fine diversion. And as my doctor friend had said about heroin in pure grades, it was not addictive. After my supply finished, I felt no further need for it; it was about as painful as giving up eating bananas.

* * *

Multan is one of the world's oldest cities, beginning during the Indus Valley civilisation some four or five thousand years ago. The complex tangle of ancient streets makes Multan one of the most difficult places to navigate I have ever encountered. In summer, it is a viciously hot dry place, surrounded by desert. My interest in Multan involved *kashi*, the Multan Blue pottery, one of the best-known pottery styles in Pakistan, available through shops in many centres. The most prominent use of the blue pottery is in tiles. These can be seen on many beautiful mosques and tombs around the city and elsewhere in Pakistan. Especially in the drier areas of the country the blue and turquoise decorated tiles stand out in stunning contrast to the dry dull brown desert colours.

Multan *kashi* has a white slip and clear glaze, with cobalt blue and turquoise copper coloured decoration. This ware is based on ancient technologies going back to the origins of glass making in Mesopotamia. This early glass was made by combining ash from burning salt bushes that grow in the desert, with silica from various sources. When heated until it melts, it becomes glass. Some Islamic alkaline glazes were also made from similar mixtures. Multan pottery allowed me to study this most ancient ceramic technology. Because of their significance in the history of technology of both glass and ceramic glazes I needed to go out into the desert and collect samples of these plants for analysis later, in Washington.

* * *

I took the Wagoneer into the Cholistan Desert, travelling with Azizullah Khan Khalil and a local guide. From Bahawalpur, we headed south-east towards the Indian border around 100 kilometres away. I planned to collect samples of the type of desert saltbush burned by the Multan potters to make ash they used in glazes.

The daily top temperature varied from around 38^0C (100^0F) in the cold parts of the plains to around 50^0C (120^0F) in the desert. The average temperature in the Cholistan desert at the height of summer is around 55^0, average indicating that the temperature is often higher. This is the real desert of myth, empty desert, with sand and more sand, sometimes raised into gently rolling dunes rather than massively steep ones. With low tyre pressures to prevent sinking into the sand, the Wagoneer did the trip with no dramas. Had we been forced to stop nobody would pass by; the chance that a nomad might appear on a camel was non-existent. We had no radio or other means of communication. We were totally reliant on the Wagoneer.

I had seen nomads in the harsh Waziristan desert, dressed in loose flowing clothes, covered entirely from head to foot, with only their eyes showing. The reason they dressed that way soon became obvious. As we moved further into the Cholistan the temperature rose to the point where any air movement past skin caused blisters to develop; the skin was literally being slow-cooked, beginning to bubble. Driving with all the windows closed, the temperature in the vehicle, which was not air conditioned, was almost unbearable. After an hour, perhaps an hour and a half, we found some plants that looked like they might be the ones, low saltbush. I took some time collecting samples, bagging and labelling them.

While I was doing that, I heard a piercing shriek from the east, unlike anything I had ever heard before. Something was approaching, moving extremely fast. Then in the sand maybe a kilometre away there was an eruption of sand into the air accompanied by a loud explosion. It took a while to work out it had been an artillery shell. Then another came, maybe 100 metres closer. Followed by more, one each minute or so, each a hundred metres closer again. My ability with arithmetic has always been a bit rough but a quick calculation told me that we had about seven minutes to get the hell out of there—or have an artillery shell explode right on top of us. We were well away by the time seven minutes had elapsed. The Indian artillery-wallahs on the other side of the border were having a bit of a practice run for the war that was coming with Pakistan. Poor old Khalil was probably silently wishing he had never seen us mad Westerners.

That same saltbush gave me more trouble later in Israel. Travelling along a road in the Jordan Valley mostly used by Israeli military vehicles I saw some similar saltbush in the near distance, maybe fifty metres off the roadside. I stopped and walked over to collect some samples. While I was pulling up some bushes an Israeli military jeep stopped and the driver yelled something at me. I ignored him for a while. I was never in a mood to respond to Israelis yelling at me. He then tried English and the word 'mines' was very distinct. I was in the middle of a minefield. I am not using the cliché expression often used to describe a difficult situation. I was in an actual minefield; where things blow up when you walk on them and you become dead or maimed. I have never so carefully trod in my previous footsteps, to get out of there. There were actually signs in Hebrew, Arabic and English along the roadside warning about mines when I looked later. I had stopped in between without registering them.

* * *

Going back to the Cholistan: clearly the rumours were correct and India and Pakistan were shaping up to fight a war. My little episode in the desert was part of the preliminaries. The rhetoric was getting louder. The *Pakistani Times* carried patriotic messages and warnings about the evil neighbour. As we travelled, the increasing traffic of military vehicles was obvious. These were not just Chinese-made trucks and jeeps but tanks and artillery pieces, serious military stuff.

The main source of the war was increasing unrest in what was then East Pakistan, now Bangladesh. In the division of India during the departure of Britain in 1948, Muslims had moved both east and west to form East and West Pakistan. But apart from religion there was no cultural connection between the two Pakistans and increasingly the East wanted independence.

The political reality was shown to us in the full horror by A K Brohi (known to all as AK), at his office in Lahore. Because our trip was facilitated by the US Consulate in Karachi we had some diplomatic privileges, one of which was meeting Pakistani politicians and administrators. Brohi at that time was the minister responsible for censorship in the Pakistan government. An entertaining and interesting man, he told us his political career had alternated between terms in government and spells in jail, depending on who was in power at the time.

Brohi showed us some films that he had banned from circulation. These showed the West Pakistan military operating in the East. Bulldozers had dug trenches, maybe 20 metres wide and up to 200 metres long, and some five metres deep. East Pakistan citizens were lined up along the sides of the trench and machine gunned, and when the trench was full bulldozers then covered the bodies with earth. Estimates now of the number of people killed in this little-known genocide range between two and three million. Along with the Armenian massacres (1914–1923) it is one genocide often forgotten.

India supported Bangladesh in its aspiration for independence, and their war of independence was the source of the India Pakistan war. India was in turn supported by Russia; and Pakistan by what now seems the unlikely combination of China and the United States.

Back in Karachi, a man did the *'mind if I join you?'* approach in the canteen of the US Consulate. Our discussion ended with him asking me if I wanted to join a fishing trip that he and some other foreigners made each weekend. My idea of fishing was walking along small creeks and rivers back in Australia, in the Snowy Mountains; his turned out to be more impressive. It involved a large ship 35 metres long, with a dozen passengers, travelling out 30 kilometres into the Arabian Sea. The sea was glass smooth; the air was staggeringly hot. We caught many fish. Most of them were large by my standards, maybe five or ten kilos each, and I had no idea what kind any of them were. Each had to be hauled six metres up the side of the ship to get them in.

I was distressed that so many people were going hungry and we were going to have far more food than we could possibly use. But when we got back to Karachi the fish, which had been packed in ice, were delivered to a local orphanage for several hundred boys. All of which created the impression in me that was intended: I decided that this was a bunch of good blokes. By this sophisticated devising the man who had invited me became someone I could talk to easily.

Only later, I became aware that he was the local CIA man. He was grooming me to provide information about military movements. I was travelling freely around the country, in an excellent position to observe and pass on information about what I saw and where I saw it. Doing so was my rather innocuous contribution to the CIA. In return he gave me an exact time when the war would start, so we had plenty of warning about when to leave the country. He specified that the serious hostilities would begin at 4am on one specific morning. That later was proved precisely correct: 3 December 1971. We had left for Teheran in early November.

* * *

Exposure to random artillery fire was not the only consequence of the upcoming war for us. Don and I were in Sukkur, one of the oldest towns of the Lower Indus Basin, located on the west bank of the Indus River with its 'twin' town of Rohri on the opposite bank.

An ancient tradition of wooden boat building thrives in Sukkur. The elegantly beautiful wooden vessels, quite distinct from the Arab *dhow*, are mainly intended to ply the Indus rather than the open sea, although the larger ones would be well seaworthy. We had been working around the boat builders, making notes and photographing their work, and the general surroundings. Then, totally unexpectedly, soldiers surrounded us. One who looked officer-like told us in an unmistakable command, clearly not just a request, to go with them. Don was not amused at being ordered around like that and started an angry tirade. He went silent very quickly when another order was issued in Urdu and the soldiers began fixing bayonets. That process makes a metallic noise easily remembered.

We were marched across the Lansdowne Bridge, a 19th century iron structure designed to carry trains and other traffic across the Indus, spanning from Sukkur to Bakhar Island, and to Rohri on the other bank of the Indus. I had, following my daily custom, been indulging in some high-quality NW Frontier hashish. That helped magnify the sound of hobnailed military boots tramping behind us on the iron bridge. At first it felt like something from a movie, but it became vividly real when I hesitated, and was encouraged to step up the pace by a poke in the back with the point of a bayonet. I discovered just how agreeable and accommodating to someone's wishes I could be at that point.

Taken into the 800-year-old Bakhar Fort, still in use by the Pakistani military, we were directed to sit together at one side of a desk in a small room. A powerful light, aimed directly at our faces came on as someone entered the room. He sat on the other side of the table under the glare; we could not see anything of him. No movie could have been set up better. He barked questions at us, based on the assumption that we were spies, working against Pakistan. We finally managed to get him to check with local municipal authorities who knew about our official status, and our purpose in being there. Before releasing us, he explained that our original sin was photographing the fort, which was a military installation. Photographing any military installation was punishable by jail, especially when tensions were high. Apart from being a lesson in being careful where I pointed a camera, this was a good lesson about when and where to be stoned.

* * *

What did I learn from this Pakistani experience, this complete change from anything that had gone before? The answers must come from memories, some of them now not retrievable. Above all, I remember constantly being with the same few people. Small niggles were magnified out of any normal proportion, especially in the often-difficult circumstances: constantly on the move in remote and alien places, in danger at times; long exposures to heat and cold, and occasional illness. Travel was stressful, with early morning starts and unconventional and uncomfortable transport, such as being cramped up in the back of a jeep already filled with luggage, for a full day at a time. Uncomfortable sleeping arrangements and strange food added to the mix, and we tired of the constant meetings with officials. All of these situations were totally different to leisurely holiday travel.

The whole experience built up my confidence about travel itself, having survived some pretty lawless places, where there were real threats; not like something you see in the movies, but real and immediate. There were days when my first waking thought was that today I might die, on roads with the ever-present possibility of falling from great heights. Sometimes it was difficult to decide whether it was an adventure or a folly, with the sheer remoteness and the impossibility of getting medical aid. Even facing shellfire—having survived all that certainly led to facing life with considerable confidence. Travelling anywhere else later inspired no fears at all; just walk around like you own the place.

It was a practical introduction to working with photography, something I have used ever since for both work and play. In relation to equipment, cameras had to be durable, because nothing that broke could be repaired. Some brands with the best reputation did not last long. An old German Contax and a cheap Minolta served me well. The more delicate Nikons and Canons died from the cold or the heat or the dust or the bashing about. Electronic flash units did not last long and rather than taking one or two of the most sophisticated ones as I had on the first trip, on the second I took many cheap ones, throwing them away as they failed. Cliff Evans told me that film was the cheapest part of the work so I used endless amounts hoping for at least some good results. That still applies in this digital age; take many and select few; always watching and waiting for the vital moment, for the fleeting image that says it all.

My work in ceramics has been strongly influenced by the idea of working in simple ways. Think of a man who made a kiln by digging a hole in the ground, maybe 30cm in diameter and 60 deep; then digging another down to the base of the first hole at an angle of around 30 degrees; then using the clay he had dug out to build a circular wall about 60cm diameter inside and 75cm high around the hole. He then had a kiln. It could be fired with wood down the stokehole he had made. The ware was stacked in the middle of this updraft kiln and covered with broken sherds. The total cost was a day's hard labour. Is it necessary to buy all our equipment and materials rather than making it or finding them?

Experiencing how these traditional potters worked, not only in Pakistan but later in other countries as well, had the feel of looking directly at the distant past, like a time traveller, seeing techniques that probably were used thousands of years ago. This direct experience is completely different to reading about history, or looking at ancient pots in museums. It brought the full sensation of being inside a tradition, creating a rich context later for my work, an awareness of continuity through time. What we do is the result of many tiny evolutionary changes, not great creativity.

Conversely, it created an awareness of the shackles of tradition, of not being able to change and develop, always doing it that way because *'my father did it that way'*. The danger of continuing a tradition, as culture and the material environment change, is seen with traditional potters all over the world. It eventually becomes redundant and finally extinct. The danger is the same for contemporary potters who admire some ancient tradition and attempt to replicate it.

It was not all danger. Memories linger of the delightfully exotic. Lingering over green tea in open air tea shops on snowy mountainsides. The sounds of that strange lingua franca Urdu, a mix of Persian and Hindi language, with English words thrown in seemingly at random. And, where most women were dressed in the burkha, with only their eyes exposed, learning about the deeply erotic qualities of eyes alone. Coronavirus has reminded me of this.

Working in remote areas with no other Westerners, unable to speak the local languages, was an extreme test. Exposure to a different culture, or more accurately many different cultures in one country, demonstrates what we as humans have in common. Ever since the Pakistan experiences I have disliked the politics of difference and hatred of others, so commonly practised now. I am more interested in what we have in common, not in our differences. We all care for our children; we all need food and warmth and we all mourn the deaths of those close to us. This attitude makes it harder to demonise an enemy. True, some individuals are dangerous and even some cultures are dangerous but normal people are not the enemy; they are us.

My awareness that we are part of something larger than ourselves evolved from feelings of total inadequacy in dealing with the extent of poverty and need; for food, for medicine, for comfort in a poor country like Pakistan. I was initially overwhelmed until understanding that it was impossible to help everyone; but it was possible to help some people. That process of awareness of how small we are in a large world has, I hope, helped me keep my ego in check. As Ivan McMeekin would say, others will decide our importance. People who have a large ego problem amuse me, the ones who have an over-inflated sense of their worth. How silly and pathetic. Each of us is just a tiny asterisk in an immense story.

9
SHORT STOPS

Broad, wholesome, charitable views of men and things cannot be acquired by vegetating in one little corner of the earth all one's lifetime.

— Mark Twain

After Pakistan we each had been given a round world ticket by the Smithsonian, with the main destination Washington, and eventually Sydney. Don Godden, his wife Deanie and I travelled together. In Washington, at the Smithsonian Museum of Natural History, we met with Cliff Evans, the man in charge of the Ancient Technology Program. Cliff offered me a postdoctoral fellowship at the Smithsonian, in the Museum of Natural History, starting after August 1972; my response was *'Why not?'*

* * *

Before that, told we could write in as many stops as we wished on the round world ticket, we had been expansive. For our first stop we flew into Teheran late at night. A travel agent in Karachi had booked us into what he described as the 'newest and finest hotel in Teheran'. The Teheran taxi driver was extremely reluctant to take us there but some persuasive bullying by Don led to us arriving at a rather grand building site. The hotel was new indeed, so new it was still being built. The taxi driver, now a little more animated, told us that his brother had a little hotel, with very reasonable rates. We were sceptical, but tired at that late stage of night, willing to be conned for one night, for the sake of somewhere to sleep.

What eventuated was a wonderful stay in a warm family environment in a building garlanded by flowers and bushes, with friendly and hospitable people. I know where the expression 'the kindness of strangers' originated; with someone who had stayed in that place. Apart from seeing some mosques and a museum, and the view of the Alborz Mountains protectively bordering Teheran, I remember little else about the time other than that hotel. One lifelong result is that I have always felt great warmth towards Iranian people. I regret not having got to cities like Isfahan and Shiraz and especially to some rural areas in Iran.

The one jarring episode at the hotel came on the last night. The family put on a going-away feast for us. The first course was sheep's eye soup. Sheep's eyes, real ones, floating in a watery liquid. I could not. I just could not. Forever since I have had a policy of not eating anything that is looking at me.

* * *

On we went. Next stop Istanbul. It soon became another of my favourite cities. Compared with Pakistan it was distinctly European in character. And later, compared with real European cities, it was exotically Oriental. It was a true mix of the two kinds of civilisations. I walked and walked, soaking it all in. Having been fascinated by the tiled mosques in Pakistan my main aim was to visit the Blue Mosque. I walked in. There was one man inside praying. I was there for hours, photographing its endless tiles, absorbing its majesty. A few other people came in and out.

The last time I saw the Blue Mosque, in 2010, it was necessary to buy entry tickets, after queuing for an hour in a line of several hundred people. The line slowly moved forwards, one step and stop, one step and stop, and finally I was inside the mosque, after a long wait in the hot sun. It was almost impossible to move without bumping into someone; it was crowded with humanity. Istanbul had become a tourist destination, a city increasingly Westernised. We go to distant beautiful places because they are beautiful and our going there progressively makes them less distant and less beautiful.

Next door to the Blue Mosque is the Hagia Sophia which to me is the most evocatively grand building anywhere. Massive walls, the massive round dome topping it, mysterious corridors leading to unexplained places, shadows and light, a wonderfully indescribable colour that once may been a soft iron red. How did they build it way back then? It has had several iterations, originally built as a Christian cathedral in Constantinople, it became a mosque in the 1400s, a museum in 1935 and was declared a mosque again in 2020.

* * *

Next, Athens. First impressions, music sounding from doorways of small eating places in the Plaka; and surprise at how beautiful Greek women were, after seeing few Europeans for so long. The Parthenon was stunning in brilliant sunlight, so unlike noble buildings in dull overcast countries. Then on to Rome, from which I remember little—perhaps the Colosseum—because we were there only a few days, ending one morning with a serious hangover from episodes forgotten even then. I recall being pushed into a taxi to the airport and flying off, eventually recovering in Switzerland. We took the train from Zurich to Biel where we stayed with some friends of Don and Deanie, who had for a time lived next door in Paddington in Sydney. Biel is on the dividing line between the German and the French parts of Switzerland and mixes both cultures.

One of our entertainments was a day trip with our hosts, up along a valley above Biel, to visit a friend of theirs who made schnapps. This alcoholic drink is made from various fruits including apples, pears, plums, and cherries. We were invited to try a glass of each. After sampling his full range, we were well impressed with his products and beginning to be well impressed with ourselves. This feeling of well-being increased when he pointed out that Hans further up the valley made a slightly different form of each drink and we should really try Han's output for comparison. Actual comparisons became increasingly difficult and ultimately proved impossible when we finally got to the varieties made by Willi, even further up the valley.

A different entertainment, one which I recommend to anyone (I hesitate to recommend the schnapps form of entertainment) was to travel up into the mountains to Kleinne Scheidegg. At least—in deference to my schnapps-dimmed faculties on the day—I think that's where it was. It might well have been Grindelwald. From a hotel balcony, gently sipping a hair of the dog, the spectacular view of the North Face of the Eiger, and two other mountains Mönch and Jungfrau spanned the sky in front of us.

That balcony was one of the prime locations for watching climbers on the North Face of the Eiger, the German word for Ogre, a famous challenge for the best climbers; a fine place to get into various forms of trouble and die. More than sixty climbers have done just that. The first successful climb, reaching the summit of this vertical rock face took three days. In 2011 it was climbed by Daniel Arnold from Switzerland solo in

2 hours 28 minutes, almost running up parts of the seemingly impossible ascent; and in 2015 by Ueli Steck in 2 hours 22 minutes.

I learned that in Switzerland you can buy food anywhere; at the finest restaurant or from a street vendor outside a railway station. Regardless of the source the quality will be excellent.

* * *

We moved on relentlessly. Vienna, Frankfurt, Hamburg, Copenhagen, Paris, London and New York. Not a bad trip for a pair of Aussie lads from the bush and a surprisingly tolerant wife of one of them. Most details are long forgotten. I do remember waking up one morning and becoming aware that I could not remember the name of the hotel. Then to my consternation I realised I was not sure what city I was in. Thinking that the country name would give me a clue, I finally realised that I had not the faintest idea what country I was in. Constant travel can do that. A call to hotel reception, answered by someone who seemed disconcerted that he might be speaking to a madman, finally helped me out with all the necessary details. *'Excuse me sir, but what country am I in?'*

It was Austria. In Vienna's world class Kunsthistorisches Museum, for the first time ever I understood the meaning of the word transfixed. The museum galleries have multitudes of significant paintings. Six Rembrandt self-portraits are hung along a short corridor. These are small, not much bigger than an A4 page. Standing before one I was literally welded to the spot, immovable, stunned by it. That must have lasted just a minute or so but I seemed more like five, ten, fifteen minutes.

It's an experience not often repeated. I had it once years later, in the museum in Peshawar in 1977, seeing a fasting Buddha (*Siddhartha*), the most powerful sculpture I ever saw. The closest I have been to that state of immobility with other sculptures was with some Stephen De Staebler ceramic figures in the de Young Museum in San Francisco.

In Germany we met Jörg Schäfer, at the Institut für Klassische Archäologie in Heidelberg University, an authority on archaeological ceramics. Heidelberg, on the river Neckar is fascinating and beautiful, everywhere mellowed mediaeval buildings and around every corner a stunning view of something. The University is the oldest in Germany. A commonly told story is that Heidelberg only retains its ancient character because a US general invading Germany late in World War 2 had been a student there, and instructed his troops to go around the city, forbidding any damage to it.

In Paris we did the usual, the Louvre and such. I engaged with a young lady for quite a reasonable fee in Montmartre. I was a young man too long celibate and had decided that Paris might be just the place to break the drought. And in London I followed up the phone number I found in my pocket after Rome, but that led to very little. More importantly, I found a place to stay in Earl's Court, the Australian ghetto in London. The Aston Court bedsitter was to play a role in many of my later visits to London.

And so to Washington, and meetings at the Smithsonian that were to set up the rest of that decade with many fine adventures.

* * *

In 1972, on my way to Washington to take up the post-doctoral fellowship I took the counter-intuitive path, round the world again instead of across the Pacific. This reminds me that funds were vastly more available and accessible then; leading me to wondering why such things are impossible now, if the politicians are right and we have benefited so much from their efforts at creating a fabulous new trickle-down economy? Why is it that institutions of learning had plenty of money back then and are deprived now? Why has the trickle bypassed them, flooding elsewhere? How can a trickle go up instead of down?

Bangkok, Cairo and London were stops on the way to Washington. Bangkok is somewhat of a blur beyond recalling eating food that was so violently chili-hot that one mouthful was enough; and being ill for days after a dose of bad tucker somewhere. I still have no love for Thai food; please do not invite me to join you at your favourite Thai restaurant.

On to Cairo. I was able to spend time with traditional potters working in Old Cairo, and gathered enough information to publish an article about them later. It was one of the first articles I ever had published.[3]

I stayed in Shepheards Hotel in Cairo. It served well as a base for seeing the Egyptian Museum, an erratically organised collection of ancient wonders including beautiful early Egyptian glass; and the pyramids, of which Cheops is massively large close up, much larger than any photo can realistically document.

The virtue of the hotel was that my room overlooked the Nile. The activity on the river made it easy to imagine the dim past. The disadvantage was the casino in the basement. Having read about casinos, this was my first chance to see a real one. At the roulette table the punters pushed forwards stacks of chips. After the spin the croupier raked most of them off. Several Saudis in full Arab attire and three Japanese dressed in Western business suits were gambling. Chips were stacked again and raked again. A close look at at the designation of the chips revealed that each was worth ten thousand American dollars. Each spin of the wheel involved a million dollars, more sometimes. I moved on.

The blackjack tables seemed a little more reasonable. On the last night in Cairo, leaving aside the detail, the end result was losing all my cash. The hotel bus took me to the airport next day to fly to London. Arriving at Heathrow the first step was to make a phone call to Jeff Eagleson, who had been my next-door neighbour in Bronte in Sydney, asking for help. It was not the best re-introduction to London, a city that would become important to me later, arriving broke and chastened.

* * *

Doug Nye the motoring writer reported that when racing driver Phil Hill first went to England in 1949 'He found himself in this stunningly shabby and war-battered country where seagulls were coughing into the fog and people went about their business looking pale and broken'. By the early 1970s the seagulls were cured, people were for the most part were less broken but no less pale, and fogs still happened. But I developed a warm affection for what seemed to be such a backward place, visually and socially. Before travelling around England, I had thought Turner's epic paintings of the landscape lacked colour and clarity. After, I realised he was portraying his land accurately. The light is that dull. And socially the English class system was shockingly real.

My base was the Aston Court, a B&B in Earl's Court. It seems to no longer be there; at least Google cannot find it. The gay couple who ran it had theatrical and musical friends and it became a lively place late at night when they would turn up for a drink after work. Dusty Springfield was a good friend of one of the owners, Tony, and she came around frequently. There was no need to go out for entertainment. Many more visits followed and for a while London was my favoured destination.

My overall impression of craft ceramics showing in galleries and shops in 1970s England was that the work was skilfully made and technically sound, but dull and unadventurous. I gradually became much more interested in what was happening with ceramics in the US where there was much greater diversity.

10
UPS AND DOWNS

Gliders, sailplanes, they are wonderful flying machines. It's the closest you can come to being a bird.

— Neil Armstrong

One of my pleasures, from the 1960s into the 1980s, was flying. I was not the only one to combine ceramics and flying: Bill Samuels and Vic Greenaway both had pilot licences. My pleasures were split between flying gliders myself, and flying in small aircraft as a passenger with my brother Dick, who in adult life managed to combine work and pleasure through his love of the sky.

My interest in gliders began at Cherbourg in Queensland when I was working there as the pottery instructor. There was not a lot for a young man to do at weekends. It was a dry town, no alcohol allowed. Going to the pubs in nearby Murgon did not appeal. And the delights of nearby Kingaroy were restricted to the movies and an occasional dance, something at which I never excelled. Discovering that there was a gliding club at Kingaroy gave me an answer. I learned to fly gliders.

A glider is a means of transport that has no practical purpose whatsoever, and has limitations as a means of achieving pleasure. Its usable only when the weather is benevolent, mainly in summer. For me, every flight ended where it had begun, at the same airstrip. Some might consider that a pointless exercise, getting nowhere; but the interval between taking off and landing was an entertainment, and a commitment, like no other. Flying alone, I mused that others would love seeing and feeling what I was seeing and feeling. Like John Magee I slipped the bonds of earth; but never got quite high enough to touch the face of the Gods some people imagine are up there somewhere.

Gliders have no engine. One of my instructors told me that the difference between powered aircraft and gliders was the difference between rape and seduction. The usual method of getting up in the air in a glider is to be connected by a rope to, and towed up by, another aircraft with an engine. At Kingaroy this was a retired crop-duster, a Pawnee for those who know aircraft. Getting off the ground required some help from other people. The gliders had but one wheel, situated below the pilot. This meant that while stationary, the end of one wing rested on the ground. After getting strapped in and organised the pilot gave a signal and helpers outside attached the towrope, held up the end of one wing so the glider was level and ran along holding up the wing for the first twenty metres or so of the take-off, until the glider had enough airflow to support the wings.

The glider took off before the tow plane, flying slightly higher. When the towplane was in the air, the glider was kept lower and about 40 metres behind. The trick was to maintain formation, looking up at the tow as it climbed away to the heights. It's much easier than you might guess, as simple as driving a car behind another car, but it was still a nice fantasy to imagine I was in the Roulettes.

When we were high enough, one or two thousand feet up, then came the spectacular release. Pulling back on the stick, the pilot first climbed the glider up above the tow plane; then, using a lever in the cockpit released the tow rope, watching it snake away in the sky, still attached to the tow plane. The glider then climbed and banked to the right, and the tow plane dived and banked left. From the glider what you saw was spectacular, the bottom of another aircraft very close by, engine roaring, dropping out of the sky. Exciting stuff, especially the first time you experienced it, but carefully calculated to be safe. The instructors concentrated at all times on what was safe and what was not.

The first twenty or so flights in the two-seater glider, student in the front seat and instructor in the back, did not go well. I was airsick every time. That was predictable, because travelling in the back of a car often made me feel ill. A tendency to motion sickness combined with the initially weird movements of an aircraft created the ideal conditions to make good use of the sick bag. I learned little tricks like not eating an orange beforehand—the acidic sensation when it came back up again was not pleasant.

The tight confines of the glider interior did not help much, especially on a hot day. The glider was designed to present as small a frontal area as possible, meaning inside it your shoulders touched the sides, your head was very near the canopy, and your legs stretched away into the long nose of the aircraft. I could move my arms and legs freely enough to use the controls, but there was no excess room for much else. Maybe scratching your nose.

The aircraft movements, that had initially seemed so madly random, gradually became predictable and understandable. They were caused by movements of the air itself and I began to understand the basis of gliding—reading the air. Increasing awareness created the necessary relaxation and calmness for the illness to stop. Understanding helped banish fear and discomfort. It was almost like being a young child again, seeing new wonders, seeing the world below revolve as you turned, looking down from an entirely new angle at miniature houses and roads and animals, like looking through the wrong end of a telescope. Constantly moving across the landscape in an entirely new way was totally unlike flying in a large commercial aircraft where everything shrinks into distant obscurity.

There was a deep satisfaction also in learning the skills needed to control the glider, beginning to feel just how much pressure to use on the controls, coordinating them to fly smoothly, and learning how to land. My pilot brother had said, 'A landing is anything you walk away from'. But I wanted elegant, feather-soft touchdowns.

There were two ways to go about it, each meant for a certain type of personality. One was for the technically minded, using the instruments, minimal as they were; flying according to their messages. A rate of climb indicator told me I was entering a thermal and how strong it was. An altimeter told me how far above the ground I was, provided I had set it carefully at the airstrip. The other way appealed to me more though, feeling more poetic. That was to use my senses, to read the sky, to make judgements based on being as observant as possible. I learned to judge altitude above the ground accurately. This was most useful in landing where the procedure was to fly along parallel to the airstrip, joining it halfway along at six hundred feet; to go past the strip a certain distance and turn ninety degrees left at four hundred feet onto the 'base leg'; and turn again at two hundred feet onto 'final'. From there you aimed at a spot on the end of the airstrip where you intended to touch down the single wheel underneath you. Being able to judge the altitude reliably made all this relatively simple.

With no engine, the glider is kept afloat by air movements, caused by temperature variations in the sky. The only means of staying up there is to fly in air moving upwards. Heat from the sun is absorbed by dark colours on the ground, such as a dark green crop, but it is reflected by light coloured bright areas such as a bare patch of sandy ground. This reflection produces thermals, circular patches of warm air moving upwards that can carry the glider upwards with them. How do you find thermals? Cumulus clouds are useful indicators, forming as moisture condenses at the top of a thermal. Seeing faint traces of dust and moisture in the thermal aided defining them; polaroid glasses helped. The main joy I took from gliding was learning to closely observe the ground and the sky, being aware of the local microclimate. The risk of having to land somewhere unpleasant helped focus the awareness.

Early on I delighted in the one instrument that helped most in coordinating the controls for smooth flight. That was a piece of cotton thread about ten centimetres long, taped to the outside front of the perspex canopy, in the pilot's sightline. When it was blown parallel to the fuselage by the air moving past you were flying 'straight'; and when it moved to one side or the other you were sideslipping, using the air inefficiently and losing height. I loved the almost clownish simplicity of it and understood exactly how it worked, the only instrument about which I could say that.

After a couple of months practicing every weekend, it all started to gel. Flying became easier than driving a car—partly because there were far fewer obstacles. I learned about clouds: so many types and variations, stratus, cumulus, cirrus and that true stairway to heaven for the glider pilot, the lenticular. Flying in cloud was forbidden because of the danger someone else might be flying in the same cloud; not hitting anything came down to avoiding the only thing you could hit, another glider.

Like a World War 2 Spitfire pilot (well that's how I liked to imagine it) you constantly turned your head watching for other aircraft. Seeing another glider was not always simple either, because front on heading towards you there was not much to them. The fuselage was like a circle considerably less than a metre diameter, and the long thin wings were less than twenty centimetres thick along most of their length. Constant vigilance, as they say, was the price of living.

Flying became more difficult as I learned more from the instructors, because they put me through increasingly more difficult tasks. Taking off flying straight into the sun, releasing at low altitude, being made to use strange landing techniques simulating a failure of some control, and other tricky tests were constant. Then after one flight the instructor climbed out and casually said— 'It's all yours'; and walked away.

One of the most intense moments of my life had arrived. I was about to go solo. At no time in my life have I ever been more responsible for my own well-being. There is something about being up in the sky alone the first time that is different to anything else in life. If things get dodgy in a car or boat you can stop and think about it. But in the sky, you have to get back on the ground at some stage. How you do that carries a meaningful prognosis, well described by Antoine de Saint Exupéry: '… *I want you to remember that below the sea of clouds lies eternity*'.[4] And Guy Murchie in one of my favourite books ever, *Song of the Sky* says: '… *the sky is more primitive, elemental, and somehow fiercer than the earth below. In the sky you cannot stop; to stop is to die*'.[5]

At the time though there was not much of that thinking going on, consciously at least, and not much emotion. I had to be practical and think clearly. The helpers got me started quickly. That meant concentrating on getting off the ground with no trouble; and up there, watching for thermals, watching for other gliders, planning where to go and how to get back to the airstrip. My mind took over leaving no space for fears. The training did its job perfectly well—except for one little incident I had not trained for. The glider had controls called air brakes, one in each wing. They could be opened up vertically to break up the air flow over the wings so the glider could descend faster. They were mainly used in landing to control the angle of descent. When you opened them more, you came down steeper and when you had them open less, shallower. When they were shut the glider was flying most efficiently.

As I came in to land from that first solo, I pulled on the lever for the airbrakes a little to begin opening them, and then, turning onto the final descent, let go the lever. The force of air suddenly blew the air brakes open, with a hell of a bang. It sounded like someone had bashed the aluminium glider with a sledge hammer. That gave me the instant adrenaline rush that hits you with a physical jolt. I thought the wing had fallen off or something equally bad was happening. To make it worse the open air brakes caused the glider to drop rapidly. But then the training came in and I grabbed the lever to close the air brake. The descent became tranquil again. I never told anyone in the gliding club what had happened. Lesson learned, I was alive to fly another day. One instructor had told me early on that it was not necessary to go looking for excitement in aircraft, that it would come and find you.

Learning the process of flying these things with an instructor in the back seat had not been traumatic, a salute to the instructor's professionalism. But doing the first solo trip and landing well was fraught enough that it brought the biggest single confidence boost in my entire life. It helped me feel that I could take on anything, and manage any venture into the unknown. What a wonderful feeling it was later to go up there and just enjoy it.

Gliding has poetic moments of serene beauty. It is also termed soaring, a perfect word for an experience that reaches the heights and lifts the human spirits. I was once circling in a thermal, a cylindrical patch of rising air, to gain height and an eagle joined the opposite side of the circle. We flew round and round, each with our head tilted, watching the other, just a few metres apart. Up and up we went until the glider could go no further, the lift diminished to the point of ineffectiveness. Just to show what was what the eagle went on up another 500 feet. I could guess what it was thinking.

And I will never forget flying five thousand feet up, along the face of a large storm front coming in, a solid body of cloud angled up at 45 degrees from ground level, stretching across the countryside in a straight line to the horizon. Warm air rose in front of it as it moved along the ground and I could climb in the lift that provided, a hundred feet or so away from the front. On the cloud surface the air boiled and swirled, but out where I was everything was perfectly smooth. I could look away down the face of the front, as far as I could focus. I was part of a grand piece of nature, right in it, a stunningly beautiful weather event seen and felt from close up.

After leaving Queensland I did very little gliding. A few goes at Warrenton in Virginia later, when I was living in Washington DC, and six months or so with the Canberra club when living there, flying along the escarpment above Lake George. I gave it away without any great regrets, considering it another thing that was better to have done than to just think about.

* * *

There was a seven-month gap after finishing in Pakistan, before taking up the fellowship in Washington. I arrived back in Australia just before Christmas 1972, with little money and no immediate prospects. My brother Dick was driving trucks for Patrick Mould and persuaded him to take me on as a driver. The trucks were loaded up with road metal, the fine stones that go on bitumen roads, at Bolairo near Adaminaby. We then took it up into the mountains, past Cabramurra and down into Tumut Pond dam. Those old trucks, carrying a heavy load, exaggerated the steepness of the roads. The brakes were next to useless; on a fully loaded truck one heavy brake application was the limit. Then they faded so there was no stopping at all. Being young and oblivious to consequences was a useful job skill.

An experienced driver gave me advice about going down those steep hills with a heavy load. Lock in the lowest gear and allow the truck to run at about 2–3mph with my foot off the accelerator. Leave the driver's door ajar so it could be opened fully very quickly; and if the speed started to go up near 4mph, open the door and jump out, trying not to fall down a steep mountainside; leaving the truck to manage its own demise.

The loaded trip, slow up every steep hill, was thinking time, with bird sounds thrown in. Two, sometimes two and a half hours. The return was frantic—who would set the record? I would not be surprised on some corners to see the black lines we left, still there.

* * *

During that time flying of a different kind became important. Dick had been having flying lessons with Stan Birtus, a Polish pilot who had flown Spitfires in the Battle of Britain and who had settled in Cooma aiming for a quiet and peaceful life.

Dick bought his own aircraft, an Auster, a small workhorse that could take off and land in short spaces; like a four-wheel-drive of the air, used in World War 2 as spotter aircraft, also for flight training. This one was the source of one of those endlessly told family stories. Where money was concerned Dick had that old hole in the pocket syndrome, but he had uncharacteristically saved up some money, urged on by Carol, his love-life at the time, who wanted to get married and buy a house. When Dick saw the Auster advertised, he could not resist, especially as he had the money in the bank. He bought it. When Carol found out she was seriously annoyed, and said *'That money was meant to be used to buy a house. Why did you waste in on an aeroplane?'* and he, looking at her as though she was deficient in the obvious logic, said *'Because you can't fly a fucking house'.*

Soon after that came the end of his involvement with Carol, but the beginning of a lifetime involved with aircraft for Dick. That lifetime eventually turned out to be short. Most people had thought that his flying habits would lead to a shortened life but finally other events intervened.

In the beginning his flying was all about pleasure, some of it closer to the ground than the authorities recommended. The Auster served a variety of purposes. One was an assignation that went wrong with a woman who was not known to Carol, shortly before she departed permanently. I had a phone call asking me to—discreetly—come and pick him up, along with his companion, from a river bank where he had landed and run a wheel into a rabbit hole, damaging the strut.

One day in the Berridale pub, after the truck driving job evaporated, Dick and I were discussing the almost non-existent state of our respective finances, and what might be done about it. We were joined by another bloke who was also short on prospects. He suggested we might be able to invent jobs based on our skills. We went through these, which did not take long. Looking at my skills, making pottery would have taken too long to set up, and ethnographic recording was not promising on the Monaro. I did mention that I could take photographs and in fact had cameras. Dick had little beyond the ability to fly a plane and actually had one. Our friend said that in the past he had also been a photographer but due to his constant drinking habit that was not practical anymore; but he still had a darkroom and could possibly develop and print images. The solution was obvious; we went into the aerial photography business.

The plan was to fly over farmhouses around the district and photograph them, using black and white film; colour film was too sensitive and unreliable for the basic shooting conditions. Dick's Auster, because it had

been designed as a slow low-level spotter plane, was perfect for the role we gave it. It had a high wing so there was no obstruction in the way of the photos. It had removable doors. Before we took off, I would remove the door on the right, my side. Strapping down the seat belt as tight as possible I could put my foot out on the wheel strut and hang half in, half out of the plane, giving a completely clear field of view.

I would set up the camera beforehand, with exposure and aperture on a fixed setting, and leave them alone while we flew. My only job in the air was to push the shutter release button. I could see very little anyway, my eyes streaming from the wind. Pushing the button often as we circled around later gave us a choice of many images, with the hope that one might be ok. Some were in fact excellent.

We would then make A4 prints, take them around to each farm and offer to sell large poster sized black and white prints. We drank tea with the farmers and their wives as they commented on features in the photos; then almost all ordered a large print, framed. In our favour, if the farmer hesitated the wife usually said yes. I have seen some of those photos still hanging on farmhouse walls fifty years later. Our alcoholic colleague had moved on by that stage but we made an arrangement with a fine gentleman, Mr Schoo of Schoo studios in Cooma, who made the prints at modest profit to himself and considerable benefit to us. He was a master of tinting, the art of adding colour to black and white prints and some farmers were happy to pay the extra cost for colour.

It was one of the best jobs I ever had—no bosses, no schedules, work only when you felt like it, and even then it only involved a half day a month to get all the pictures you needed for the next month's income. Anyone who has only ever flown intercity in large jets up there where the earth becomes a mere abstraction, has not had the pleasures of flying around low. Rabbits dived into burrows and cattle kicked up their heels and ran. Moss on the rocks and water grasses in creeks were plain to see.

Farmers working on their tractors waved to us. If they were on my side I could wave back, if not a wave of the wings sufficed. Anywhere we felt like going was just over there.

I did more flying around with Dick between 1974 and 1983 when we both lived in Canberra. By then he had graduated to a Cessna 172. The old Auster rattled around the skies like an early model Land Rover, the 172 cruised like a Holden or Falcon. The 172 was basic transport, practical without luxury, good for getting four people from one place to another; or five if nobody official was looking. The Cessna allowed much longer trips than the Auster, while still being basic enough to allow traditional methods of navigation such as following roads, or dropping down close to railway stations to read the signs on platforms.

Flying with Dick was not anything like flying with Qantas. He was near blind in one eye. In one memorable landing at the busy Bankstown airfield in Sydney he was wearing sunglasses with one broken lens that made seeing difficult. That was over his good eye. His method of passing the annual eye test, to keep his pilot's licence, was to go along with a mate of his who did the test first, memorising the letters on the test chart. He then told Dick the sequence to recite when it was his turn.

Later he decided to start regular airline flights between Cooma and Sydney. His airline motto was to be *'You can chance it with Ansett or risk it with Rye'*. Unfortunately, the authorities who granted licences for such ventures doubted his capacities. When that idea failed to materialise, he decided to buy two old DC3 aircraft and start a business flying racehorses around. The name of that airline would be Orsair. Another idea stillborn.

In the 1980s he did finally graduate to serious flying business. He had a partner Bill, a proper qualified aircraft engineer. They started off by buying a few planes that had crashed, repairing them and then selling them. This eventually became the aircraft maintenance and sales business, Aerotechnics, set up at Canberra Airport. Dick was the salesman and Bill the engineer. They specialised in selling Cessna 185s, a sophisticated version of the old Auster designed as a bush aircraft that could land on any short rough dusty strip. In the final year of 185 manufacture Dick sold more than anyone else internationally. The Cessna management in the USA offered him the last 185, specified any way he liked. He asked for it to be finished with a polished aluminium skin; the sun glittered on every magnificent surface.

Aerotechnics was taken over in the mid-1980s by other businessmen. Dick got involved in crop dusting and cotton spraying, both jobs for young men. The cotton spraying seemed to me especially fraught and funky. It involved flying at night, in the dark, close down above the crop, at an altitude of about four to six metres (fifteen to twenty feet) above ground, maintaining the height by using a downward light on each wing, keeping the two lights overlapping. The saying that there are old pilots and bold pilots but no old bold pilots, seemed highly relevant to this job, that required skill and a measure of caution. And according to Hamish Brunton, one pilot I met who worked with Dick, a few shots of whisky beforehand to calm the nerves. Hamish had an odd manner of walking, kind of crablike. He had broken virtually every bone he possessed in an earlier crash.

Ultimately lack of caution was his Dick's downfall. A conversation with someone in the Australian Air Force in a Canberra pub gave him the idea that he could sell Australian ultralight aircraft to some foreign military forces, to use as spotter and patrol aircraft. The argument was that they could replace helicopters which cost millions of dollars when shot down, with ultralights that were only fifty thousand. He had trips to Burma and Thailand and was successful in selling some of these aircraft, destined to do border patrols.

Somewhere in his discussions with military types, he found out about some military helicopters in Ecuador that he decided he could buy and resell. As a novice in arms dealing, he was not aware that whoever wishes to buy military equipment has opponents who wish to prevent them from doing so. The end result of these activities was that in 1988 he died in Quito, ostensibly from a heart attack, but his body came back to Australia battered and bruised, in a lead-lined box.

* * *

A cloudless black night with all the stars bright and sharp was followed by a frosty July morning. Later, on that day of his funeral the sky became vivid blue, as blue as it ever becomes. The sunshine was strong and everything around was crisp and sparkling. It was the kind of day you see only in July, only in the mountains where the air is clearest. From the Berridale cemetery you could see way across the edge of the treeless plains, past the Cooma airport; and you could hear the Beaver take off, the big radial engine roaring. As he passed over the cemetery and flew away the pilot gave a wave of the wings. Never was there a more appropriate goodbye. The women dabbed their faces with handkerchiefs and the men lowered their heads so others could not see their eyes glisten.

A part of me permanently died along with my brother, the part that was surrounded by music, and laughter at the most dire situations, the fun of doing silly things for no good reason except for the laughing that accompanied them. Now when I see a small aircraft pass overhead he is alive to me again for a few minutes; but all the fun of our lives together has gone forever.

11
THE FELLOWSHIP

Washington is a very easy city for you to forget where you came from and why you got there in the first place.

— Harry S Truman

Arriving on Mars would have not been much different than arriving in Washington DC—after driving trucks with no brakes on steep descents in isolated mountains, and taking photographs of farmhouses, hanging half in and half out of a fragile aircraft with eyes streaming, shirt flapping furiously. Here I was in a city of world interest. The White House that every newspaper mentioned every day was just a short ramble down the street and Richard Nixon had recently become the main resident. I lived in DC for eighteen months during 1972–3.

Have you ever tried to read an ancient book where the words seem to be vaguely familiar but the font and the use of language are strange enough to inhibit understanding? That's how I felt at first. The difference between America and Australia was totally unexpected. Before going to Pakistan, my first trip out of Australia, it seemed obvious that the culture and environment would be different to home, and it was. The whole country was exotic, even overwhelming at times, but I felt no culture shock because that was expected; I was almost comforted by the anticipated differences around me. In the US I was shocked by the differences because they were so unexpected. In the cities a constant visual bombardment of neon signs and all the enticements of commerce were far more evident. A flash of awareness came one day, driving in the countryside. When I was not concentrating, the trees and fields looked familiar, but taking a proper look and concentrating on the details, absolutely everything, every detail, was unfamiliar.

Some of the accents from the deep south, especially of the African Americans, were difficult to follow. In reverse, many people had no idea what I was saying to them. The more urbane *'loved my accent'*. *'Are you British?'* they asked. *'No, Australian'*, I replied. *'Oh, now that's near*

Germany, isn't it?' was a common response. My educated colleagues had a well-developed world view but the average American I met had little or no concept of the world outside. In the first year there, Australia was mentioned only twice in the Washington Post, supposedly one of the more worldly papers.

* * *

Each Smithsonian fellowship holder was assigned a mentor. Mine was Cliff Evans, chairman of the anthropology department at the time. Cliff and his wife Betty Meggers were best known for their role in South American archaeology, supporting a theory about how the Pacific was populated from South America, a theory that met with little support from their colleagues. Cliff and Betty were kind, generous and supportive, almost like substitute parents, which was understandable in that they had no children themselves. They took an interest in the work of those around them and paid caring attention to the personal lives of their colleagues.

Cliff was on a three-year stint as chairman of the Anthropology Department. A somewhat unwilling administrator, he was more interested in his work on archaeology than administrivia, which he approached as a pragmatist. He asked me one day if I could write with my left hand. Seeing my puzzled expression, he explained that sometimes he needed signatures from people who were not around and perhaps I could help out by forging them. He assured me that there was no dishonesty involved, just the need to satisfy silly rules and regulations.

He looked down on most people, physically if not temperamentally. Unlike some bosses who are built large, he did not use his size to intimidate anyone. Quite the opposite, he persuaded rather than intimidated, usually with a slightly sly smile that suggested entering into a co-conspiracy.

Because of his likable character I was entirely surprised when Cliff told me his war story. In World War 2 he had flown as a bombardier in aircraft doing daylight bombing raids on Germany. When the bombs were about to be dropped, his job as the bomb-aimer was to take control of the aircraft, looking intently into a shrouded instrument in front of him. On his last run he was totally engaged—when there was a loud explosion. When he looked up there was no aircraft. He was out in mid-air, alone. After parachuting safely, he was interned in a prisoner of war camp for the duration.

Betty was rather slight and lean enough for me to worry that she was undernourished. Her demeanour was generally stern and serious. She looked puzzled when someone told a joke. I remember her mainly as an achiever, finishing whatever she started. She was active in many areas, among them as a member of the National Geographic Committee for Research and Exploration. That was helpful when I later applied to the Committee for—and was awarded—funds to work on my Palestinian project.

Betty's support for me continued on after the fellowship ended. She organised and published a series of books on technical subjects related to archaeology, written by specialists on things like pottery, basket weaving (significant in the US context), and studies of ancient skeletons. My book on pottery studies was published later, in 1980, and was still selling well into the 2000s.

Their life was not all work. They had three season tickets to the Kennedy Center, to attend concerts. One ticket was intended for taking along a friend, and occasionally I was the friend. I was quite stunned to hear the swelling bursting power of the National Symphony Orchestra, right there, something I had not experienced before. Cliff and Betty had a similar ticket arrangement for the National Playhouse and attending plays there started off my interest in theatre. I followed up later at many plays in London, said to be the world leader in theatre. Over several stays I saw the best: Olivier, Alan Bates, Gielgud, Guinness and Michael Redgrave; and others on their way up including Marianne Faithfull in *The Collector*.

A poignant memory of Cliff lingers. In the 1980s I was teaching the history of ceramics at the Canberra Art School, and asked Cliff for some slides of indigenous North and South American ceramics. Betty told me later he assembled the collection over two days. The next day he went down to mail room and mailed it. A few hours later he died from a heart attack. Mailing those slides to me was one of the last things he ever did.

* * *

Cliff suggested Hartnett Hall at 21st and P streets for accommodation. Until its demise in the late 1970s Hartnett Hall was a large complex that rented rooms at reasonable rates, and included meals and a housekeeping service. It was close to Dupont Circle, an area of Washington with many embassies including the Australian. It was not far from Georgetown, a varied suburb; one area was the centre of nightlife; another housed wealthy people living in genteel safety in tree lined streets.

Other parts of the District of Columbia were not safe. I was there not long after the riots of 1968 that followed the assassination of civil rights activist Martin Luther King Jr. The population of DC was around 70% black. King's death was a source of deep anger and frustration. In some areas of DC best avoided, the riots had resulted in burned out and destroyed buildings, many of which had not been rebuilt.

The crime rate was high. Muggings were common, and shootings frequent. During my six months in Hartnett Hall two of the women who worked there were shot and killed. Knowing where to go and where to avoid was essential. Sometimes it felt more dangerous than the wild tribal areas of Pakistan. There people might kill you, but for a reason; if you obeyed local custom you were pretty much safe. In DC the violence was dangerously random and unpredictable.

Day to day living was pleasant though. My daily walk to work at the Museum could take in many of Washington's famous sites including the White House. Taking a different trek each day eventually allowed absorbing all the famous sites including the Ford Theatre, where Lincoln was shot. It's just up 10th street from the Museum.

I frequented the neighbourhood corner store across the road from Hartnett Hall and became friendly with the black owner. My washing was done via his dry-cleaning agency. One time I attempted to explain cricket to him and he tried to explain gridiron football to me. We both failed. Among his many and varied items on sale were second hand books, and one day he recommended, and I purchased for one dollar what became one of my favourite books of all time, Conrad Aiken's *Preludes*.

The residents of Hartnett Hall came from many countries and many parts of the USA. I dined and talked with Negros and Navahos, with Pakistanis and Dutchmen. After-meal common room discussion roved round a wide range of subjects. I especially valued the company of a young Navaho man who had been sent to Washington, funded by the Navaho nation, to learn the white man's law so it could be used against them. His manner of speech was more like poetry than prose. And I marvelled at the unique theories of one slightly deranged black man about all kinds of issues. His theory about alcohol in excess leading to brain damage was that alcohol was lighter than blood so flowed naturally to the top of the head and finally built up to the point where it created a damaging pressure on the brain.

One of the contentious issues at the time, leading to some heavy-duty differences of opinion, was the Vietnam War. I was vigorously opposed. That created a profound dislike for the international policies of the US, and for the weakness of the Australian government in trotting along behind like an obedient pup. Those attitudes were cheered on by some of the residents and jeered by others.

Mahomed Ashraf Aziz, another resident, and I became good mates. His father was born in Pakistan but his family moved to Uganda and he had taken citizenship there. The family was expelled by an Idi Amin decree and their citizenship revoked, resulting in Aziz becoming stateless. He is the only stateless person I ever met. He had applied for residency in the US, and was waiting while the bureaucracy bumbled around making a decision, finally in his favour.

He was a multi-talented man. Drawing was one of his skills, leading him later to become involved in medical illustration, and he is now a professor at Howard University School of Medicine. More important to me at Hartnett Hall, he was the film critic for the *Washington Star*. We had sessions at the Biograph where we sat for twenty-four hours, with few breaks, as their entire program reeled past.

At a poker game one night we ended up with everyone else's money as they gradually dropped out. We decided to play one more hand for the lot. A large group of spectators had gathered in deep silence, outside the circle of light on the table, watching intently. I turned my cards face up and then he showed his winning hand. I looked at him intently and said, '*Kali haram zada*'; meaning approximately, '*You black son of a bitch*'. He was the only person in the room who understood. He roared laughing.

* * *

The stay in Washington was not all about fun and games. There was work to do—that's why they gave me the fellowship. The plan was simple enough. Write a book about the traditional potters of Pakistan. I was allocated an

155

office—a room about eight metres square. It was normally occupied by Gus Van Beek, an archaeologist who was excavating a site near Gaza in Palestine. He would be away from Washington the entire time I was there. The office was on a corner of the museum, overlooking the Washington Mall, which extended three kilometres—from the Lincoln memorial to the Capitol Building, on a hill overlooking the city. Through the window to the right from my desk, I felt important, looking straight at the Capitol about 400 metres away.

It took little time to get into a regular work schedule, exploring what was available. One of the privileges of working at the Smithsonian was access to the Capitol library, although after a few visits I decided it was too large and too intimidating with too many head-turning distractions.

The writing was made easier with access to all the collections we had made in Pakistan, stored in the museum basement. Whatever was requested would be brought up by one of the assistants. The museum library was a few doors down. All the facilities were there to make the work easy and everyone was helpful, from the librarian to the museum photographer, Vic Krantz, who photographed pots and other materials I had collected. Vic was a slow talking Texan. I learned to say hello and then get a few things done before turning back to Vic for his reply.

If I felt tense I could go down to Vic's studio for a chat, returning to my office entirely relaxed. His slow talking style was quite hypnotic. So was the quality of his black and white photography; he was an absolute master. Most of his studio photography was done with a century-old wooden box camera, with large single sheets of film in a holder slid into a space in the back. The only control was a lens cap. To make an exposure he would remove it, count for a while, then put it back on.

Most of the research positions in the Museum of Natural history were taken by men. This was not such an issue in the early 1970s as it would be now. Fortunately, there were females. One young librarian visited my office frequently and subtly offered more than the usual friendliness. She was smart and well put together but suffered from a voice that would grate ironbark.

Hartnett Hall had a reputation for being a highly efficient marriage bureau, because it housed young single males and females from around the world. There I met Sandra Lantz, and we joined the club, starting off with long interesting conversations and ending up with marriage. Sandra was a journalist. Having a strong interest in politics, she had worked with a Senator on an election campaign, as her initial impetus to move to Washington from Kansas. She then worked for the *Washington Star* newspaper and later, before we left Washington, for Voice of America broadcasting service.

We moved out of Hartnett Hall and settled in a tiny house in Arlington, Virginia, two doors down from a high-quality ice-cream shop. While living there I experienced snow in a city for the first time. I was reversing from my driveway when a car came past at an impressive speed, travelling backwards and continued on downhill through a red light. I drove back into the driveway, parked, and had the day at home.

We then moved to Maclean, to mind a house rented by Smithsonian archaeologist Dennis Stanford who was going on a field trip for six months. Maclean has one area made up of large blocks of land. Ours was five acres. These were mostly owned by the very wealthy; a nearby property was owned by the Kennedys. Our block of four houses was owned by a woman known to us only as Granny. She lived in the last house down the back of the block. The other three were rented. Granny was not inclined to welcome visitors and was known to fire a shotgun over the head of anyone who approached her house too closely. We waved to her from an acceptable distance, but never managed a conversation.

One neighbour Bill, an eccentric man living next door to Granny, worked for Delta Airlines. Bill occasionally threw a party and invited a large number of female air hostesses but no males, with no apparent success in setting up a relationship. He decided one day to dig a basement at his house, using a large machine to excavate a large hole outside the kitchen. The house ultimately began to fall in the hole and from then was propped up with long poles. His father, wealthy from prospecting oil and gas wells, visited once. I came home to find a large purple Kenworth truck parked near Bill's house. When I asked the father about it he said he had bought it that day. I asked him why and he said that he hated the colour so he bought it to have it painted white, and then resell it.

Our closest neighbour Bob Humphrey, an anthropologist who taught at George Washington University became a good mate. Travelling around with Bob in his Morgan sports car was a regular event; each Friday night we headed off to the local Pakistani Pizza shop. Pakistani because of the proprietor; the pizzas were regular Italian style. Bob was a tall jovial man, with a neatly trimmed beard. One of his skills was cartooning, an art at which he was talented. A collection of his cartoons was published in 1990 by the Friends of the National Zoo.

In his earlier cartoons he was fascinated with the theme of boomerangs as things that came back to bite you. That inspired our plotting to be the first people ever to throw a boomerang around the Washington Monument. I made a large one, almost a metre long, having earlier been taught the secrets in Cherbourg in Queensland. Off we went one night around midnight, accompanied by Dennis Stanford who was back in DC for a brief visit. Dennis was dressed impressively in a quality suit and tie. His job was distracting the security guards while I threw the boomerang, by telling them a long story about how he was from the *Guinness Book of Records*.

The monument is enormous. Square, at the base each side is about 17 metres long (55 feet). The boomerang had to travel more than seventy metres around it. When I threw it there was a long silence, then the boomerang clattered against the monument high above us. Success. By that time the guards had caught on that we were what we were, trespassers. After retrieving the boomerang, we ran in three separate directions to escape from the guards. Fortunately, they were a bit disinterested about chasing us. Bob later had the boomerang mounted on a maroon velvet background, and framed—I wonder where it is now? He is no longer with us, to ask.

* * *

Living in Maclean, Sandra and I went to work each morning in Dennis's large Ford Galaxy convertible, with the top down if the day was warm. We travelled along Chain Bridge Road, past the CIA building at Langley, past the Watergate building and across the 14th Street Bridge onto which, in January 1982, Air Florida Flight 90 crashed, after taking off from nearby National airport. We often stopped beside the Potomac River in the mornings, watching the aircraft come in at the rate of about two a minute to land at National; one moving off the runway, one stopping and one touching down all at the same time. The opposite happened in the afternoon when they were all leaving. Sandra liked to have breakfast out—she never had it at home—so I would either join her, or drop her off at a café and head on to the Museum.

The Watergate hearings into Nixon's dodgy behaviour were happening while we were in Maclean and Sandra attended the hearings, freelancing as a journalist for the *Washington Star*. On those days there was no need to listen to the news, she would come home at night and tell me what had happened that day.

Sandra and I were married in late 1973 in Bob Humphrey's house, appropriately decorated for the occasion. We all wore stylish velvet in some form and thought ourselves quite elegant as we sipped champagne from cut crystal.

* * *

I started my fellowship with no real idea what happened in a museum. Like most people not involved in them, I thought they were places to visit on Sunday afternoons, where stuff was displayed in order to educate and entertain, like the Hope Diamond and the dinosaur skeletons in the Natural History museum. That is true; but I soon discovered that the public display is just a minor part of their reason for being. In reality museums exist to promote research, and to maintain collections that assist that research, collections that I had contributed to from the research in Pakistan. In order to advance our knowledge, the most sophisticated collecting activities require deep research; and to further extend that research more collecting is essential.

A visit to the Pitt-Rivers Museum in Oxford, England, stays in my memory for its eccentricity and the apparent randomness of its displays, cases stuffed with ethnic exotica from around the world. The Smithsonian museums in Washington DC are at the other extreme, for the grandeur of their aspirations and the diversity of their interests. Anyone visiting the USA should see the Smithsonian museums as a first priority. The Smithsonian is the world's greatest *wunderkammer*, cabinet of curiosities, for ultimately it is man's curiosity that drives research. Francis Bacon, in the 1594 *Gesta Grayorum*, said: '*The compleat learned gentleman would want to compile a goodly huge cabinet, wherein whatsoever the hand of man by exquisite art or engine has made rare in stuff, form or motion; whatsoever singularity, chance or the shuffle of things has produced; whatsoever Nature has wrought in things that want life and may be kept; shall be sorted and included.'*

Over six months' worth of lunchtimes I saw everything on public display in the nearby National Museum of Art, and the Renwick Museum. Apart from its art collection the Art museum had the best cafeteria, in the basement. On more recent visits to Washington I have been engrossed by the Air and Space Museum, a collection of the actual objects or exact replicas of them, that have been in space or on the moon. The size of some of the rocket engines amazed me. The Hirschhorn Museum of Sculpture is nearby, a magnificent work of architecture with superb displays. Neither of these existed in my early Washington days.

* * *

Some of the world's most knowledgeable specialists worked in the Smithsonian and to my initial amazement, they were easily accessible. Once you were an insider you could call on the internal phones and ask the world's expert for an opinion, or ask a question and receive a friendly response. Even better, it was simple to knock on someone's door and be ushered in for a discussion. Whatever your specialisation you a member of the elite and had easy access. Nowhere in the world was it easier to learn from the best.

Saul Reisenberg, a dignified elderly gentleman whose office was just a few doors down the corridor was one of the world's experts on Polynesian navigation. I relished talking with him, learning how the Polynesians navigated their big twin hulled canoes, sailing across vast distances of open sea. I remembered Saul later when it became real, and I was travelling on a twin-hulled sailing canoe in Papua.

T. Dale Stewart, the museum forensic anthropologist was doing a post mortem analysis of an Egyptian mummy and he invited me to have a look. Imagine a bleak institutional room with grey walls and harsh lighting and a small long dead person laid out on a stainless bench, with someone carving into them; shiver-creating, but difficult to look away from. That was in the FBI headquarters, the J Edgar Hoover Building, just over the road from the Museum, the building you see in all the movies about the FBI.

People in the museum's Mineralogy Department used their specialised equipment to analyse my samples of glaze, glaze materials and fired clay. The electron microprobe was essentially an extremely high-powered microscope that allowed analysis of tiny areas of a sample. Bill Melson, head of the mineralogy department, was interested in my work and soon became a friend. Bill was a vulcanologist. He permanently kept a full set of his research gear, clothing and other supplies, at nearby Andrews Air Force Base in Maryland. From there he could be flown to a volcanic eruption anywhere in the world immediately after it began. Of more immediate interest to me, he was studying samples of moon rock brought back from the recent Apollo 14 mission. In the minerals lab one day, he tossed me a small piece of rock. It looked like a piece of basalt. I gave him a questioning look. He explained it was a moon rock that they had finished working on, giving me the unforgettable and exceptionally rare experience of holding a piece of the moon in my hand. With Brian Mason, Bill later published the textbook, *The Lunar Rocks*.

The Smithsonian is highly respected in America. Working there gave many formal privileges. One was access to diplomatic baggage, allowing access in other countries, or re-entry to the US, without any inspection by customs. It would have been unconscionable to misuse the privilege. It made some travel much simpler, such as entering and leaving Israel, forgoing their prolonged searches of everything.

Another privilege was easy access to people in other institutions who might normally be difficult to meet. I had a day in Boston, at Massachusetts Institute of Technology (MIT), with Cyril Stanley Smith. He had worked on the Manhattan Project, developing the atomic bomb during World War 2. In common with many of his co-workers there, he finally realised what they had done. Robert Oppenheimer summed it up: *I am become death, destroyer of worlds*, quoting from the *Bhagavad Gita* (XI,12).

No more bombs for Smith. He worked for the rest of his life as an historian of technology. It was in that role I went to visit with him, feeling that my work at the time might have something in common with his interests. To my great surprise he did almost nothing all day but ask me questions. He made no effort whatsoever to demonstrate his genius. He seemed to have no ego, just deep curiosity—the most important indication of intelligence. He was interested in learning; even from a novice like me who had only limited experience of the world. I admire him for that lesson. As a small thank you at the time, I bought his lunch. He invited me to lunch, his shout, and led me to a vending machine. When he went to pay he discovered he had no money and asked me if he could borrow five dollars.

I also went to visit Fred Matson, a specialist in studying pottery excavated by archaeologists. He said he had just returned from Germany. I asked what he had been doing there he told me he was so harassed at Penn State University by commitments and committees that he was unable to make time to finish a paper he was writing. He went to Germany for two weeks and stayed in a hotel room. Nobody knew he was there, so he had time to think and to finish it.

Jim Adavasio, the Post-doctoral fellow in Anthropology the year before me, invited me to the University of Pittsburgh to talk to his students about my work. I arrived in Pittsburgh during a snowstorm and Jim gave me a considerable fright by driving his powerful car fast on the icy roads. At home he offered me several strong drinks, followed by a suggestion that we should try samples of his collection of hashish from different parts of the world. We did the job properly and sampled them all.

I came to the next day to discover I was sitting at the front of a room full of expectant students, being introduced by Jim. To this day I have no idea what was discussed at that event; and I only resumed normal consciousness several days later. I was reminded of that experience many years later when Mitsuo Shoji invited me to talk to his students at Sydney College of the Arts. Mitsuo suggested we have lunch and a few drinks before the talk. In both instances I was forgiven and treated kindly by students who plied me with coffee and reassurance that they had seen it all before.

* * *

Near the end of my time in Washington I was offered jobs in the USA. My marriage to Sandra qualified me for a permanent residency visa, so there would be no problems of that kind. There was talk of assembling an archaeology research group of technical experts at Massachusetts Institute of Technology, one of the world's prime research institutions. Each member would have experience in an area that would help to interpret archaeological material; pottery, human and animal skeletons, basket making and cordage and other exotic specialisations. The group would work together on projects anywhere in the world. That appealed to me, having learned what it was like to work with the best people in a well-funded and highly regarded research centre, in a but in the end it never came together. If it had I might still be in Boston. If is a small word, sometimes with large consequences.

Another job in the US that was offered in 1972 involved working in a group where each person was identified as a 'creative thinker', developing methods of using the sun as a source of power, solar energy. The basic idea was that lateral thinking might produce something novel whereas anyone trained in engineering and physics might just follow conventional thought processes. Not that any of this mattered, the whole idea was alien to my psyche and it took only a short while to say no. I am pleased to say that the harnessing of energy available from the sun has proceeded acceptably well without me.

Any ongoing stay in the US involving a job would have to wait anyway. My Smithsonian contract was coming to an end in 1973 but I was determined to finish the book on Pakistani potters. Time had been lost visiting Israel to start work on a new study of traditional Palestinian potters, following on from the work in Pakistan. It was my first book, so it was extremely important to me to get it completed and published. Cliff Evans had extended my Smithsonian fellowship, and its income, beyond the limits of even his administrative ingenuity and could not do any more to help me stay in Washington. He did help me apply for a grant that would allow living in London for four months. The grant was given on what was really a fairly flimsy excuse that I wanted to continue my research in the India Office Library and in the Indian collections of the Victoria and Albert Museum. The truth was I just wanted to finish the book; and London was then one of my favourite cities.

* * *

Early in 1974 Sandra and I began a four-month stay in London. We found a top-floor flat in Harrington Gardens, near to Gloucester Road. A round blue ceramic plaque on the outside of the next-door building said it had been one of the homes of W. S. Gilbert, Sullivan's mate, of *The Pirates of*

Penzance and *Mikado* fame. I would take a bet that when W.S. was at home he had more salubrious surroundings than our claustrophobic attic of a room. Still, it had a bed, and a chair and a table, and some facilities for preparing meals and washing bodies, so it did the job.

The contrast with working in an office in the Smithsonian was dramatic. At the museum I had been a tiny part of a grand institution, with every facility anyone could ever want for pursuing research, and a building full of fascinating colleagues. In London I was a loner, knowing virtually nobody. Whether I worked or not, and what I worked on, was a matter of total disinterest to everyone around. Working hours were non-existent. Early morning, late night, there were no regular hours when everyone entered the building or went out again, not that the Smithsonian researchers had been quite that regular either. That suited me, independence always has. My great fortune is to rarely have been subjected to timed routines formulated by someone else.

Sandra's training and experience as a journalist meant she easily found a job. She was employed by the British Epilepsy association as editor of their magazine. It regularly went out to anyone interested in that subject. Her salary and my grant income meant we lived quite well, helped by the fact that London in those days was one of the cheap cities to live in. Food, rent, clothes, all the necessities were much cheaper than in the USA, so much so that once when I was living in Washington and needed to buy new clothes it had been cheaper to fly to London and buy them than it was to buy them in the USA. Not only that but in those days of Carnaby Street fashion the London fashions were much more interesting than the dull polyester offerings available in DC.

* * *

The old India Office Library on Blackfriars Road in East London was established in 1801. Its character had not changed much in 1973. The books and documents were not dusty but looked like they should have been. This colonial remnant was well hidden away from the world on the top floor, eleven up in a plain ordinary building. It held documents from the British in India, and journals and books relating to Indian history. They rarely contained information about ceramics, but it was a usefully quiet place for writing, using only pen and paper.

I found pleasure in the ride on the underground, the walk across Blackfriars Bridge, and the strange ambience of East London. Much later my father occupied himself discovering family history, and found that our ancestors had lived in East London; the earliest members of his family in Australia had migrated from there. That explained my mysterious feelings of connection to the area—it was implanted somewhere in the genes.

That part of London suffered from bombing during World War 2. There were remnants, vacant sites and evidence of the damage, an odd sight to an Australian who had never seen such things at home. Something formerly a distant abstract concept was converted into reality: the Germans really did drop bombs on this place. Despite the damage many buildings were untouched, including some small pubs, strange places that could fit no more than a dozen drinkers inside. I regularly had my lunch, hunched in a corner, in one that offered various kinds of sausages and chips and that nasty concoction HP Sauce.

Writing in our home attic became difficult. My eyes hurt and I often had a headache, leading me to consulting a local GP, a formidably breasted senior female with a booming voice. She asked my occupation and I told her, writing. As a cure for my ills she recommended I go out and buy a strong light, because writing in the poor light in the dim attic was the cause. Following her advice gave relief. That same light sits beside me on my desk still, rejigged with an Australian plug. She also suggested that it would be relaxing if I got naked and walked around for five minutes every hour, telling me that she did that herself, to relax. It took quite some time to erase that image from my mind.

The Victoria and Albert Museum had a collection of ceramics from old India, stored in an annex in an outer suburb of London. With all the necessary permissions sorted, I turned up to a meeting arranged there with a curator, who showed me around and introduced me to the two permanent caretakers, both Englishmen. The process of looking at pots in the collection was to find one listed in the catalogue, write its accession number on the appropriate form and hand it to one of the caretakers who would then go and find the pot and bring it to my allocated worktable. All very formal.

On the first day, when it was time for their morning tea, one of the caretakers asked me if I would like tea. I was jaw-droppingly surprised when it was duly made and placed on a table far away from where they were sitting. My natural response was to take it over and sit with them, but it was immediately clear that made them uncomfortable. It took a while for me to work out that the problem was that I was considered by them to be of a higher social class and they thought themselves unsuitable company for such an exalted being.

This was the English social system right there in front of me, my first real exposure to it. No doubt the curator who had shown me around would have taken tea separately. We got it worked out before too long though, and we eventually just sat and talked like old acquaintances. I was sorry to eventually say goodbye to them, good blokes both.

* * *

Finally, the book was all done and the manuscript sent off to Cliff Evans. In response he sent an agonised, apologetic letter saying that the Smithsonian had just adopted a new policy. Only monographs written by full-time members of staff would be published. Cliff suggested putting his name on the cover as joint author to allow it to be published. In doing so he was obviously deeply embarrassed, because this was a well-known ploy by incompetent but ambitious academics that were not doing much themselves, to associate their name with publications by juniors who had done all the work. But I knew Cliff too well for that, and understood he was trying to help, so, agreed, with absolutely no hard feelings. *Traditional Pottery Techniques of Pakistan* was published under our joint names. Otherwise it may not have been published at all.

* * *

The book was finished, the grant money was nearly gone, and the attractions of London were waning. We decided to go to Australia rather than back to the US and began looking for a job to go home to. A letter to Arthur Basham, Professor and Head of the Department of Asian Civilisations at the Australian National University, explained my interest in pots, and Islamic countries, and my wish to turn those interests into a job. Basham was a historian specialising in India so it seemed my experience in Pakistan might be a positive, might allow me to continue working there or in other nearby countries. Iran beckoned, and then there was Afghanistan, Uzbekistan and all the other *stans*. In the end there never was a reply from Basham.

Presently though along came a positive letter from Jack Golson, Head of the Department of Prehistory at ANU. He offered me a job; or more accurately, a two-year post-doctoral fellowship which from that distance looked like a job, especially considering the non-existent alternatives. It would involve studying pottery. The idea had other benefits too. My family were a short drive away from Canberra and other relatives lived there, it was familiar territory. It all looked good. My return letter explained to Jack that I could not turn up straight away, having organised to be in Israel for four months studying traditional Palestinian potters. His reply: no problem.

12
ISRAEL

Some problems are so complex that you have to be highly intelligent
and well informed just to be undecided about them.

— Laurence J Peter (of the *Peter Principle,*
Oxford Essential Quotations 5, 2017)

My experience of Jewish people started soon after beginning high school.
I went into one of the two general stores in Berridale for something. The
shopkeeper Roman Chaikovsky was intrigued. Not long before he had
a fairly vocal disagreement with my father, who had suggested where
the old man could go, and said he would never go in his store again.
Characteristic of Stanley, he never did.

Roman was puzzled. *'Your father refuses to come into my shop. So
why do you come in?'* My answer, roughly remembered, was that the
disagreement was with my father, not with me. The result was that over
the next few years we became friends. When later Roman sold the shop
and took over a business making concrete blocks, he occasionally paid me
to do some work there.

In discussions over a cup of coffee it emerged that he and his wife, both
Polish, and the first Jews I knew, had been in Auschwitz. They showed
me the numbers tattooed on their arms. He told me that he had escaped
the gas chamber three times. The first when there was some fault in the
equipment. The second when a prisoner had snatched a rifle from a guard
he then shot, and a melee started. I wonder now if it was the incident on
October 7 1944 where two prisoners assigned to staff the gas chambers
launched a brief, unsuccessful uprising. The third reprieve came later, in
January 1945, when many prisoners were marched out of the camps, and
guards began murdering the remainder, but left soon after leaving many
prisoners still alive. Russian soldiers entered the camp soon after.

Roman loved trout fishing which he often did at Eucumbene Lake at
night. Returning home to Berridale at dawn one morning, long after I had
moved to Sydney, he picked up a hitchhiker who shot him in the head,
dumped his body in a ditch and stole the car, a 220S Mercedes. Later it

became known that the murderer was wanted by police and had used the car to make an unsuccessful escape. It is a sad irony that Roman survived so much only to end up murdered anyway.

* * *

Two cities have intrigued me more than any other: Jerusalem and Peshawar. I loved Peshawar in the 1970s because of echoes everywhere of the mediaeval city it once was. And I loved Jerusalem because of—because of what? What a difficult question to answer. Its old city, primarily, fascinating in its rich complexity, its narrow laneways stepping up and down, its stalls selling all manner of goods, and its complexity of cultures spread over four quarters (Muslim, Christian, Jewish and Armenian) before the Israelis began taking it all. In the 1970s the Israelis had begun the process of encircling the old city by the profound ugliness, visual and political, of the new Israeli box-structured buildings aimed at claiming total ownership. Their term for this was *'facts on the ground'*.

What I savoured in Jerusalem was the intricacy of its history, reflected everywhere you went. Reach out on one side of a laneway and you touched a building that had been there two thousand years. Reach out the other hand and you bumped against an Israeli soldier with an assault rifle at the ready. Jerusalem sits on a junction between Africa, Asia and Europe where invaders through history have passed. The impossibility of its politics now is just a continuation of its past; it has ever been so, and so it will be.

The land around Jerusalem (*Al-Quds* in Arabic), is central in the history of three of the world's great religions, Islam, Christianity and Judaism. The region is known to most Christian westerners as *The Holy Land*, to Muslims as (in Arabic) *Al-Ard Al-Muqaddasah*, and to Jews it is *The Promised Land*; the latter concept the source of present-day conflict. Each of the three religions has sacred buildings or structures within Jerusalem's old walled city. The Temple of David (and its remnant Wailing Wall) is central to Jews, the Church of the Holy Sepulchre to Christians and the Dome of the Rock is where Muslims believe Muhammad rose to heaven. These three religions have fought over, and alternately ruled over the area. Each has strong claims to it, or at least strong arguments about its significance to them. Any rational person would suggest they should all have some share in its politics and administration. Instead, there is no part of the world that allows less rationality.

* * *

My first trip to Israel was in 1973. The three weeks in August finished not long before Israel's war of that year with Egypt and Syria. I planned to locate where Palestinian potters were working, and how many there were. I stayed in the old city of Jerusalem with John Landgraf, an American who was also interested in Palestinian potters.

The second trip, with Sandra, was a four-month stay in 1974 following our time in London where I completed the Pakistan book. We lived in the apartment with Al and Lois Glock in Ali Ibn Abu Taleb Street, off Salah ed-Din Street, opposite the Israeli District Court where Palestinian prisoners were brought on open jeeps with calico bags tied over their head. Salah ed-Din Street was the ancient main road to Damascus, something like an equivalent of Sydney Road in Melbourne.

My final visit, in March to May 1977 with Brenda, my wife from my third marriage, came when we were both working at the Prehistory Department at ANU in Canberra. It started for me with a brief stay, cared for by Irish nurses, in St Joseph's Hospital, with serious stomach problems. We lived in Beit Hanina (between Jerusalem and Ramallah) in an apartment rented from Setrak Balian, an Armenian potter. Beit Hanina was originally a small village. Now it is surrounded by Israeli settlements aimed at ultimately excluding all Palestinians; part of their long-term plan to remove all Palestinian Arabs from Israel.

* * *

Most of the Palestinian potters I saw worked in the old traditions, making unglazed wares used for water, for cooking, for storage and other purposes. A distinctively different group of Armenian potters in Jerusalem made glazed ware. Setrak Balian, our hospitable and amiable landlord, told me how they had arrived there.

The Dome of the rock (Mosque of Omar) is one of the best known and the most photographed features in Jerusalem. It was completed in the 7th century, built on the site from which Muslims believe Mohammed ascended to heaven. It was damaged during the First World War and in

1918 Armenian potters were brought from Kutahya in Turkey to repair the damage, one of several renovations during the 20th century. Setrak Balian presented me with an original tile made by his grandfather for that purpose but not used. It is one of my valued possessions.

Later the Armenian Pottery (known as the Palestinian Pottery in the 1970s) was established on Nablus Road, near the then US Consulate. Another workshop, the Jerusalem Pottery had been set up on Via Dolorosa in 1965. Visitors to Jerusalem will have seen the coloured tile street signs and house numbers in the old city and in East Jerusalem. All these were made by the Armenian potters.

Balian told me that Kutahya potters originated in Persia and moved to Turkey in the 15th century. The inhabitants of Kutahya were lucky to have the sympathy of the local Turkish administrator so there no massacres of Armenians there from 1915 on.

∗ ∗ ∗

The house John Landgraf was renting, where I stayed on my first trip, was like something from a fantasy. It was in a dead end, off an alley, off a lane, off a minor street in the old city; it was easy to get lost trying to find it. It had four stories on a narrow frontage. Each level was five hundred years newer than the one below it, making the ground floor two thousand years old, more or less. We often sat in the tiny courtyard beneath the cooling branches of the lemon tree, drinking tea made from its leaves. Lemon tea was very palatable and refreshing for a few minutes after brewing and then became increasingly bitter and undrinkable. John was a seriously committed vegetarian. He spent half a day shopping, half a day chopping and a few minutes cooking and eating.

I soon adapted to the rhythm of Jerusalem life. Siesta from about midday to 2 pm; there was no point in going out because nothing happened anyway. Business resumed mid-afternoon and continued into the early evening. In the warmer months everyone went out for late evening walks and the streets were quietly lively. It seemed wise for me to respect the religious days each week; Muslim Friday, Jewish Saturday (Sabbath) and the Christian Sunday, by taking that day off.

My favourite eating place was the Golden Chicken in Salah ed-Din Street. Diners could recline like a Roman emperor on couches if they wished, although for me trying to eat lying down was too uncomfortable. The chairs were more practical. Many a 40-salad was consumed there, that being a meal that consisted of forty tiny portions of different delicacies; followed by their chicken that was golden indeed.

My working base on each trip was the Albright Institute for Archaeological Research, known generally to all as the Albright. Originally established in 1900 as the American School of Oriental Research in Jerusalem, it was a beautiful old stone building in Salah ed-Din Street. A quiet haven secluded from a busy urban setting, it had accommodation for visiting scholars and a welcoming cool courtyard that had witnessed discussion between many esteemed residents. Having tea in the courtyard seemed just so civilised. I became friendly with Jörg Schmeisser, a printmaker and resident there. He made superbly detailed prints, working as an illustrator for an archaeological dig. Jörg later taught printmaking at the Canberra Art School.

* * *

My work in Israel originated at the Smithsonian, more or less by accident, the kind of accident in life that happens in the right place at the right time with the right people. I was friendly with another Fellow there, Bill Potts. Bill was Jewish, short and sturdy, black haired and bearded. He was interested in the archaeology of the Middle East, especially Israel, and knowing about my work in Pakistan, Bill felt studying Palestinian potters would be a natural development.

It was easy to get research funding then. Bill had contacts with Dr Al Glock, an American archaeologist living in Jerusalem. Al offered to contribute funds to help my work. Cliff Evans helped me apply to the American Philosophical Society for money for the 1973 trip. Later in 1976, Betty Meggers was on the Committee for Research and Exploration of the National Geographic Society so it was easy enough to organise a grant from them for my 1977 trip, which was also supported by the ANU Department of Prehistory by giving me leave with salary.

My plan in 1973 was to find all the Palestinian potters still working in a traditional way. Bill Potts had previously done archaeological work in Israel and given me a general briefing, but I went there with virtually no knowledge of the region apart from some place names remembered from my enforced attendance at the Berridale Anglican church as a child. I had heard about Jerusalem, Nazareth, Bethlehem and the Sea of Galilee. I had no conception of the history, or of modern-day realities. I still feel a twinge of embarrassment when I remember seeing the street sign for the Via Dolorosa and asking Al Glock, a man steeped in the history of the region, why the road signs were in Italian? I had even forgotten about the Romans and the crucifixion, all information that then (and now) had little value to me.

* * *

Al Glock was not as I had imagined before meeting him. He was the complete opposite of an Indiana Jones character; as in reality most archaeologists are. When we first met, he was still a Baptist minister associated with the University of Chicago. He had a quiet speaking manner and he could walk past you in the street without being noticed. He was an ordinary looking man dressed in ordinary clothes, with a slight stoop as he began to age. If you stopped to talk to him you might find he was not interested in many subjects, but that his mind instead was focused on his archaeological work and the controversies surrounding it. He was a man with a mission, albeit a mission that had evolved into something very different to the one that had first brought him to 'The Holy Land'.

He first went to Palestine in 1962, and was later resident for 17 years until his death. As an archaeologist, he was known widely in the region, but less well known in his original role as a Lutheran minister and missionary. He abandoned these responsibilities over the years, although he retained his Christian beliefs. His initial interest had been Biblical archaeology, a form of research with a long history, intended to illuminate and even prove the truth of the Christian Bible. To this same end, various archaeological schools with a heavy emphasis on biblical studies had been set up in Jerusalem: in 1900 the American School of Oriental Research (later the Albright); in 1890 the École Biblique et Archaéologique Française de Jérusalem; and the British School of Archaeology in Jerusalem, set up in 1919 by the Palestine Exploration Fund. The latter is now the Kenyon Institute, a broader based institution renamed after Kathleen Kenyon, excavator of the ancient city of Jericho.

Glock soon realised that archaeology that was based on evidence often contradicted and sometimes denied the biblical accounts. As one example the Kenyon excavation of the Jericho mound in the 1950s showed that Jericho was uninhabited when the Israelites were supposed to have been there, an error of around 150 years. The myth of Joshua causing the walls to fall is contradicted by evidence of many earthquakes in the area. Biblical 'scholars' range from obvious nutcases, to well-meaning individuals attempting to better understand the Bible, to proper academics, the latter who mostly publish only in narrowly focused literature.

As Glock became more involved in understanding local life and politics, particularly through involvement with Palestinians, he moved from biblical archaeology, which focused on faith-based hypotheses with a narrow view of the history of the area, to open minded evidence-based archaeology. This change in approach canvassed many issues: how to separate fact from fiction, belief from reality, delusion from rationality, legend from observation? How could lumps of fact be rescued from this murky soup of myth? In the final reduction the issue is the conflict between faith or belief, and evidence—something that has become a common theme of modern civilisation, even modern politics worldwide.

Glock's ideas about conventional archaeology were developing when I first worked with him. His role in local archaeology was developing in parallel. In 1970 he had been appointed as research professor at the Albright Institute, where in 1978 he was made Director, a prestigious appointment.

Al expected that my knowledge of pottery techniques would contribute to studies of pottery from his excavations. Previously pottery was classified according to the shape of vessels and any decoration applied to them. A Byzantine pot had a certain appearance, as did a Mycenaean pot. Think of it like this. Can you look at a pot and recognise who made it? This requires highly specialised awareness, and previous study of a large number of pots, knowing who made them. As a modern example: a Janet Mansfield pot is quickly identifiable by the characteristic form, and from the surface which results from her methods of firing. Some archaeologists developed a reputation as 'pottery experts' based on this kind of knowledge and experience of excavated pottery.

Al was looking for more sophisticated classification methods that might allow assigning the sherds to more precise time periods, and might allow more information to be derived from the sherds. He had looked at evaluating minerals displayed in thin sections cut from pots as a new method of classification, a method that Bill Potts had suggested. But this proved far too complex to be useful generally. My job was to look for other methods. I decided to look at techniques used in making the ancient pots, to see if that could help. This research was later summarised in my book *Pottery Technology*, first published by Taraxacum Press in 1981.

Later, when Glock was teaching at Birzeit University, the Palestinian institution near Ramallah, he developed the idea of ethnoarchaeology, the archaeology of ordinary people rather than the archaeology of rulers and warfare. Our discussions of my work in Pakistan, and Wulff's in Persia helped develop this thinking. The ideas were first applied to studying pots excavated by Glock at Tell Taanach. The general idea was for me to study traditional potters still working in the region, and see how knowledge from this could be applied to learn more from excavated pottery.

A *tell* in this part of the world is an isolated mound or hill, sometimes a hundred metres high or more, often flat on top, and several hundred meters around the base. Tells are man-made, not natural, and have been built up over many years by successive destruction of buildings and erection of new ones on top of the rubble. Tell Taanach is one such. North of Jerusalem, it overlooks the Plain of Esdraelon, the valley of Jezreel, prime agricultural land Israelis took from the Palestinians beginning in 1967.

The first builders of Taanach were the Canaanites roughly 4000 years ago; the area has been occupied one way or another ever since. When I visited there was still clear evidence of Jordanian military trenches and other structures from 1967 on the top, on the north side.

Taanach is a few kilometres from another tell the Israelis call Megiddo, better known to us as Armageddon. I regret not having sat on Taanach, writing a letter to someone beginning: '*I am presently close to Armageddon*'. Following Glock's excavations of Tell Taanach he worked in the Palestinian village of Ti'innik, situated at the base of the Tell, aiming to develop an understanding of recent Islamic residents and how they lived; an aim that did not endear him to the Israeli authorities.

The archaeology of the Islamic heritage in the area was in the past neglected in favour of Christian biblical issues. Under Israeli rule it is now actively discouraged or even forbidden. Israeli archaeology is more political than religious, aimed at establishing 'ownership' through ancient connections mainly with the Iron Age, the period when the Jews believe they came out of Egypt into what is present day Israel, or at least parts of it.

A major method of Israeli archaeology has been to deliberately destroy the upper (Islamic, Christian) layers by bulldozing them aside, until reaching evidence of ancient Iron Age Jewish levels. Then they began careful excavation. Al told me it was common knowledge among visiting American and European archaeologists that an Israeli excavation would be conducted in that manner. This destructive approach, obliterating Palestinian heritage was discussed by Katherine Lamie in a 2007 article *The Life and Death of Albert Glock.*[6]

Destruction is not new here; few areas on earth have been subject to so many invasions and takeovers, mass murders and destruction of previous cultures. It is the crossroads between North Africa, Europe and Asia. Throughout history invaders of one necessarily passed through here from another, giving the area high strategic value. As an aside, presumably the first humans to enter Europe from Africa also travelled through this region. Each phase of occupation of this land has established its own landmarks for the next to destroy. The Israeli destruction of Palestinian culture is but the latest in line.

Anyone working in this region has to decide where their political loyalties are placed. Glock decided that if his work would inevitably involve him in political disputes, he would begin to concentrate on archaeology that helped the Palestinian cause. This crystallised when he started teaching part time at Birzeit University in 1976, while still at the Albright. Birzeit is the main Palestinian university, established in 1975 in Birzeit town near Ramallah. Its symbol is the olive tree. Glock moved to full time work at Birzeit in 1980.

Birzeit University had a policy forbidding cooperation with Israeli academic institutions, and there was antipathy towards Glock and his aims by many Israelis. Despite being caught in the middle, Glock had good contacts with various Israeli professionals. Such contradictions are an integral part of the irrationality in this part of the world. One of these Israelis, Dan Gill, told me that if you wanted to operate in that part of the world, it was necessary to make your views clear so everyone knew what they were dealing with. Nobody cared what attitudes you had, there was a full spectrum; but they liked to know how to deal with you on a day to day basis, whether to reveal secrets or keep them, whether to invite you into their home or keep you at a distance.

Paradoxically by our standards, but befitting local irrationality, Glock also received opposition from many Palestinians who for their own reasons decided that his work was helping the Israeli cause. He faced hostility from all sides. His life was further complicated by attempting to conform to UN regulations about occupying powers, regulations ignored by Israelis. According to the UN, an occupying power is a temporary manager with responsibility for preserving cultural heritage, and it is illegal to carry material across international boundaries. Israel did not see itself as an occupying power but as a rightful owner of what they term 'the promised land', so does not recognise the boundary between the West Bank and Israel as an international boundary.

Israeli policy is that finds from digs in the West Bank must be deposited in an Israeli Museum. Conversely, Jordan considered the West Bank, although occupied by Israel, as part of Jordan. Their policy was that permission must be obtained from Jordan for any archaeological activities in the West Bank. Again, Al was caught in the middle. He elected to obtain permission for his dig in Tell Taanach from the Jordanian Department of Antiquities in Amman, where he made regular visits, partly to renew his residency visa and partly to consult with the relevant department and to organise funds to carry on his research.

Everyone who knew him had a view about what Glock was up to. One common one was that he was a spy. Some believed he worked for the CIA, some thought for the Israelis. This idea may have arisen from the fact that in order to function at all he had to have communications with Israelis; or from the common view from all sides that any foreigner who spent any time in the West Bank was probably a spy. Another view was that he was dealing in antiquities. This may well have arisen from the common idea that archaeologists search for treasure, an idea popularly developed in fiction and movies about archaeology and not helped by popularisation—think of Tutankhamen and his golden heritage.

The idea that Al was dealing in antiquities may also have derived from something much more prosaic; that the history of people is in part preserved in museums. The Rockefeller Museum in East Jerusalem,

Palestine's major museum before 1967, held a strong record of Palestinian history and culture, until it was taken over by Israelis who then imposed their priorities on it and moved some major items to other Israeli museums.

As a result, Glock was extremely interested in establishing a collection of Palestinian antiquities and indeed modern objects. Along with Al and John Landgraf I was involved in collecting Palestinian pottery in villages, both modern and old. While we may have been dealing in antiquities because we were buying them, the purpose was as honourable as the aims of any museum; to preserve evidence of Palestinian culture. They were to be housed in a future museum of Palestinian culture. The Israeli authorities may well have considered this illegal; they were only interested in getting rid of Palestinian culture.

The big problem with my collection was where it would reside. I have no idea what happened to the 100 or so pots. They were originally stored in the house of a Palestinian employee of the Albright Institute. I fear that if they were found during a house raid by Israeli soldiers that they would have been smashed. I hope they ended up at the Albright Institute which is relatively safe, or at Birzeit; although Birzeit is far from a safe place because it is subjected to constant Israeli closures and curfews.

* * *

Back to the beginning. On my first trip I needed to travel the whole West Bank and Gaza, to locate all the traditional potters. The language difficulty was solved in a way familiar after my long stay in Pakistan, by using an interpreter that Al organised for me. This was a young man who said 'call me Mike'. He was not willing to talk about his reasons for being involved, but they gradually emerged. Discretion was necessary because he was a recruiter for Al Fatah, the main Palestinian political organisation, founded in 1959. Yassir Arafat was its leader. Like Sinn Fein in Ireland, it had a political wing and a militant wing. Mike was carrying messages, and recruiting people for, the militant cause—active in resisting Israeli occupation and its humiliations '... *this life which has destroyed our cultural, moral and political existence and destroyed our human dignity*' (Helga Baumgarten).[7]

My pairing with Mike made sense for both of us. With Palestinians it gave me credibility that I was not an Israeli spy or agent, so I would be at the least tolerated and at best welcome in Palestinian villages and towns. To Israeli intelligence it provided the cover that he was travelling with me as an interpreter.

It was not a comfortable relationship. Mike was young, and despite his quiet approach in public he was simmering with passionate rage. As with many Palestinians, he had developed a sense of extreme injustice about their treatment by Israelis, and abandonment by the international community. It is painful to say that was back in 1973 and as I write this many years later the only changes are for the worse, as the intensity of Israeli oppression keeps increasing.

Mike had not the slightest interest in my project and often became unresponsive, even angry after a few minutes of translation. Obviously to him it was a waste of his time. I was more supportive of his project than he was of mine. It would have been easy for me to become frustrated and angry; but I was neither, instead happy enough to get the minimum result. Knowing the names and locations of all the Palestinian potters and having met most of them was the main aim, and that was successful. Understanding their work could wait till next time.

* * *

For the second visit, Sandra and I came in from London in 1974. The three months then were far more productive. I studied potters in the main pottery centres: Gaza, Hebron in the south and Jenin in the north near Nablus, and many other locations in villages, working with John Landgraf, a fluent Arabic speaker and an excellent interpreter. We were able to discuss any confusion and sort it out with ease. John had also taken a strong interest in Palestinian pottery traditions and had been making his own records, so he was pleased to further his knowledge. We were both equally immersed in the work.

John and I had completely different personalities and temperaments but we travelled together with no discord. John's experience expanded my planned travel itinerary, taking us for example to Haifa where Christians made pottery more modern than traditional. We traversed the coast around Haifa (old Jaffa) and later drove to the Sea of Galilee. Christians would be either delighted or annoyed that we camped on the supposed

LEBANON

SYRIA

GOLAN
HEIGHTS

HAIFA

NAZARETH

TELL
TAANACH

JENIN

JORDAN

MEDITERRANEAN
SEA

NABLUS

WEST BANK

BIRZEIT

BEIT
HANINA

JERICHO

JERUSALEM

QUMRAN

ISRAEL

HEBRON

DEAD
SEA

GAZA

AL ARISH

location of the sermon on the mount. No fish were multiplied.

Travel then, only a few years after the 1967 war was not impossibly restricted by Israeli roadblocks and checkpoints as it is now. We could go virtually anywhere we wanted in the West Bank or Gaza, unobstructed. There were exceptions. Gus Van Beek from the Smithsonian, who was excavating a site not far out of Gaza, asked me to help interpret a kiln he had excavated. His crew were staying about ten kilometres from the dig. Driving to and from work, we were led by a truck with a device on front flailing chains onto the road, to destroy mines or what are now called IEDs, improvised explosive devices.

It was not all work; we looked around widely from El Arish in the South to the Golan Heights in the north, from the Dead Sea in the west bordering Jordan, to Haifa on the Mediterranean coast. From Gaza, we drove south-west along the Mediterranean coast, to visit Bedouins that John knew, camped in their magnificent tents in the desert near El Arish. Sitting with a group of these dignified people, we were given coffee. The most distinguished guests are given the longest brewed, strongest coffee and refills. I buzzed for two days.

Between us John and I got the information we needed. Our ultimate aim was a book on Palestinian potters. We decided to divide the task. John would write about women potters who used hand building methods to make their work and I would write about the male potters who made their work on potter's wheels. For a multiplicity of reasons neither book was ever completed although we had each done a draft. After John died in 2018 his wife Elizabeth has overseen completion of a combined book.[8]

Sandra and I travelled around also, into areas where there were no potters; but fascinating places to see. We traversed the area of the Jordan Valley, past Jericho and the Dead Sea. I particularly valued our visit to Qumran, the village established by the Essenes, members of a Jewish religious sect who escaped from the Roman occupation and established Qumran as a sanctuary. They created the Dead Sea scrolls which they hid in nearby caves, to be discovered again in the 1940s. A highlight at Qumran for me was seeing two Roman style kilns that had been excavated, one of which was almost complete, allowing clear understanding of the kiln size and design. These kilns were by modern standards quite small—the domed chamber where pots were stacked was about 60–70 centimetres across and about the same height.

On another excursion we swam in the Dead Sea, if floating around on the oily looking salt saturated surface can be called swimming. The ancient Jordanian site of Petra immediately over the other side was hidden in the haze. We moved on to Masada, the location where it's claimed that almost a thousand Jews committed suicide rather than be captured by the Romans in AD73.

Later we had a day trip to the Golan Heights, where the ground was strewn with metal, shrapnel from artillery and tank battles in the 1973 war between Syria and Israel. Quneitra was a town destroyed, with not a square metre of any remnants of building free of damage from bullets or shrapnel. Walking around was difficult because the ground was completely covered with fragments of metal.

* * *

In 1977, in a potter's workshop I often visited, a man came in sometimes and sat quietly in a corner, watching, not speaking to anyone. He was almost bald with just a little short hair on each side of his head; not all that tall, and a little portly. Everyone seemed to know him but for some reason nobody acknowledged him. His eyes were on everything, taking it all in.

One day he said to me, in perfect English: *'Do you want to see some old pottery?'* I did. Travelling in my Kombi van, we went off, briefly on a main road, then along a side track for a few kilometres, and finally down a rough track to a large modern tin shed, much like one that can be seen in any Australian industrial area or farm. Inside I was immediately astounded. On racks, the metal shelves were loaded with ancient pots, in every direction, thousands upon thousands of them.

'Where did you get these?' I asked him. *'I made them'* he replied. I caught on straight away. I was in the presence of The Forger, the mythical man everyone knew about but nobody knew. The archaeologists knew about his existence, the gift shops knew about his existence, the antiquities dealers knew about his existence. But nobody I had ever met knew who he was; or if they did, they did not tell. I don't know why he decided to trust me. *'Look around,'* he said, and I did for half an hour or so, looking through the amazing range of pots from all periods of history, perfect in their 'as excavated' replications. Most of them seemed to still have traces

of the dirt from which it appeared they had been dug.

He did not at any stage ask me to keep it confidential. He had introduced himself so I had his name and location. I was there presumably because he felt that he could trust me, or perhaps he had talked to others who had said—correctly—that I could be trusted.

He knew I was working with archaeologists based in Jerusalem. His *piece de resistance* was his story, illustrated by showing me some of the actual pots and a copy of an article in an archaeological journal, about how he had studied archaeological literature of the area very closely. He had identified a problem archaeologists had with the early Bronze Age, a gap in the chronology. One style of pottery had been succeeded by another quite different, with a distinct time break between. He had worked out what a *'missing link'* might look like, and made a range of pottery that fitted the image. The pots were then suitably aged, and then hidden in a cave.

Through some well-staged choreography, he then had the proverbial shepherd boy lead an archaeologist to the cave and discover the horde. Subsequently the archaeologist published his findings in a prestigious journal. The forger showed me a copy of the article, something in which he took great delight, rocking back and forwards with mirth as he told the story. Even stranger for me, I knew the archaeologist involved, an American I saw quite frequently; and could not in conscience tell him the story. I still suspect he would not have believed it anyway, although scientific testing of the pottery for age would have shown clearly that the pots had been fired recently.

As we left the warehouse the forger reached out almost randomly and tossed a small pot to me, saying *'here is a little souvenir of your visit'*. Later when I was leaving to go back to the US, I realised that the little Hellenistic style pot might be judged by the airport authorities to be real rather than a copy. Taking it out of Israel necessitated a certificate from the Rockefeller Museum certifying that it was not a rare and valuable antiquity. I left it at the appropriate museum desk; and went back a few weeks later, to be told that I could not take it out of the country because it was quite rare.

That created a small conundrum. I hated leaving it because of its inherent story and associations. I could not say it was a fake. Israeli experts had said it was not and they knew best. There was no point in questioning their superior knowledge. Finally, Al Glock provided me with a reference on Albright Institute letterhead, in his role as director, saying I was working on important archaeological research and the piece was critical to my studies in Australia. The experts gave me permission to take it with me. I still have it. I still show it to visitors to my house sometimes, and retell the story for the thousandth time.

* * *

Albert Glock was murdered on January 19, 1992. He had been working at the Birzeit University Archaeology Institute sorting pottery. He left there, intending to visit a close female colleague. He parked his car on the road near her house, but he never made it to her front door. From the front garden, concealed from the road, a young man wearing a black and white *kaffiyah* head scarf and dressed in a dark jacket, jeans, and white tennis shoes shot him three times.

Who killed Al Glock? That is still unproven. Englishman Edward Fox wrote a book based on that question. It was an assassination rather than an everyday murder. Glock was the first American to be murdered in the Occupied Territories.

Various theories exist about his death. One points to Palestinian villagers objecting to Al's archaeology, partly through fears that if archaeology was conducted in their area and brought up evidence of earlier Israelite occupation then the military would seize the land and they would lose it forever.

Another theory attributes the murder to rivals and disaffected colleagues at Birzeit, especially one from whom Glock withheld a position the applicant felt he deserved. Glock became the foreigner taking a job a Palestinian should have had. Hamas has also been implicated, for reasons not clear, although it was said they considered the murder would disrupt peace talks in Oslo. A strong argument against Palestinians being involved is that most foreigners who were active in the West Bank or Gaza were sympathetic to the Palestinian cause. It was difficult for any visitor who travelled around to see the reality of what was going on there and not take that side.

The most likely killer was a member of Israeli death squads instructed to remove someone who was beginning to put forward dangerous theories contradicting Israeli heritage claims to ownership of land. There is no rule of law in the West Bank; it is subject to the whims of the military occupation. Murder of Palestinians is an everyday act by settlers and members of the Israeli military, both doing as they please without retribution, with no fear of ordinary justice as we understand it being applied.

Israeli logic leading to the disposal of Glock may simply have been to create fear in Birzeit University. Educated Palestinians are considered dangerous. Fox quotes Gabi Baramki, past head of Birzeit, about the Israel censor banning books that contain a Palestinian perspective on history, or geography; anything related to Palestinian villages pre-1948. Edward Fox said: *'Recording the Palestinian past was considered an act of sedition'*. Israel has closed down Birzeit many times especially during *intifada* periods. The usual excuse for any such action is security, or prevention of terrorism, weasel words meaning *'we know this is illegal or at least immoral but we will do it anyway; and get away with it'*. Call someone a terrorist and you can do as you wish with them. Israel does not in general worry too much about foreign outcry condemning acts that would be criminal in more civilised countries: the saying is *the dog barks, and the wagon moves on.*

One argument against the Israelis being responsible for the Glock murder is that Al, like all non-citizens, was in Israel on a visa that had to be renewed every three months. Had the Israelis wanted to get rid of him they could simply not renew his visa. That argument is seriously weakened by considering the value and reach of published information. The best way to stop people publishing what they would see as anti-Israeli propaganda is to kill them. The Israelis have a long history of not just retaliating but of *'giving a lesson that will never be forgotten'* to anyone they wish to discourage.

The IDF, Israel Defence Force, has well-documented death squads, undercover units whose work involves killing anyone who *'threatens the security of Israel'*. A powerful argument for Israel committing the murder is the method of the assassination. One of their standard execution methods is to fire a first shot from behind into the back of the neck to destroy the spine, paralyse and disable the victim; then to turn them over and place the second shot or perhaps third into the heart to ensure death.

That is precisely how Al was killed. Killing an elderly archaeologist would have been an easy assignment for the person given the task.

So—who killed Al Glock? I agree with Edward Fox—the final conclusion will never become general knowledge. Someone knows but they will not tell.

* * *

What remains now of my experiences in Israel? Not much of the archaeology, I have not kept up with developments. Something of the work with potters; the book which John Landgraf and I wrote is finally being published and I am delighted to be associated with something that portrays Palestinian culture in a positive light.

Most vivid is my sense of the profound injustice that is the lot of the Palestinians and the profoundly ugly treatment of them by Israel. After experiencing the realities first hand, and following events now for more than forty years through reliable sources other than the main media, it's clear that my understanding when I first went there was extremely naïve. It had been prejudiced by sophisticated and effective propaganda. In this form of communication, Israel is the world leader. The propaganda is viciously enforced; anyone publishing anything not fitting the propaganda line is harassed so completely that they give up trying to present the truth. Finding truth is not easy; to that end what is not published is more important than whatever is.

I learned that what you see depends on where you stand. All views are strongly, passionately held on all sides. My original views before going there were entirely reversed by direct observation. Put simply, in a conflict where nothing is really simple: Palestinians are victims and Israelis are the aggressors. The occupation of Palestinian lands involves complete injustice towards the Palestinian people.

That is the truth; but I am aware of not only the history but also some of the complexities. Edward Fox, in his book *Palestine Twilight* said: *'Palestine has a strange psychological effect on people. Everyone who gets involved in it either has—or acquires—a sense of mission, a feeling that they have become protagonists in its history, promoting a view that must be borne like a battle standard, and which is in contention with other points of view that are wrong.'* [9]

186

* * *

Getting in and out of Israel has never been simple. Security checks are the most intense in the world, especially for travel on El Al, the Israeli airline. To the normal baggage search, they add reviews of intelligence reports. When leaving from that last trip, the security man we asked if we had spent any time in the West Bank or Gaza, or had contact with Palestinians. My reply was yes, there had been some time in those areas and some contact.

The security man told us to wait and went away for some time. He came back holding some papers and commenced to read through them aloud, in English. They listed everywhere I had been, in detail, with times and names of people I had contacted. It was a better diary of my travels than I could have kept, and at no time had I been aware of being watched so intensely.

13
CANBERRA

The best thing about Canberra is that you only have to travel for 20 minutes in any direction to be in Australia.

— Barry Humphries

Leaving Israel, Sandra and I arrived in Sydney in late 1974 and stayed with Don Godden in Paddington, intending to be there for a few days. I phoned Jack Golson about his offer of a postdoctoral fellowship in the Prehistory Department at the Australian National University (ANU). Sounding apologetic, he said the Professorial Board had recently decided that department heads could no longer simply employ new staff, but they would have to go through a formal interview process. Would I mind doing an interview? No, I would not mind, although implicit somewhere in that was the vague threat that things could go wrong. The threat was not from Jack but from increasing concerns about an income. We were broke, seriously so; it was a time of uncertainty and strains. Jobs had been offered in the USA. Here nothing was certain.

Finally in Canberra—the interview. After being introduced to a gaggle of people dressed—shall we be polite and say casually—sitting around a large table, Jack said we should get on with the interview. He had one question for me: could I bat? I suppose I looked a little puzzled so he explained that the department had a cricket team, and that the bowling side of things was pretty well covered but that it would be handy to have some new batting talent. I said I had played cricket for my high school, and had got a few runs at times, but had no experience since then. Jack looked satisfied, and asked if anyone else had any questions. Nobody did, so he suggested we all adjourn to the Staff Club to celebrate the newly employed staff member. That was the nod to new university regulations.

The post-doctoral fellowship carried through 1975 and 1976 and my stay was extended when appointed as a Research Officer from 1977 to 1980. Those years were to include some intense experiences.

The Prehistory Department administration appealed to me because there was very little of it; bureaucracy was minimal under Jack Golson's leadership. Right at the beginning I asked him what the job involved and what he was expecting from me. He said '*We employed you to do what you do; so do it*', bringing back memories of Frank Harvey at Diana Pottery. That left me free but confused, needing to find out what went on around there. I felt a little like a fraud, not knowing anything about Australian prehistory, or the archaeology of the Pacific, the two main interests of others working there.

The truth was I knew virtually nothing about archaeology anyway, never having formally studied the theory. In Washington I had heard in passing about the American Indians, and had picked up a bit about biblical archaeology in Jerusalem, somewhat unwillingly, having no interest in the Bible. The Israelis had demonstrated that archaeology could enrich political propaganda. But that, and whatever else had transpired in Jerusalem seemed no use at ANU.

ANU was unlike any other Australian university. It was originally established in 1946 as the centre of international exchange between Australian and international researchers in all fields. The research schools, in which Prehistory was placed, were the core of ANU. Each Research School had few tenured staff, and a larger number of visiting staff on fixed term contracts; with no students apart from a few PhD candidates. The aim was to keep up a turnover of new people to maintain awareness of new developments. The other part of ANU comprised the teaching schools which functioned like other universities, teaching students.

Given its international role, ANU was not a place to publicly demonstrate one's ignorance. I kept mine to myself, becoming a good listener, practicing the art of nodding wisely. The Prehistory department was known around the research schools as the piranha pool. The regular Prehistory seminars were an intellectual *Schützenfest* where the intention was to refine ideas until they could be refined no further, by a process of fierce argument and debate. I often struggled with concepts beyond my immediate reach, feeling like the intellectual equivalent of a small mahout trying to ride an enormous elephant. Reading the literature was not much help because I did not understand the jargon or the point of it all.

Sometimes the Prehistory Department was an interesting place to be;

sometimes dull. I was put off by the intensity of some of the others; faced with their relentlessly narrow obsessive focus, it seemed to be impossible to have a normal conversation with them about simple everyday things. Listening to a long and convoluted presentation of some minute detail felt like trying to walk in big unlaced boots through deep mud. Passionate interests are only tolerable when you share the passion.

It's easy now to feel nostalgic affection for those past times when you could be given a responsible and well-paid job whilst having not the faintest inkling of what it was about or what the other people involved were doing. Those were the days of learning on the job. It's unlikely anyone with my lack of experience would be employed now because it is necessary to have all kinds of complicated (and expensive) qualifications; and an excess of people have those qualifications.

To complicate things, research from the department was highly regarded and had good standing internationally. We had visitors like Richard Leakey. The Leakey name was known to every archaeologist. His father Louis Leakey of Olduvai Gorge fame, discovered skeletal evidence of early human evolution of our ancestors in Africa.

The department's reputation was based on several factors. Some developments in Pacific research were world leading; as an example, Jack Golson had discovered evidence of some of the world's earliest cultivation of plants in the New Guinea highlands. Australian aboriginal prehistory was distinctive, studying the world's oldest surviving culture where often the evidence was minimal. In an obituary for Rhys Jones, Les Hiatt said *'Rhys Jones's professional life coincided with what will surely be seen as the golden age of Australian prehistoric archaeology'* and that the Prehistory Department Rhys worked in made *'an institutional contribution that had brought Australian archaeology to the forefront of the world stage'.*

How that had happened was the subject of tearoom discussion one morning. The tearoom ritual was well established. Everyone met there at about the same time each day. The latest ideas received blessings or were consigned to the bin. This alongside normal workplace discussions about who was doing what with whom, or the last cricket match. The subject of the department's respectable reputation came up one day, and someone asked why it was so. After everyone paused to ponder, Jim Allen suggested that we should look around the room at each person one at a time. There was Rhys Jones, whose parents had been respectable academics in the UK and who had grown up with that solid example. But as Jim said, 'Rhys is an exception. Most of us come from the working class and we don't know how to behave'. This makes sense. A good mind with little knowledge can throw up some wrong and eccentric ideas, but sometimes some inspired and creative insights emerge. In a world where it is increasingly compulsory to have 'training' in everything we have lost some of that creative nonconformity and unorthodoxy.

* * *

I learned slowly, listening carefully to conversations, absorbing jargon and insider assumptions at weekly seminars, gradually building a general idea of what was going on; also gradually becoming aware that while I understood very little about what they were doing, they conversely understood very little about what I had been doing. In a way we were on equal terms. My responsibility was to find some points of useful interchange where both sides learned something. In Jerusalem I had learned how to combine my interests in traditional potters with the questions raised by excavations. That type of research was gaining some wider attention. I began to see that archaeology is not like the hard sciences, where there can be 'facts'. Often it involves speculation based on a small amount of evidence. It's difficult to disagree with someone's speculations when there is no evidence with which to disagree.

Outside of the university life was going well in the first months in Canberra. I liked living there. My family in Berridale was not far away, my brother Dick lived only a few minutes away. The poverty problem was no longer with us; I had a good salary and Sandra was working as a research assistant in the Geomorphology Department at ANU. The general work ethos of the Prehistory Department suited me perfectly. It was possible to take a day off for any good reason. Being ill was one. Equally, going to a cricket match, going fishing or attending to family matters were acceptable. ANU theoretically had procedures to follow for such things as having a day off, but they seemed like a nuisance and generally everyone in our department ignored them. Filling in forms was a waste of time. This was good for morale, which was excellent, and we probably achieved far more than we would have done working in an environment where everyone had to answer to someone else for everything they did.

Jack's strategy for dealing with staff was that he was the head of the department but never the boss. The focus was almost entirely on getting research done and only minimally on management. The quality of research in the department vindicated his approach. His management style, involving occasional informal discussions with staff was disrupted one day when he was instructed by some administrator that he must have formal staff meetings. When he told us about this in the tea room he said he had decided that one a year should be enough.

Our annual meeting discussed money. Each person had to say what they were planning to do, why they were doing it and what it would cost, as briefly and clearly as possible. Not in the kind of bureaucratic jargon that later appeared in universities but simply as an aid to practical planning. The requested amounts were added up and compared with the total amount the department would receive in our research budget. We then decided who got what and to me the result seemed almost organic, almost natural; everyone got a fair go. Such experiences stayed in my mind later, particularly in Monash where dictatorship was in vogue; where nobody knew the meaning of the word collegiality and had they known they would have rejected the concept anyway.

* * *

The early glow of good living ended in an instant. Sandra's pregnancy ended badly. In 1975 the baby was born with the umbilical cord wrapped tightly around his neck; a condition known as a nuchal cord. The obstetrician in charge was at home and not, in his words, available, to do an evaluation before the birth. His unavailability continued for some time after. The baby's irregular and weak heartbeat before birth was a concern. He was born dead. I was there, helpless. Sandra was in shock. The tiny boy was silent, with a disturbing grey colour. The medical people worked quietly but urgently to revive him. He started breathing after what seemed an hour; time had stopped. He was placed in a ventilator to aid his breathing. We decided to name him Nicholas after a mutual friend we had in Washington; he needed a name so he was not just 'baby'.

The obstetrician finally appeared. He called me aside and asked me to make a decision. *'The child'*, he said, *'is in life support equipment. His brain has been permanently damaged and it is unlikely he will ever live a normal life. He may not survive the next few days because the brain damage has an effect on all the other organs. His respiration for example is very weak. Please decide before tomorrow if we should keep him on life support or remove it.'*

I drove to Weston Park and sat on a park bench, on a deserted slope overlooking Lake Burley Griffin. Making a decision was impossible. How do you decide to kill your son? It was not my decision anyway—there were two of us.

The next morning the obstetrician came in, and told us Nicholas had made his own decision—to live. He did, for two years. But our marriage did not survive. There had been too many earlier complications and not enough closeness. The strain of having no sleep and caring for someone who could die at any time became too much. Nicholas's respiratory problems were a constant. His lungs could fill with fluid, rapidly. We were both taught how to recognise that. When it happened he had maybe ten minutes to live. The hospital was close by, the emergency department a five-minute walk. Sometimes it took four. They were pre-prepared and knew what was up as soon as we walked in. He survived several episodes. The stress lingered.

Life was lived in a fog of tiredness. We decided to split. Sandra moved out, into a small apartment; it was more practical for Nicholas to stay with me most of the time, with the help of a day carer, Mrs Thomas, a kindly Welsh woman. My workmates were understanding. If the office door was closed, I was probably asleep. Despite the intense difficulties there were tiny rewards. Nicholas did recognise us both. He would sometimes look closely and then reward us with a smile when we were close. But his injuries meant constant pain and constant crying.

He went with Sandra when she returned to the US and was placed with carers in California. I visited there once, and left satisfied the carers were good people, lightening much anxiety. He died aged two. On one trip to the US I stopped over at Wichita in Kansas and took a road trip south, passing the nodding oil well pumps on the way to the small town of South Haven near the Oklahoma border, where Nicholas is buried. The cemetery is a quiet place on open, flat land with a far horizon. I placed a small badge on his headstone with combined flags of America and Australia, and stood there with my thoughts, cooled on a warm day by a slight breeze.

* * *

When my two-year post-doctoral fellowship ended in 1977 I was re-employed and given the title of Research Officer, which at ANU was a support role to the real archaeologists, a 'specialist' in my area of pottery studies, one of several specialists in the Department. Some of my work was independent, such as studying the effects of and reasons for wetting clay with seawater by some Papuan coastal potters, and some was tied in with work on excavations.

My pottery knowledge was not much use in Australian prehistory research. Australian aborigines did not make pottery although they were responsible for the earliest examples of deliberately fired clay. John Mulvaney showed me some samples from Lake Mungo of fired clay hearthstones, used for setting up cooking fires. These may have been around 40,000 years old. There was no stone in the area that could be used for the same purpose. But my work was about pottery, so I concentrated on the Pacific and specifically Papua.

I mainly worked with Jim Allen. Like many archaeologists Jim had one major site that he would become associated with as his. That is Motupore, an island in Bootless Bay, off the coast about 15 km SE from Port Moresby. In 2014 the Lonely Planet Guide noted that there were zero things to do on Motupore Island. That judgement seems a little harsh. The island has in the past been quite lively at times and now is a research station mainly for marine studies, run by the University of Papua New Guinea.

There had been plenty of local activity in 1942 and 1943. American and Australian soldiers were posted around Bootless Bay. Wartime remains visible now at low tide include a B-17 and B-24, both American bombers, that emerge from the water at low tide with an eerie presence and submerge again like some giant slow-moving marine creature as the tide rises.

Motupore Island is a protected cultural heritage archaeological site. One part of it is a traditional burial ground. This was excavated in the 1970s by a group led by Alan Thorne, the physical anthropologist (someone who studies ancient skeletons). Alan became well known around Australia in 1989 for his *Man on the Rim,* a television series about the people of the Pacific Rim. In 1976 a group of us stayed in the main house, a conventional building in most respects except that it had fly wire mesh walls instead of the more usual kind; practical air conditioning that worked well in the hot humid climate, especially at night.

Weeks of careful excavation of the burial site produced a fragile yield of skeletal material for Thorne to take back to Canberra for study. On leaving, the carefully wrapped and packed bones were gently placed in a Toyota Landcruiser which Thorne 15 minutes later crashed off a cliff onto the rocky platform below. Fortunately, he survived the experience, the main injury being to his dignity, and the bones were in good enough condition to eventually serve their academic purpose.

On another visit to the region, I rented a small tinnie with an outboard motor and muddled around Bootless Bay studying the land for potential sites of past settlement and potential clay sources, finding a number of both. This fitted neatly with my boyhood fantasies of exploring in exotic places. As someone who is congenitally unsure about anything involving lots of water I was impressed with my handling of the boat. Any experienced boatman might have been less so.

Jim joined me for several day trips, one up river in what felt like a scene from a movie, perhaps *Apocalypse Now.* The air was hot and humid, the slow-moving brown river water surrounded by dense jungle foliage. A loud penetrating buzz overlaid everything, produced by multiple types of insect and who knows what else. Jim very politely held the boat still whenever we stopped at a likely site, so I could get out first. After some time, I asked him why he always wanted me to get out first. He pointed out that there were reports of a dog being taken by a crocodile, nearby, a few days earlier; and if either of us was going to be attacked by a crocodile it was not going to be him.

The Port Moresby area did not appeal to me and I would never recommend it as a place to visit. The climate was viciously hot and humid. The crime rate was high, the likelihood of having a house burgled almost certain. I drove from Port Moresby to Bootless Bay each day while I was doing the survey, and a few times was faced with a group of aggressive looking locals standing right across the narrow road, blocking it, with machetes in hand. Stopping was not an option. The simple choice was either turning around and not getting the job done, or carrying on driving and taking the risk that they would get out of the way. The more serious risk was that they would not move. Local custom was that if you injured someone, or even worse killed them whether by accident or intent, then revenge would follow as soon after as possible. You would receive whatever you had committed with a bonus severe penalty. I was fortunate to make my way through each time with no consequences and deeply relieved when the job was finished.

Another far more pleasant trip involved a three week stay on Mailu, a small island roughly two kilometres long and half that wide, situated about ten kilometres off the Papuan Coast along towards the eastern end of the Papua New Guinea mainland. Less than a thousand people live there. It is isolated and rarely visited by foreigners, who need to establish some purpose considered worthwhile by the island council before being given permission to visit. It has traditionally been the location of a significant pottery making industry; the pots were traded widely. My interest was seeing the pots being made and measuring temperatures as the pots were fired in small open bonfires—by women wearing grass skirts, made from very dry grass, a combination that appealed to my sense of irony. Somehow, they never went up in flames. Later in art school I showed slides of this to students and told them they could have their degree on the spot if they could emulate the Mailu women.

My transport to Mailu consisted of a flight in a small aircraft from Port Moresby to the dusty Amazon Bay grass airstrip, followed by a half hour walk to the coast, then a half hour trip on a big double hulled sailing canoe, a wonderfully evocative way to travel. Geoff Irwin, a New Zealander doing his PhD in the Prehistory Department had been there a few years earlier studying the potters.

My stay was made a little easier by the Mailu locals knowing what I was planning. I was assigned to a hut on stilts—the only form of local house—sharing with another single man. Each house was strictly located, and inhabited, according to the occupants' relationships to each other person on the island, so my placement was quite formal.

I loved it. The reality was like some South Pacific fantasy movie. Vivid pale blue-green sea, clean sand, palms swaying in the breeze. It all seemed unreal. Because visiting was highly restricted it was easy to imagine it was

the same as it had been hundreds of years ago. My first walk around the perimeter of the island took less than an hour, but in later trips I became more sensible and slowed to the local pace so the walk became an amble that could occupy a half or even full day, stopping to watch groups of women gathering shellfish, all the while singing in harmony. While they sang, I could sit under a palm tree and think about nothing in particular.

The food, cooked in the earthenware cooking pots made by the island women, consisted of a stew made with fish, shellfish, coconut and a type of banana that after stewing had the taste and texture of our regular eating bananas. Sometimes travelling in remote places involves some pretty grim interpretations of the concept of food, but I would be happy to have Mailu food any time.

The first few nights were less than fantastic though, sleeping on a thin woven mat on a wooden floor, feeling restless in the strange environment. Rats running around on the same floor made me far more nervous. I imagined waking up in the morning with large bites taken out of my legs, or worse. Every now and then a rat would take a big run up and jump straight over my head. Eventually I decided none of them were actually landing on my head, but simply using it as bar to challenge their jumping abilities. After the first few nights I slept peacefully, rats or no rats.

Showering was different. Each afternoon about an hour before dark it would rain. Large drops of warm water, like you would get from a big old-fashioned shower head, covered the island. Everyone would place their towels under their huts, remove their clothes—most of which were minimal anyway—pick up their soap and walk out on the beach to scrub away for a few minutes. A communal wash on a grand scale. In five minutes or so the whole population would be clean and fresh and ready for another meal and a refreshing sleep.

When it was time to leave, I had collected about thirty cooking pots, some of which would fit in a 30cm cube, some bigger. Getting them back to the mainland was no problem. Just load them up on a twin hulled canoe and hop on for the trip. In ancient time pot trading along the coast would have happened the same way. The canoes would easily hold several hundred pots so mine was a tiny load. We pushed off, and immediately the sail was up and we were under way all ten locals on the canoe lay down and went to sleep. I wondered how this fitted in with Saul Reisenberg's theories about Polynesian navigation across vast areas of the Pacific. Still, they woke up as we approached the mainland. The bush telegraph had worked and there was a large group of porters there to carry the pots to the airstrip where they would be stored away in a rough shed. A fine colonial sight it was, a long line of porters moving along a path through the tall grass; all you could see was a line of bobbing heads each with a pot on top, and me following along behind like some colonial master. Leaving the pots stored in a rough shelter at the airstrip, I flew back to Port Moresby on a small aircraft, the regular connection.

Later at ANU, I had the problem of working out how to get the pots to Canberra. I remembered Bill Melson's stories at the Smithsonian about cooperation with the military for transport, how he could call up Andrews Air Force base and one of their aircraft would soon have him on his way to the latest volcanic eruption anywhere in the world.

It was worth a try. Phoning the Fairbairn Air Force base at Canberra airport, I asked for the commander, and was most surprised to be connected. Thinking ANU would seem respectable to him I told him I worked there, and went on to tell him about my collection of pots at Amazon Bay airstrip. He was still listening so I moved to the next step and asked him if they did training flights; if so would he consider bringing my pots back? He said they certainly did training flights, which had to go somewhere, and Papua was as good a destination as any, so he would put on a training mission for a Hercules transport plane, and I would have my pots in a few days. And so it was. A Hercules was despatched to Amazon Bay, to what was probably a quite heroic landing on the short grass strip, and loaded up with primitive pots bound for Canberra. I am still amused by the thought of this large aircraft that could probably carry battle tanks, flying all that way to pick up a few pots that probably weighed a total of fifty kilos. It all fitted with my family motto: '*There is no harm in asking*'.

* * *

My trip to Mailu was part of my main project in the prehistory department, to study trade. Jim Allen and I were interested in the annual *hiri,* trading expeditions along the Papuan coast in the big double hulled Melanesian canoes. Our general aim was to try to understand what voyages took place and what contacts had been made. The Pacific is the biggest ocean on earth and the people who lived on its islands knew how to navigate, sailing great distances to their destinations. Throughout history one main reason for travelling to faraway places has been to trade something you had, that other people wanted, for something they had that you wanted.

Wal Ambrose, a colleague in the department had done a study of obsidian, a kind of glassy volcanic rock that was traded widely around the Pacific because of its suitability for making stone tools. He located obsidian quarries used in prehistory, identified easily by the waste materials left behind when shaping the obsidian tools. Wal analysed their chemical composition to characterise each specific quarry. Then by analysing obsidian from archaeological sites, he could identify where it originated. In this way he began to discover trade routes, and who was interacting with whom.

I tried doing the same with clay, aiming to locate and analyse clay deposits, then obtain fired pottery from archaeological sites and identify any matches, indicating trade. This started with the concentrating on the area around Motupore, where Jim had excavated, combining two jobs—looking for archaeological sites and collecting clay samples at each.

The next step was to have the clay analysed for chemical composition. To do this, I ended up at Lucas Heights, location of the nuclear reactor HIFAR (later permanently shut down in 2007). In 1978–79 I had research grants from the Australian Institute for Nuclear Science and Engineering (AINSE) to do this research. If that sounds other-worldly, I can assure you it was.

The Prehistory seminars had sometimes been befuddling. The nuclear scientists at Lucas Heights were entirely incomprehensible. I have never been among a group of people whose discussions I understood less. They seemed to be speaking some alien language not previously recorded on Earth, but they were welcoming, friendly and congenial. Again I did a lot of wise nodding, and very little talking.

My clay analyses were done by Peter Duerden. Luckily Peter was capable of some normal conversation and we got along well. One of his regular subjects was the two-hour commute to and from work, something I found astonishing. Peter was expert in the process known by the rather cute name of PIXE (proton induced x-ray emissions). I never understood how it worked, but did understand the end result, the chemical analyses of my clay and fired pottery samples. The time at Lucas Heights was rewarding in its novelty. I had looked into the HIFAR reactor and seen the fuel rods immersed in—was it heavy water? It looked like water. This was certainly another world, one that most people don't get to see.

Back at ANU, the results were complex and frustrating rather than enlightening. Clay is complicated stuff. Even in the one deposit its composition varies so doing comparisons between different deposits was not simple. Some useful results were obtained but I was getting caught up in something that inevitably involved statistical analysis. About that I had no knowledge or experience and even less interest.

As might be expected, ANU was an early user of computers, and we had access to one (one!) in the Prehistory Department. I had my first go, beginning with no understanding of how the thing worked and ending up with little more. It required some knowledge of computer programming and I was a slow learner. My work also required some knowledge of statistics, not a strength of mine. I had done a short course in statistics as an undergraduate and failed the exam. The lecturer had let the several students who failed do a deferred exam, which I failed. He then let us do an oral exam, and at the end of that I was the only one still failing, so he kindly gave me a conceded pass. Not a good basis for doing sophisticated analysis.

The basic problem in my study was that Wal's obsidian at any individual source was all more or less the same, having the same chemical elements in roughly the same proportions so that any difference from other sources stood out clearly. Clay deposits were variable and complicated. And pottery, fired clay, lost various elements when heated, so matching clay to fired pot was not simple either. All this made it difficult to see whether I was actually achieving anything or not. Jim Allen got some value from my work, but I got depression. Statistics made my head hurt. It was all too unsatisfying.

* * *

The last year in the prehistory department was for me the most productive, involving skills and knowledge that I did have. At the annual staff meeting that year it was agreed that I could have 1979 to write a book. This would be about how pottery was made and fired, and how archaeologists could use that information to enhance their studies. It had been commissioned by Betty Meggers in the Smithsonian. She planned to organise and edit a series of books on archaeological analysis, mainly written by people associated with the Smithsonian, to be published by Aldine Press in Chicago.

The book had been planned over a few earlier years so the content came together relatively easily. The writing went well because of my new approach to the discipline of it—an approach I have used since then. The method came from an unlikely source, a small sixteen-page booklet found at my local newsagent, cheaply printed on newsprint quality paper. It was titled 'How to Write'. It contained the suggestion that a long work like a novel could become bogged down if you thought about it constantly day and night, that a more disciplined approach would work better and be more efficient. It suggested doing a limited number of either hours or words each day. To make it easy I chose four hours or a thousand words. As soon as either the time or the word limit was reached you walked away and forgot the thing completely until next day. It worked then and it has worked since, a good system that makes life much less agonising.

The book was finished, edited, and about to be published—and the planned publisher Aldine Press went out of business. Betty, not short on innovation, set up as a publisher herself, under the name of Taraxacum Press. Taraxacum is a genus of plant known commonly as dandelions. I am not sure why this connection appealed to Betty—maybe something to do with spreading seeds of knowledge? A dictionary meaning of taraxacum, one which Betty almost certainly did not intend is: The dried root of the dandelion, used as a laxative, diuretic and tonic. One hoped that the book would not have that effect. Perhaps Betty was aware that the blossoms can be used to make wine.

My book was first published in 1981 and was still selling copies in 2013 when Betty died, so I take some pride in that. I consider it the main achievement from my time in the prehistory department. Along with other publications from my time working on studies of traditional potters, and with archaeologists it contributed to being awarded the 1999 Society for American Archaeology Award for Ceramic Studies, an honour that had been earned through making the most of some hard times. I was invited to Philadelphia to receive the award but was unable to attend because of work commitments and lack of funds at the time—ups and downs again.

* * *

I might still be involved in that kind of work if it had been possible to continue working with archaeologists in the Middle East. There the history of pottery was much more varied and interesting. My other book that was planned, on Palestinian potters and the Taanach excavated pottery might have been finished much earlier. Who knows what then? What-if questions cannot really be answered. It became clear, thinking about this in Canberra, that continuing in that type of work would involve looking for a job in the US, because none existed in the Middle East, at least no paying jobs. There were none in Australia. Internal conflict developed—how sensible would it be to abandon one field where a good reputation had been developed, for some unknown other whose future was uncertain?

Two more conflicting thoughts about future possibilities were constant. One was that archaeology dealt with the past and that immersion in what had happened a long time ago was gradually becoming less appealing, less interesting. The other appealed more—living the life of a potter. I had occasionally made pots again soon after starting at ANU, in difficult circumstances. For the first two years I had a potter's wheel in the laundry in the small house rented from ANU, in Garran. Washing clothes became difficult; there was little room to move. There was nowhere to dry pots or store them so I clogged up the tiny space even more by having a ladder leading up to the manhole in the laundry ceiling. This allowed me to take work on wareboards up into the ceiling space and store it there. The arrangement was far from ideal but better than nothing.

* * *

Brenda Jacobs began working as a research assistant in the Prehistory Department in 1976 and we became involved, moving in together later in that year. In 1978 Lois White, secretary of the Prehistory Department, and her husband Bob were off to Europe for a year. We were given the job of minding their house in the suburb of Mawson. Bob, a painter had just held an exhibition based on the then-popular recent book *Poor Fellow My*

Country by Xavier Herbert. Bob's painting studio, in the house, had a tiled floor and was a good space for setting up a potter's wheel. I built a temporary gas kiln outside and the clay work started to move along slowly.

In 1979 we bought a house in Fisher, a southern Canberra suburb. I looked around at tin sheds suitable to build in the backyard as a workshop. Then a friend introduced me to a builder who had retired, but was taking on small jobs to help his son finish an apprenticeship. He offered to construct a proper building from concrete block, which could later be turned into a flat, all for the same price as a tin shed. The condition was that he would work when it suited him and not at other times. No problem. The end result was perfect, with one enclosed room for making, that could be heated in the cold Canberra winters and opened up in the hot summers. The back area had walls on two sides. I applied for and got a grant from the Australia Council, something that can only be imagined now their concept of art has moved on and ceramics is of total disinterest to them. That allowed me to build a gas kiln especially designed to fire high temperature porcelain to 1480^{0}.

As the work improved people began to buy it and a few galleries began to take an interest. My main supporter was Norma Shields. Norma, who had earlier been a student at the Canberra Art School, opened a gallery she called Potters Place in 1978. It was upstairs above the Boot and Flogger, a wine bar/restaurant in Green Square in the Canberra suburb Kingston. I had two exhibitions there in the late 1970s. Exhibition openings always featured food served on the platters and dishes available in the shop. Pottery back then was almost always about functional ware.

I liked Norma. She was friendly and well suited to the job of running a gallery. I was distressed when she contracted cancer. One day in Mawson there was a knock on the door, and when I opened it Norma was there with a bottle of wine. She said *'I've come to say goodbye and have a final drink'.* She died soon after and I have never forgotten that wonderful gesture.

* * *

Towards the end at ANU, one memorable day I was sitting in my office in the Coombs Building, a labyrinthine web of strangely angled corridors and unpredictable twists and turns. There was a knock on the door so I yelled *'Come in'.* When I looked around Gough Whitlam was there, looking a bit flushed. After 'The Dismissal' in 1975 and leaving politics in 1978 he had been given a fellowship at ANU to write his memoirs. When I asked *'Can I help you?'* he said *'I hope so. I'm lost. Where am I?'* I said *'You are in the prehistory department'*. And he said *'Oh God no, I am trying to forget about the past. How do I get out of here?'*

* * *

The lead-up to the end of my contract had brought a state of complete uncertainty about the future. Should we sell up and find a place in the country somewhere where I could make pots for a living? The dilemma was simple: making enough to survive by selling pots looked pretty precarious; making house payments in Canberra was increasingly a problem with interest rates climbing and a national economic depression on its way.

Brenda's job at ANU had finished some time before. She was pregnant with Thomas, who was due to be born in 1980—the year we were married. There were no job offers on the horizon for me, or for her. Depression had set in, to the point where I was receiving occasional Vitamin B injections from my GP.

Finally, my five years in the Prehistory Department was up at the end of 1979. I decided to finish with archaeology; finishing my book was the appropriate finale. Everything I had learned went into it; there was no more to offer. Over the next few years, I was invited to speak at archaeology conferences in Nice, France and other exotic locations, but I had moved on. My archaeology days were gone, never to return.

Vere Gordon Childe, the famous archaeologist, wrote: *'For myself I no longer believe I can make further useful contributions to prehistory. I am beginning to forget what I laboriously learned. New ideas rarely come my way. I see no prospect of settling the problems that interest me. I have no wish to hang on the fringes of learned societies or university institutions.'* Childe committed suicide. I went to the Canberra School of Art.

14
THE BIG SIDESTEP

It is never too late to be what you might have been.

— George Eliot

My teaching career started by accident and finished by design. The accident arrived through a chance meeting with someone who became my valued friend, Alan Peascod. The design (some readers will appreciate the pun) was much later precipitated by someone who became a focus of my disrespect at Monash University, John Redmond.

Underlying everything between the 1960s and the early 2000s was my desire to have a workshop somewhere and make things from clay, with no distractions. The desire, always there, was tempered by the need for income. Looking back now I was to wait thirty-four years to start on that romantic life I live now. The work with archaeologists was a diversion, but beyond question not a waste. It had given me travel, adventure and an acquaintance with the world at large.

I had no interest in making an income from pots by repeated production of standard lines. The answer was there right there early on, tapping me on the shoulder as I spoke to McMeekin. He was being paid by the university to teach people how to make pots, earning his income from teaching. That freed him to experiment as he wished without the worry of having to sell work constantly.

* * *

In the prehistory department one day in 1979, near the end of my tenure, I was idly pondering my past and wondering about my future. There was a knock on my office door, and when I yelled '*come in*' Alan Watt appeared. Alan was the head of the ceramics department at the Canberra School of Art. I had not met him before so I was a bit puzzled. After some preamble he asked if I wanted a job. It was one of those situations where if I had said exactly what I thought the real answer would have been '*Don't be bloody silly, of course I want a job*'. The real answer, after I had found out that the job involved teaching about glazes in the Canberra School of Art ceramics department, was a simple yes; especially because it held the promise of time and encouragement to be making claywork.

I have always assumed, without actually asking anyone involved, that Alan Peascod had recommended me for the Canberra Art School job, doubting that Alan Watt or any of the others at the art school would have known anything about me. Peascod must have been persuasive. I had met him at an exhibition opening at the Watson Arts Centre in Canberra, in the mid-1970s. A sharply dressed stranger came up to me and said, *'They tell me you are the bloke who is interested in Islamic ceramics'.* I said *'Yes'.* He said: *'So in Australia that makes two of us. I'm hoping we can talk sometime.'* And talk we did, until the day before he died.

* * *

So began the third major transition in my life. The first was the move to Sydney to attend university. The second was becoming involved in archaeology and anthropology. The third came at just the right time. Wanting change, I had lost interest in studying the past and wanted to get back to making pots, to building up a daily coating of clay on my clothes. The job teaching glaze classes at the Canberra School of Art (CSA) promised salvation.

In 1980 my son Tom was born and family life was looking good. We had bought a house in the southern Canberra suburb of Fisher. A studio was built in my backyard, complete with kilns—by then a second, woodfired chamber had been added to the gas kiln and was working well. Once again there was a future. We were happy to stay in Canberra; many would not be. My view, as a resident of ten years, is that anyone who came from the country, or from any country town, would enjoy the benefits of living in Canberra, with all the facilities unavailable in smaller towns. Anyone who came from one of the larger cities might dislike the lack of some attractions available there.

The art school was only 100 metres away from the ANU Coombs Building, my workplace for the past five years, so I could go to the same bank and eat in the same places. It was easy, everything was familiar. The art school had no connection to the university then, but all the Prehistory people would still be near and accessible for socialising. Alan Watt told me that the job would start off on a part-time basis, three days a week, but that a full-time job was coming vacant soon and he had put my name on it.

That led to many years of quiet resentment towards Alan, thinking he had deceived me, because when the job did come up it was given to Hiroe Swen. Many years later I discovered that Udo Selbach, then director of the art school had been responsible for insisting Hiroe was employed, overruling Alan's protests. This was not my first time misjudging someone. In retrospect Alan gave me the start in teaching that destined everything since, and I am extremely grateful to him for that. Any trace of that undeserved resentment has long gone away.

* * *

Canberra is a town of cliques. Your work determines your friends and your social network. As an academic your social network consists of academics. The transition from the Prehistory Department at ANU, to the Canberra School of Art meant a complete and somewhat confusing change of life in quite profound ways.

None of the people I had worked with for five years knew any of the people I was now surrounded by. And the people in the art school had not the faintest idea of the life I had been living, and the people in it. It felt like a real-life giant game of snakes and ladders. I had just landed on the biggest snake and slid down, needing to start again from the bottom.

Gradually I became the art school glaze man—with a massive case of culture shock. Working with academics and scholars at the Smithsonian and in the ANU Research Schools had not prepared me for art students. In both those places I was among some of the world's most intelligent people. In the art school there was the full range from intelligent to dumb, mirroring society as a whole. I felt like I had just had one beer in the pub with a group of people who were all on their tenth. It took a while to fit in.

I started off in my naiveté with the McMeekin method of teaching about glazes, using the Seger formula. Most of the students had no concept of chemistry and no grasp of calculations although the few that did were enthusiastic. It took some time to work out methods that would not only be understandable to the students but would produce useful results. In some ways I was learning more than any of the students—mainly about teaching. That process has two ends, the thrower and the catcher and a bad throw cannot be caught even by the best catcher. I was not explaining the chemistry well; and the lack of earlier learning about such things did not equip most of the students to understand. It was a few years in before it began to come together and I was quite happy to abandon the Seger method and work more intuitively from a better understanding of how the materials used in glazes functioned when they were heated.

My greatest difficulty in teaching was with beginners and this continued later in Gippsland. I never did develop the capacity to inspire enthusiasm with them in a way that was possible with more advanced students. I didn't have the patience, the acting ability or in truth the interest. It all seemed too much a one-way process. Anita Macintyre was an excellent beginner's teacher. She somehow instilled them with enthusiasm that followed them through into later years.

Independently of glaze teaching, I was concerned then—and even more so now—that ceramics students around Australia do not receive any worthwhile teaching about the history of ceramics, ancient and modern. This concern led me to organise a history course at CSA, bringing in someone once a week to talk about their experiences—for example, Tim Moorhead talked about his early experience of California Funk. I assume the history course disappeared when I left.

* * *

Whether real or imagined, it felt like I was being classified by my colleagues as a technologist, not an artist. Resentment followed, mainly because of the accuracy of that judgement. No negative criticism is as painful as that which you know to be correct. Instead of developing my ceramics I had been involved in archaeology and had not worked enough, made enough, exhibited enough and been around long enough to compete with the established ones. Their work was in magazines and books, and mine was not. They were exhibiting in respectable galleries and I was not.

My inability to change the situation quickly enough did not help; it would take years to build up some kind of reputation, not knowing at the start whether that could be achieved anyway. What if it all went nowhere? In the midst of all that I was working hard at making pots, and dissatisfied with the results. Over time my understanding developed that Canberra was probably the worst place in Australia for me to begin trying to achieve recognition. It was like living in a big fishbowl, with everyone looking in and making comments about the inadequacies of most of the fish, leaving only a limited few open to admiration.

Colum McCann, in his book *Zoli*, said: *'The worst burden in life is what others know about us. But maybe there is a burden worse than this. It happens when they don't know about us, it is what they think about us when, in silence, they force us to be what they expect us to be.'*

Far from being all negative, it was a job, of a kind, and provided a meagre living. Looking back, a much larger positive was that I shared an office with Alan Peascod. We had many discussions about the world in general, and some of the people in it. He was impatient, like a child who wants it 'now'. One morning I came in early and he was standing near the big electric kiln, looking despondent. I asked him what was wrong, and he muttered as he walked off, *'Mate, I've got technical problems'*. When I looked in the kiln, he had blown a complete kiln load of biscuit ware into small pieces by heating too quickly. It was not a beginner's mistake; it was the result of pure impatience.

There was a level of freedom to experiment without being burdened by the OHS stuff that came later. Alan experimented with all kinds of materials and processes. As an example, he ordered a cylinder of every type of gas sold by CIG at the time and blew each into a kiln near top temperature to see what happened. Much of what he did, and I admit to sharing some of the experiments with him, would now be illegal and 'unsafe'; but resulted in some valuable learning.

* * *

Another positive at the art school was the kiln known to all as the Bizen kiln, built by Bill Samuels when he was teaching there. The design was based on kilns in Bizen in Japan. That area is the source of a chocolate-coloured woodfired ceramic often having red flashes on the clay, or sometimes displaying organic markings where the pot had been wrapped with salt-soaked straw before placing it in the kiln. Sometimes flame-like markings appeared, created by small flames licking around the pots, from charcoal placed near them as they cooled.

Like many others around the world at that time I was fascinated by Japanese woodfired pots from Shigaraki, Bizen and particularly Tamba.

There were none available in Canberra to see in real life, but published photos were enough to help me decide to make work like that. The CSA Bizen kiln was like a gift from Prometheus in person, allowing me to start off in a direction I have followed ever since, firing kilns with wood, connecting me directly back to my childhood experience with preparing firewood and burning it.

My first firing in this kiln was shared with Terry Kirk, my friend from undergraduate days, who was teaching ceramics at Goulburn CAE. Terry had not had time to make anything so my work filled the kiln. There was a plentiful supply of wood available near the kiln but it had not been split to usable size. We had not thought about that before starting the firing. We fired for four days, alternating shifts: four hours wood splitting, four hours stoking. I had never been so exhausted in my life as at the end of that firing. I slept for most of a day, maybe twenty hours. The results of the firing were acceptable, so it was well worthwhile. Pots that are still with me from that firing provided some valuable learning. They show some bright flashing colours. It was obvious that different parts of the kiln gave different results so the methods of stacking work in the kiln needed careful consideration. The two most important lessons were that I should continue with this style of work, and next time should be well prepared for the long firing to make it as physically easy as possible. An important part of the preparation would be recruiting more people to help.

There were several years around this time where we had groups of excellent students, potentially talented and universally enthusiastic. Most of them are still working at ceramics and some became teachers themselves, Simone Fraser for example, and Sally Cleary who eventually became head of ceramics at Royal Melbourne Institute of Technology, RMIT. Daniel Lafferty and Yuri Weidenhofer were the woodfire duo who made maximum use of the Bizen kiln, beginning their life in woodfiring.

* * *

In 1980 the Crafts Board of Australia Council gave me a grant to build a gas-fired kiln that could fire to 1480^{0}C (Cone 17), the firing temperature of my high-temperature porcelain body. Glazes were quite simple, because just about anything melted, but almost all ceramic colours burned out. About the only one left was cobalt oxide, which produced a kind of greyish blue. This is the reason the Meissen porcelain factory in Germany, firing to similar temperatures, used enamels fused on to the fired glaze surface in a later lower-temperature firing, to produce a range of colours.

The gas kiln was modified by building a second chamber so its flue conducted heat into this back chamber. When the gas kiln had almost reached top temperature, wood was stoked into the second chamber until it reached Cone 9. That allowed me to experiment with many types of glazes, in a preview of the way I am working now.

When I left Canberra my high temperature kiln was bought by a company that made robots to sharpen surgical blades. They used it to fire the sharpening medium, alumina, to 1430^0C, its point of maximum hardness. When they no longer needed the kiln, Hugh Legge bought it from them.

* * *

One of the problems of working part-time at the art school and living in the suburbs was that well-meaning people would decide that because I was at home they should come and visit. That often broke up my rhythm of work and had some implications for my income. A dilemma ensued. The visitors were mostly people I liked and I did not want to tell them to stay away; I just wanted them to come when I was not working.

My marginal income from teaching was supplemented by selling pots. Large porcelain platters made from commercial porcelain clays, and fired in the gas kiln, sold for what seemed to me to be the phenomenal price of $40 each. But gradually woodfiring took over from porcelain as my main interest, contributing to my increasingly poor financial state. Woodfired work was very difficult to sell then.

The payment system used by the art school did not help finances. Part-time lecturers (later termed sessional, more recently the profoundly misleading term casual) were not paid sick leave, holiday pay, or any of the other advantage payments made to full time staff. There was no income outside of teaching times, including a three-month break over Christmas. The worst problem came after any break. Payments would not start for anything up two months after resuming, meaning up to five months with no pay. Even then further payments had erratic and unpredictable timing.

As a paid-up member, I consulted the ACT Teachers Union; they were useless, no help eventuated. In 1982 Toni Robertson and I formed our own union, determined to do something about the pay situation. Toni was a lecturer in printmaking and photo media at the School of Art and a strong-minded woman. By sheer persistence, despite total disinterest by officials in the ACT Education Department, we finally achieved a hearing in the Federal Arbitration Court. The Teachers Union joined in more as spectators than participants. The female judge heard both sides patiently and then launched a scathing attack on the Education Department spokesman who she labelled a dissembler at best and a liar at worst, and found in our favour. From then on we were paid on time—which is all we had asked for.

Some extra income came from teaching one day a week at Goulburn College of Advanced Education (CAE) with my good mate from student days, Terry Kirk. The road between Canberra and Goulburn was hazardous, narrow, rough and bumpy and every time I went along it there was a crashed car somewhere. The road was so bad that the Holden car company had duplicated sections of it for their Lang Lang proving ground suspension testing track. Still, I made some friends and the students in Goulburn were universally enthusiastic and friendly.

* * *

Money worries aside, ordinary life in Canberra was satisfying. My second son, Mike, was born in 1984. There was plenty of entertainment for kids without needing to go to organised events; picnics in the countryside or by the lake for example. Much family life can be enjoyed without needing to spend money.

I had played rugby league as a schoolkid and enjoyed going to Seiffert Oval in Queanbeyan to see the Canberra Raiders in their early days. Someone at the art school asked me rather snootily why I liked such a thuggish spectacle and I said it was the only place I knew where you could stand and shout abuse at someone and everyone around would agree with you and join in. It cleared the mind, a bit of good shouting. Eventually Anita McIntyre, whose husband John was the chairman of the club, organised that I could watch from the committee box. No more standing in six inches of mud; instead there were chicken wings and beer laid on, and the politicians who attended, especially Fred Daly, were lively entertainers.

My other main entertainment was trout fishing. I had started going out with my father at a young age and loved being out in the hills along with just the soothing sounds of running water. I used to go trout fishing at Yaouk (pronounced Yi–ack) near Adaminaby, leaving home around 4 am and getting to the Yaouk Creek just before dawn. Through the fishing season I went there most Fridays, ensuring that I never saw anyone. Robert Hughes in his book *A Jerk on One End* wisely described fishing as best a solitary activity.

The main attraction of such fishing had nothing to do with catching fish although that was a bonus. It was being there, alert, alive and alone in the mountains with the sun and the breeze, watching the underwater grasses waving in the current, seeing the eagles soar and feeling a sense of bliss unobtainable in civilisation. The actual fishing involved some fancy techniques. The narrowness of the stream and the constant breeze made casting a line into the water challenging, and I liked to use the lightest, most gossamer line and a light rod, and superlight lures which all meant that skill was paramount. Floating a light dry-fly down the ripples into a deep hole worked well, as did dropping a wet fly over the edge of a high bank into a deep hole and allowing it to sink slowly and naturally.

Once on the Maclaughlin River, on that unique occasion I went fishing with my brother Phil, I caught a big trout. At the very least a five-pounder, a hook-jawed brown. The slow and careful process of bringing it close was followed by lifting it out of the water a bit too suddenly, only to feel the line break, and to see the fish splash back down onto the water and glide away soundlessly to some underwater haven of dark invisibility in deep water. Something like this has happened only twice in my fishing career and each time an instant feeling of loss has afterwards been replaced by a wish that the cunning old fish would live out its days with no further intrusion.

Trevor Shearston, the novelist, his then-wife Ursula and I were friends and we had a few sessions of fishing together. Trevor took me out in Moruya catching bream, about which I knew nothing. I reciprocated by taking him to Yaouk to catch a trout, of which he had no experience. In that peaceful valley I told Trevor that it would be a beautiful place to live. *'It would be a prison,'* he replied. Isolated fishing for a day now and then is refreshing, but a permanent and enforced isolation would be unhealthy.

There is a distinction between choosing isolation and enduring it.

* * *

On my most memorable fishing trip, John, my neighbour in Fisher, joined me. I liked John. We had intelligent conversations—far more than I had with the previous neighbour, a large man with a large moustache, who smoked large cigars and drove a large Jaguar. His trade was making porn films in Fyshwick. He never acknowledged my presence with more than a nod as he drove past, without even looking at me; not a word ever passed between us.

John was different. He moved from Tasmania hoping the world might open up to him, assuming that in Canberra lawyers would be consulted frequently, rather than rarely as in Tassie. He dressed neatly. He was careful about what he said, and was, in the words of those days, a little uptight. His wife Julie was his conduit to the world, a warm, friendly and funny woman who perfectly understood perspective and keeping him within it.

When he discovered I went fishing on Fridays, John asked if he could go with me one day. I asked him if he had done any fishing and he said yes and we left it at that. He did admit later, long after our joint expedition, that he had only been once, with his father, on a boat off the Tasmanian coast. He had caught nothing. But before our adventure I assumed he had some experience, and when he asked me several times for specific information about fishing gear, I was happy to show him mine and explain its use.

He finally decided to take a Friday off work. We were set to go. I knocked on his back door at 4 a.m. He came out looking bright and shiny under his porch light, dressed in an immaculate white business shirt and a pair of shorts that looked like he had bought them in one of Canberra's gentlemen's boutiques. A newish looking hat, long socks and shiny brown shoes completed his attire. His fishing gear looked new and unused.

When we arrived at the river, he seemed a bit unprepared so I helped him get ready and explained to him that I moved all day and did not just fish in the same spot. He decided to spend some time where we started, but on the opposite side of the creek. So off I went. I saw him in the distance occasionally. Later he caught up, having, as he said, crossed at a shallow point. I could see that because the only place you contacted mud was at shallow points and he had obviously gone in face first. His immaculate appearance had taken a pounding. Not only had he fallen in the river but he had lost his hat. It had been blown away by the wind and he had the beginnings of a nasty sunburn. He had scratched his face, arms and legs many times on prickly bushes.

Not noticing my obviously incredulous expression, he asked me what bait he should be using at that spot. I saw that he had lost his lure and just had the free line dangling. We chose another lure. Then he asked what knot was recommended so I tied it on for him to demonstrate. First cast he caught the lure up in a bush and broke it off. He tied on another himself. With a mighty cast he heaved it so that the knot came loose and the lure sailed off towards the horizon.

Once when I looked for him, he was nearly a metre in the air, with a tiger snake below him. He had reached that minutely brief interval where a man going upwards stops before he comes down again, and appeared to be considering where he might land if he had any choice, which he clearly did not. He need not have bothered because the snake, realising a very large weight was about to descend on it was getting out of there as fast as it could.

So it went. I never had so much entertainment fishing, and Bozo the clown at his peak never put on such a performance. John slept all the way back to Canberra, poor man, having tired himself out. Before we got back, I gave him a few fish since I had many and he had none. When I delivered him back to Julie she caught on immediately and smiled at me and led him away to the necessary remedies. She told me the next Monday he slept for nearly 24 hours and, as he had the first coffee he said to her, meditatively and after some thought, '*You know, I think I just had the best day of my life*'.

15

GIPPSLAND

*Gippsland is not somewhere you go for fun. You go to Lorne for
fun, but you go to Gippsland for isolation.*

— Kevin Mortensen

The reasons for leaving Canberra started to build up. There were no
prospects of any realistic paid work. Brenda's research assistant work had
finished and she had decided to stay at home with Tom. Finances became
increasingly grim. Selling pots required abilities that were lacking in me:
business sense, marketing, mass production, publicity and more. The
only way forward was to start again, somewhere else.

In the new class of tertiary education, the College of Advanced
Education (CAE), ceramics art courses proliferated through the 1970s
and 1980s. Teaching jobs were available around Australia, especially
in regional centres, following government policy of strengthening the
economy of regional centres.

In 1983 I did some asking around if any jobs might be coming up.
I applied for a few that were advertised; one at Wollongong University,
and one at Chisolm Institute in Melbourne, where they wanted a head
of ceramics. The Chisolm decision about who got the job was comical,
or corrupt, depending on which predominates: your sense of humour, or
your sense of ethics. Harold Farey, head of the Chisolm art school, placed
ads all around the world. Then he and Lindsay Anderson did a round-the-
world trip to interview applicants. Their interview with me in Canberra
was the last of the epic series. Then they gave the job to Ken Leveson who
had been working at Chisolm the whole time. Looking back, I was lucky
to miss out, given the eventual chaos when it became part of Monash
University.

The art school in Wollongong University was interested, and offered
me a trip that included a day to look around the city and the art school
and a day for the job interview with meals and accommodation. My city
tour was pretty miserable; it was raining heavily, and Wollongong in those

post-industrial days was not Nirvana; it felt like the opening scene of the movie *Blade Runner*. The art school looked decidedly uninteresting and there was not much sign of activity among the teachers and students.

For the interview I was ushered into a long thin room where people sat around a long table, and formally introduced. Oddly the only one I knew was Guy Warren, the painter, who I had met as a student in Sydney when he visited our department. He greeted me warmly: *'Hello Owen, it's years since I saw you last'.* He was there as their 'impartial outside observer'. The meeting was called to order; the chairman asked that standard question; *'Why do you want this job?'* The interview came to a rather uncomfortable and embarrassing end when I answered: *'I had a good look around the city and the art school yesterday and decided that I don't want the job. Thanks for your interest.'*

But the money situation had become seriously grim. Down to my last two dollars, I checked pockets, looked through the house in small containers on shelves, everywhere some coins may have been placed; but that two dollars was it. It was not going to go far towards the regular household needs. It seemed like a better use for it to go and buy a bottle of stout, and drink that for solace. Placed in the fridge to cool for a few hours, it had built up some condensation on the outside when the time came to drink it. That made it slippery. I dropped it. It broke on the tiled floor. That was the low point. Something had to happen soon.

I applied for a ceramics lecturer job at the Gippsland Institute of Advanced Education (GIAE) in Victoria. Soon after a letter arrived from Hedley Potts, asking me to attend an interview. Around that time Hedley had organised Spotkanie, a residency event. Among others, Alan Watt and Maria Kuzynska, who I knew well in Canberra, were participating. One of the Canberra art school students, Rob Sinclair, was going to attend as a student helper so I asked him to look around and size up the place and the people, and let me know whether I should consider it or not. Rob said Hedley was a bit eccentric, indulging in performances like getting the crowd to form circles and hold hands; but the countryside was attractive especially up in the hills. That was prophetic, really, considering I am in those hills as I write this.

Norman Creighton, head of the art school, had selected my application from some eighty others for the only interview—because I was the only one with a PhD. The job, after the interview, was mine. Several locals were not at all amused. Kyoshi Ino was seriously annoyed because he had been doing some teaching there and thought himself eminently qualified, if you ignored his inability to speak English very well and his alcoholism. Peter Ries had also done some teaching and was more realistically hoping for the job. We have since become good mates, I'm happy to say.

I took up the offer of the Gippsland job, thinking that I would stay a few years and then move on to something better. That decision was made in 1984; the something better has never arrived. The move to Gippsland in retrospect was one of my life's better decisions. Now I cannot think of anywhere else I would prefer to live. Perhaps, reconsidering, some part of Queensland in mid-winter?

* * *

Like a cartoon man who walks slowly, shoulders hunched and head down looking just in front of his shuffling feet, I left Canberra at the beginning of 1985, sad and depressed. As a place to live it was well suited to family life with a couple of kids to entertain and educate, and it offered easy access to all of my wider family. Socially it was advanced, often being used as a laboratory for testing new ideas that would later be adopted Australia wide.

Compared with that, the prospect of living in Gippsland engendered little enthusiasm. I had come from ANU Prehistory, one of the world's respectable departments in that field, and from the Canberra School of Art which was highly rated—I hesitate to say over-rated—by the people in it. In reality it had some excellent people teaching in various departments: Klaus Moje in glass, George Ingham in furniture and others. In the Australian context I suppose it was a contender. Now here I was at some rural backwater—that's how it felt at first. The Latrobe Valley was like some alien place. It has no centre; it is made up of a number of towns that compete rather than cooperate.

No matter. After six months living in a house owned by the college in Churchill, after extensive research into the advantages and disadvantages of locations around the area, we bought a house in a small town, Boolarra, for what I thought was an extremely low price. The difference between Canberra and Gippsland house prices was startling. Boolarra was a friendly welcoming community and it seemed to have the best school for Tom and Mike. It was an easy move for me because I could apply what I had learned as a child about living in small towns. It was a little more difficult for Brenda because she lived in cities and had no small-town experience.

* * *

In time I began to understand the nature of the art school. It was what we made it. None of the teachers had a worldwide reputation but all were serious in their practice and most were good teachers. Euan Heng was an excellent drawing teacher, Kaye Green at printmaking, Chris Coventry for painting and Susan Purdy photography. Dan Wollmering and Clive Murray-White ran an effective sculpture department. Collectively we knew a wide range of artists, allowing the school a good visiting artist program. Painters such as Sally Smart, Stewart McFarlane and Jon Campbell were longer-term visitors or lecturers. In ceramics there were many residents: Sandy Brown and Sebastian Blackie from England, Jack Troy and Sandra Johnstone from the US among the internationals and my good mate Chester Nealie among the locals. We also ran the weekly artist forum program where visitors gave a one-hour lecture.

What did we lecturers have in common? We all practised and exhibited as artists. We worked together well enough, with occasional minor contretemps but generally for the good of the school as a whole rather than for selfish ends, supported by Norman Creighton, head of the school. Norman held regular staff meetings where issues were raised, on which we voted, and the vote was put into practice. If we liked an idea we used it, if not we discarded it. This collegiate approach gave each staff member a stake in running the school and created the feeling of belonging.

It's probably difficult to believe now, but we had plenty of money. Enough for all the materials we needed, for student outings, for any reasonable work travel, and for visitors to be paid well. The money was divided fairly, although some felt they deserved more. Again, the collegiate attitude was prominent.

For me it was a transformation in status. From being the glaze technician, the non-artist in ceramics at the Canberra art school, I became a member of a group who respected each other both as teachers and as artists. My self-confidence returned and my depression lessened.

An extremely important advantage, helping me to gain wider recognition in the field of ceramic arts, was the freedom to try anything. Build a new kiln? No problem. Here's the money, there's the space. Need some time off? No problem. Some travel money? Here it is. The working week was four days. The fifth was expected to be dedicated to artwork, away from the campus. I began working almost three days a week on developing my ceramics.

There was an understanding by all that my interest was woodfiring so that became the focus of student involvement. We built more kilns. My work soon began to move along. A small anagama kiln at the college built by Kyoshi Ino allowed several firings each year, as many as ten some years, sometimes exclusively my work, sometimes student work. We modified it, making it larger. I learned quickly, allowing me to do talks at conferences, to offer workshops, and to be involved in the international woodfire scene. I doubt any of that would have happened if I had stayed in Canberra.

In the second year there, 1986, I organised the first Australian woodfire conference, and some 100 people attended. All parts of the campus contributed: the accommodation people, the printers, the café and food people, and the audio-visual people all made the organisation relatively easy and straightforward. The administrative people in The Gippsland Institute were universally helpful and friendly, and reliable. Looking back, that woodfire conference was a significant event in Australian ceramics, not so much in itself but for what it bred. A series of woodfire events followed, generally every three years, and these still occur today. The next one after mine was organised by Janet Mansfield at her family farm near Gulgong. Subsequent events at Gulgong morphed into the now famous 'Gulgong' ceramics gatherings with international and local masters demonstrating, and a series of exhibitions, lectures and participatory happenings. I can reasonably claim to have started that whole process.

The only drawback at the Gippsland Institute was the time spent attending meetings. This would not surprise anyone who has worked in a large tertiary institution. Along with time spent in administration and extras like open days and student exhibitions, this was the part they paid me for. The rest I gave free.

Norman Creighton, head of the art school, was a man of overwhelming enthusiasms. He would develop what can only be described as a passion for a new project of some kind. That usually worried others around him because they would have to carry out whatever it involved. The compensation was Norman's support of collegiate decisions. When he put the new project to the staff for a vote, we could all say no. To his credit he would have a brief moment of disappointment but then carry on with no sense whatever of recrimination or vindictiveness. Socially he was a genial friend and a pleasure to be with, professionally he was hard work.

There were few postgraduate students in the beginning, only a few doing the graduate diploma course. My teaching mainly involved undergraduates. After the painfully narrow focus on teaching about glazes in Canberra there was a wonderful sense of freedom, covering the whole range of ceramic possibilities.

None of us had formal tertiary teaching qualifications, but that was pretty much standard in Australian art schools. I worked on developing a personal approach, setting a series of quarter- or later half-semester projects. The first year involved pretty standard kind of stuff, like making some work for a salt glazing firing, or painting on majolica. But in the second year I set projects in areas that I knew little about myself, having explained that to the students in the beginning. We were all in together trying to work out something new. My aim there was not to teach specific knowledge or skills but to have the students learn something far more important: how to learn.

We had many group discussions where everyone contributed ideas for experiments which we then tried, followed by more discussion. I felt that this kind of learning would stay on with students. They had planned it themselves and then seen the results of their planning and thinking. This applied to all aspects of ceramics, the aesthetics as well as the technical, seeing what worked and what failed, and what could be developed and improved. The end result, I hoped, was that in later life they could go into new areas of work with confidence that they could work it out as they went along. This is a most important skill for rural artists who do not have all the helpful facilities and colleagues found in cities.

I struggled with some of the students. It was easy to help those who were committed and enthusiastic. It was problematic trying to fathom anyone who was filling in time by selecting a ceramics elective because they thought it would provide an easy pass. They needed placing on a hot rock in the morning to warm them up, like lizards. Everyone needs encouragement but with the duds I believed that if their work was hopeless it was best to tell them so. I advised them to look for something they might eventually be good at.

Usually the better students were the ones we knew as 'mature age'. Many of the young ones had little discipline and few had much in the way of talent. They wanted it all to be easy, not understanding the long slog ahead of them if they wanted to become serious professionals in ceramics. With my lack of skills for dealing with beginners, it was easy to become disenchanted. I lacked the patience and whatever other qualities it required.

It was profound relief when in a staff meeting Norman said, as all heads of departments now say constantly, we are short of funds and something has to go. I did a Captain Oates and offered a sacrifice—my undergraduate ceramics course. Everyone else was relieved because their empires would remain intact; and I was happy to say goodbye to the difficulties. That attitude has since been confirmed in that almost none of the then younger ones have continued, although some of the mature age ones are still active.

Over time the school received less and less funds. At one staff meeting Norman gave us a serious talk about how pay increments would now be related to productivity gains. He asked each of what we could do to increase productivity and I offered to start using bigger words.

* * *

Around 1990 we developed the idea of a distance course for postgraduates. Euan Heng and I worked out the basic approach. We only considered postgraduates, assuming that teaching beginners at a distance would be too complicated. Beginners need to be taught techniques but communications then were by letter, fax (which most students did not have) and phone. There was no email, no easy way to send images, and no simple way to demonstrate skills and techniques. In contrast postgraduates would already have those skills; we could talk to them about concepts, about content, about acquiring more knowledge. It's interesting to note that much later distance courses for ceramics undergraduates were able to be started up in Canberra at the art school, when computerised means of communication were available.

Setting up a new course in the Gippsland Institute was simple. First decide what it would involve—in my case, ceramics, and make a rough overall plan for how it would work. Nobody expected all the details at the start, understanding that could be worked out as we went along. The professional staff, the registrar, the printing department, the audio-visual section and others worked out how they could contribute; they were there to help.

All this contrasts to the endless obstacles placed in the way of achieving anything later when Monash University took over. A tiny change to any course would have to go through several committees and could take six months. In the Gippsland Institute the whole concept of a new course was approved on the day it was presented, usually with some helpful suggestions offered. If I wanted to change something later, I just changed it.

In the beginning, before computers were common, we communicated with students by telephone and mail. Later I introduced video, and each student was issued with a video camera and made regular reports through that medium. Later, when email was available it became the standard for both word and image. I particularly enjoyed discussions on the phone and was always well informed about the weather in various parts of the country.

The Gippsland Institute was one of the CAEs in Australia offering a wide range of distance courses so ours was nothing out of the ordinary. But out there in the ceramics community it was revolutionary. It offered professionals in the field, and people teaching in tertiary institutions, a way of study that they could not have managed if they had to attend somewhere full-time. Many ceramics lecturers in other art schools completed the graduate diploma course. In time MA and PhD courses were added.

The big question in the beginning was how to do it. The immediate solution to that problem came in the form of Tony Nankervis. He wanted to upgrade his qualifications; we agreed he would be the guinea pig for trying out how to do things. Tony was a friend so we could discuss the process without any dramas. He could tell me what worked and what did not and I could adjust easily.

At first, I was concerned that he knew more than me about being a potter, but I soon realised that was not important. My job as a supervisor was not to have superior knowledge about everything. The basis of postgraduate study is that candidates select an area of research that will produce new knowledge, and develop that knowledge themselves. The important part of my role was to discuss their work with them and ask questions. They had to come up with the answers.

In following years, the word gradually spread that the course was suited to professionals wanting a formal qualification. The Gippsland ceramics courses became well known and respected. More than 70 people completed graduate diploma, masters and doctorate courses. The standard was helped along initially by selecting candidates who promised to contribute at a high standard. I respected and highly valued their commitment and willingness to move away from safety, to take risks and explore the unknown. A valuable side effect for me was that taking on a stranger often led to having a lifetime friend.

A few insisted on simply continuing what they were doing before they started. I should really name them here, arrogant sods. As John Dewey the great educator said, learning is the difference between when you started and when you finished. I could not understand why anyone would not want to learn although it seemed ego was a problem in a few cases—they could not admit to any ignorance so stuck to what they knew.

I was also unimpressed by those few who just wanted a higher qualification, preferring those who wanted to investigate something new, for the sake of learning. The better students said that the demands of the course provided the discipline to carry on their research, something they might not have done working alone. It has been gratifying to follow the careers of some who started new lines of work, continuing to develop it professionally afterwards, people like Gail Nichols, Ian Dowling, Johanna Demaine, Ray Cavill, Simone Fraser and Merran Esson.

My aim was to produce graduates who could work independently, with a distinctive personal identity in ceramics. They would know where to get information, and know how to pass on information to others. They were expected to end up competent and comfortable with both public speaking and writing.

The students came to the campus once a year for the Winter School.

This was best early on when they came in for three weeks, to work on their individual projects and as a bonus learn from each other. The winter school anagama firing ritual was a source of bonding for people from widely dispersed locations around Australia, New Zealand and even from the USA. Many friendships and working contacts begun at winter schools have continued through the years.

Later the time was shortened to one week and revolved more around talks by students about their projects. This change had been pushed along by students in other disciplines—painting, printmaking, photography, sculpture, who were not interested in working together but were focused on their personal interests. Jack Troy told me about his experience travelling on a plane somewhere and discovering the person sitting next to him was a painter. When Jack told the painter he was going home from a ceramics conference, the reply was that painters would never have a conference, there would not be enough corners for them all to sit in and ignore each other.

* * *

The move to Gippsland was the best change I could have made professionally, but Brenda suffered because of it. Most of her close friendships had started in Sydney and were easy enough to maintain while we were in Canberra. But for her, Gippsland was too far away. It was one of those situations where I could meet and become friendly with new people through my work, but staying at home with two small kids made it difficult for Brenda. She was not gregarious and not interested in joining local community organisations.

Her isolation changed when the college started up a new course in Aboriginal Studies. The course was aimed to give indigenous local youth an opportunity to advance their education, and was developed in a different manner to other college courses, to be culturally appropriate, using elders for some of the cultural teaching just as it had always been done.

When the people running it discovered that Brenda had a background in archaeology and was doing a masters degree on aboriginal sites in NSW, she was offered some sessional teaching. What seemed to be a perfect opportunity did not work out that way. There was an instant mismatch. Brenda approached the teaching as she would have at ANU or Sydney University—where she had been a student—presenting a serious academic introduction to Australian archaeology. The students were not prepared well for that approach. Some had not finished high school; most found the concepts alien and difficult. The situation became more stressful and unsatisfactory both ways. Brenda retreated into internal agonies.

Leaving aside most of what occurred, she eventually was diagnosed as suffering from a schizoid illness, similar to schizophrenia. That involved paranoia, thinking people were plotting against her, including the medical professionals who were prescribing medication that she believed was intended to harm her. Refusing the medication meant she became increasingly more detached from everyday reality. Characters on television were speaking to her. Colours took on emotional significance. Her behaviour became more problematic. My attempts to understand her new reality and be able to help failed. These were the most difficult years in both our lives. After a few years of this it was impossible to continue together. Brenda moved back to Adelaide and I became a sole parent. She eventually declined in health, suffering from early onset Alzheimer's, and was placed in a home. She described it as 'a place for people who cannot find their way home'. She died there, aged just sixty.

16
MONASH

... when he recalled bad times he seemed not so much bitter that
they had existed as grateful there had been a means of escape.
— Sebastian Faulks in *On Green Dolphin Street*

For amusement, look for quotes about the word *change* on Google. Every quote comes directly from the mouth of Pollyanna, suggesting change is good and resisting change is bad. It's quite obvious that none of the people who made these quotes ever worked in Art and Design in Monash University.

Trouble in art schools started in the early 1990s, with a revolutionary change in Australian tertiary education, initiated by John Dawkins, the education minister in Bob Hawke's Labor government. The whole College of Advanced Education (CAE) system was closed down, and most of the colleges taken over by universities. For the art schools previously in colleges, this brought profoundly difficult changes. It was the beginning of the end for many. As I write this the former Canberra School of Art is being restructured into insignificance.

The Gippsland Institute CAE was taken over by Monash University in 1992. The Monash leadership seemed to be plotting to take over the world, opening campuses in Malaysia, South Africa and elsewhere, and taking over several CAEs. It soon became obvious that Monash planned to asset strip the CAEs, moving any worthwhile courses, research projects or staff to Clayton. Monash abandoned the Gippsland Campus in 2014, mission accomplished. The campus was then combined with Ballarat University to form Federation University. Whether this is a success or not I neither know nor care; it's remote and I am disinterested.

Prior to the Monash merger we had been collegiate in campus administration, cooperating across schools, involving all parts of the campus in important decisions and administration. Monash destroyed that spirit of cooperation by linking each separate school (such as education, art and engineering) to the relevant Clayton faculty, breaking up our campus into separate units. No longer did we have any overall perspective. Gradually we lost contact with colleagues in other schools and our horizons narrowed, a serious loss.

Our distance education courses faced new difficulties. Monash academics were content to ignore our graduate diploma courses. But for masters and especially doctorates by distance mode, their arrogant view was that if they were not doing it, it could not be done. The resulting ignorance and obstacles made what had been a successful program much more difficult. Minor changes in any course required endless discussion in committee; before, if I wanted to make any changes, I just made them. Particularly with PhDs it was forbidden to run off campus candidates. Gail Nichols had a rough time because of this.

Indicating the stupidity of it all, I can say with a Gallic shrug: we had been way ahead of what was to come. Now, many current Monash postgraduate students work off campus. eLearning is common. An undergraduate student can view podcasts of lectures. Online group study is routine. Students can contact lecturers via SMS during class, while others sit in a virtual classroom taking in pre-prepared lectures. All of this is really just a technological extension of what we were doing 30 years ago when our students could be working from anywhere.

* * *

Another pressure was financial. Humanities courses were cheap to run because one lecturer could talk for an hour to five hundred students, unlike ceramics where one lecturer spent several days a week with ten students, the best way to teach art practice. Plato said the ideal number of students for effective communication was four. In ceramics, tacit knowledge could not be passed on in a lecture hall but only by the sense of touch. But the powers that be rejected our arithmetic.

Courses were structured by whatever cost least. Instead of having ceramics, painting, sculpture and so on as separate courses, eventually all were combined into something called 'Visual Arts'. All the students in one year-group would be given a project which they could carry through in any medium of their choice. Worse, governments became more demanding about what we did with the money they handed out. Trust that we knew what was best was abandoned in favour of authoritarianism.

Politicians made decisions about art.

Monash University in the 1990s embraced managerialism theory and practice, the child of market-oriented reforms: Thatcherism, economic rationalism and neoliberalism. This was the beginning of the transition of universities from places of learning, to businesses; the time when university staff began referring to their place of work as—the factory.

Monash introduced restructuring, removing permanent positions and replacing them with casual, and expanding the number, power and remuneration of senior managers. The trend was that administrators had the full-time jobs; lecturers were sessional. They invariably worked many more hours than they were paid for. The buzzword was 'efficiency'. I am unable to reconcile the Monash use of the word with its definition in the Oxford dictionary. The reality was that less staff meant each person had an extra workload, usually an overload; and each student less contact with teachers.

In restructuring Art and Design at Caulfield, those chosen to stay seemed to be selected for their ability to say yes at all times. Those selected for removal were the achievers, anyone with initiative, individuality and strength. While purging lecturers and downgrading working conditions, the remaining staff increasingly felt alienated by an environment where the management showed no downward loyalty to employees, expecting it to flow upwards only. The result was an overall dumbing down of faculty activity. Brilliance can only shine in an atmosphere where the individual is free to function as they think best. The end result of all the changes was universal low morale.

Accountability was another new concept. Previously everyone was expected to do their job and most did with no need for reminders. The new 1990s regime meant that a university lecturer would spend half the time, or less, teaching and doing research than a university lecturer of the 1960s. Like me, most staff saw the other fifty percent as a bureaucracy-driven waste of time. Anyone expecting praise, or even acknowledgement, for their increased time and effort was disappointed. Accountability required each person to demonstrate how closely their activity followed priorities, as set out in the institutional vision or mission statement or aspirations (all the new weasel words) in the five-year plans.

An extract from an article in the now-defunct *Bulletin* magazine in

2005 spelled out the results of this kind of dysfunctional management: 'An unhappy workplace, demoralised people with feelings of hopelessness, helplessness, despair, feelings of loss of value and entrapment'. The depression in each individual became the demoralisation of the group.

* * *

It's clearly wrong, and would be a little churlish, to dismiss the whole institution with negatives. Many respected academics worked there. I met some through my role as chairman of the Art and Design research committee, hence membership of the university-wide research committee. The Monash leader I most respected was the senior deputy vice-chancellor, Ian Chubb (1993–1995), who later became Chief Scientist of Australia. He formed a private advisory committee, consisting of an odd mix from all around the university. I was invited because of my involvement in distance education. Others included everyone from a gardener and a maintenance man to a professor who was a faculty head. Chubb's instruction to us was to say nothing to anyone about the existence of his advisory committee. We met only when some university-wide issue that created strong, disagreeing opinions arose. As an example, when the regular issue of pay rises for staff came around, I suggested at the meeting to discuss it that I, and potentially others, would welcome keeping the same salary but having more time each year to work on my interests. This meant forgoing extra money in exchange for free time. Chubb agreed – and that concept soon became university policy. Rarely in life is it possible for an ordinary individual to have any influence on major decisions that affect their lives.

Generally, though, the transition from a CAE in Gippsland, where an individual could shape policy and strategy, to a monolithic organisation, where the leadership appeared autocratic and the individual felt powerless, was difficult. In the past I had been free to develop and learn, to make my own mistakes and achieve my own successes. Innovation, creative thinking, seeking new developments and maintaining the highest standards were all encouraged, bringing out the best in people, encouraging them to be enthusiastic and creative and contribute to building a better organisation. But from a distance the Monash style was autocratic and management-centred, discouraging any of the previous approaches.

In the early days of involvement with Monash, when we were taken into the Faculty of Arts, the management style was benign and sometimes even helpful. But eventually when a new Faculty, Art and Design, was set up, a new Dean, John Redmond, was appointed as faculty head. He and I were – to put it as politely as I can manage – not amiable workmates. I did not warm to him from the beginning, and it was clear that the feeling was mutual. I have no wish to go into the painful details of all that transpired, but that relationship gradually became a major factor in my decision to leave Monash altogether – and finally achieve my youthful ambition to be the potter at the end of the country lane.

The problems might have gone away sooner if the faculty had the same sensible system as the Smithsonian Natural History Museum, where a chairman would be appointed for three years, afterwards never having to do administration again. Australian academics moved into administration remain there, gradually drowning in bureaucracy, oftentimes losing their ability to continue their academic work.

* * *

Form took over from substance, appearance from reality. A fancy building, a Denton Corker Marshall design, was constructed after Art and Design became an independent faculty. I called it the crooked building. It looked from outside, I suppose, modern and sophisticated, but that belied the dumbing down happening within. A form of intellectual corruption began to creep in. One manifestation that bothered me, because I was involved in postgraduate supervision, was the selection of postgraduate examiners who could be relied on to pass candidates with a minimum of evaluation, keeping up the numbers, making the faculty look good—regardless of quality. Some of these examiners did not even have the qualification themselves. My view always was that anyone who has completed a master's degree or doctorate should take pride in their achievements. Making a real contribution is an admirable achievement. The ones who got through with dud examiners should be embarrassed enough to hide their testamur in a bottom drawer rather than putting it up on the wall.

The Dean preferred clean activities like design where the designer could dress well and sit at a clean computer. He had little regard for messy activities like ceramics; or indeed other areas of arts practice. The traditional arts were downgraded in favour of the new design courses.

That transition was not unique to Monash; it became an Australia-wide development in art schools and eventually filtered down into high schools.

One example will allow some understanding of my attitude towards the Dean; I have no wish to remember more than that. He asked me to do the planning for something. I've forgotten what, but do recall it was a complex job. Complex plans were a Monash specialty. I worked after teaching hours, late at night for a couple of weeks, enduring calls from Redmond as late as 11.30 at night. One result was stress that came out in being unpleasant to my family. Mike, who was about fifteen, once said to me *'For God's sake go out and burn something, that might make you feel better'*. When I completed the job, I handed the document to Redmond. His immediate response was that they were no longer relevant; he had moved on. They were rejected with no attempt on his part to even read them. Thrown down on the table and ignored.

In the past, taking initiative had at best been praised or rewarded. In the new regime there were no opportunities for staff to work together to establish policies or practices, no collegiate activity. The transition was extremely difficult. As an example of initiative stifled, John Neely from Utah State University in the USA, Tony Nankervis from Southern Cross University in Lismore, NSW and I had been discussing setting up a three-way course relating to woodfiring. Students could move from one university to another for a time, perhaps a semester, to vary their experience. An agreement between the universities would ensure the experience counted towards the student's home university degree. Utah State, and Southern Cross enthusiastically supported the concept, but the Dean opposed it, presumably on the basis that he had not originated the idea. The concept was abandoned—although there were some exchanges between Utah and Lismore.

In the past I had strong attitudes about maintaining standards, about developing new approaches that would benefit students; but I just stopped caring about the faculty or the university. For them I had nothing to offer. Supervising postgraduates was still important, the personal connections were still important, my artwork was still important, but for Monash—*nada*.

* * *

The inevitable result was general despair, demoralisation and depression among staff. Suffering from all these, I went to a psychologist in Morwell, near our Churchill campus, to look for help in finding some way to survive. One of his first questions was 'Where do you work?' 'Monash,' I told him. 'Ah yes,' he said, 'I make a good living because of them'. He asked me why I had come to see him and I told him, at some length. Finally, he interrupted me and said 'you have talked now for almost thirty minutes about this one man. He obviously occupies a great deal of your mental time. How much time do you think he spends thinking about you?' The light came on. I was cured. I thanked him, paid his receptionist, and suffered depression no more.

Toto Wolff, boss of the high-achieving Mercedes Formula 1 team, said it well: 'Why do people perform? It is because they have the right environment, having passion for it, and they feel respect. They feel understood. They feel they have the right objectives. I am trying to provide that framework, trying to achieve a situation where nobody would want to leave the team.'

* * *

One day I sat there at my desk, looking at a pile of papers, each asking me to do something pointless. The top one was new to me: a request for details of my plans for the next year. The introduction explained that every year two documents were required, one detailing achievements in the past year, the other plans for next year. This contradicted what every creative person knows: developments come along unpredictably and it's not always possible to forecast their trajectory. What can an artist say about what they might do in the next year? Who knows what you might dream up? Who knows what exciting discoveries a postgraduate student may make and where it will lead them?

For my first lot of next year's plans, I invented ambitions for marvellous achievements on a scale previously not imagined in art schools. My submission was deliberately and completely nonsensical; winning the Nobel Prize nonsensical. At the end of that year when asked to report on achievements, I cut and pasted the previous planning nonsense, indicating that everything had been achieved. The next year's plans submitted were exactly the ones from the year before, except for a change of date. I never received any comment on this nonsense from anyone and assume it was never read by anyone—unfortunately, because it contained some quality fiction writing.

The greatest achievement of this human resources thinking was to introduce some wonderfully ridiculous new jargon. KPIs (key performance indicators), benchmarks, entrepreneurs, annual aspirations and achievements, international acclaim. I particularly liked *vision*, considering that the people who most used the term seemed to have least of that ability. Subjected to this drivel, I worried about the mentality of the people who dreamed it up, and missed the days when our main task was teaching students.

In the early CAE days, we had concentrated on teaching and practising traditional arts, painting, sculpture, ceramics and so on, encouraging extended hours in the studio. At the Gippsland art school students worked in the studios all hours of the day and night. Monash concentrated on minimizing studio time, focusing on the theoretical and conceptual rather than the practical. Around Australia, many art school teachers who were originally employed because of the high standard of their practice, were flustered. Their art, such as ceramics, printmaking, or photography, involved a heavy focus on process. They thought it profound silliness to suggest that their work should concentrate on concept at the expense of process; effectively, to minimise time involved in making art and extend the time thinking about it.

Intellectually, the fashion then for postmodernist thought made everything of equal value. The concept of quality was out of fashion and skills were ignored. Instead of originality, copying was in vogue except it was not called copying, it was called appropriation. The next phase was deconstructionist thought. This sought to reveal the concepts and influences (patriarchal, racial, elitist) that might have led to the creation of a work. Less attention was paid to the artwork itself, its effect, its beauty, its sweep, its passion, its ability to take us out of our small world and understand universal themes. Instead, deconstructionism concentrated on unpicking structure and context, on unmasking assumptions.

I understand well that the nature of art changes constantly and new approaches must be respected. But the new focus on theory over practice came into art schools at an unfortunate time. Economic rationalism required maximising student numbers and minimising time teachers spent with students, radically changing the teaching process. As universities became businesses those teachers who had difficulty with the transitions became prime targets for restructuring, which essentially meant they were fired. The positive spin was that younger, more contemporary teachers could be brought in. The destructive negative was that the new staff were employed on a casual or sessional basis, at a lower salary that the ones who had left. The employment uncertainties caused by casual appointments for only a few hours or at most one or two days a week were heightened by lack of continuity and threats of not being re-employed.

The original idea of sessional teaching had been sensible. Bring in let's say a highly regarded surgeon to the medical school for a lecture or two, or bring in artists for a one-hour talk, enriching learning. But this worthy aim became distorted by prioritising economics. Paying the minimum for teaching was just a business decision. Combining this with administrators inventing incomprehensible tasks made you wonder: why would anyone stay there? The only possible reason was not being able to get a job anywhere else and needing the money to live on.

* * *

I was overwhelmed. All ambition evaporated. The struggle to maintain standards had been lost. Everything crystallised on my day of ultimate enlightenment, sitting at my desk, numbed by some final piece of bureaucratic bullshit. Some people say they have seen the light, or have had a vision, or some other profound religious insight. I had my first epiphany watching Ivan McMeekin throw a pot and that led to a rewarding life. I had my second sitting at my desk that day, the clearest vision I will ever experience drug-free, and it came to me in words. They were: *'You are wasting your life. Being here is wasting your life.'*

I decided to leave, tired of being filled with antagonism and worse, taking it home and directing it to my family. They deserved none of it. My artwork suffered through lack of enthusiasm for anything. My loyalty at work was solely to the postgraduate students. I liked most of them as people and was generally pleased to be dealing with such a mature and dedicated group. But the university lunacy had worn me out.

* * *

Everyone I have ever met who was about to retire after a lifetime of work is apprehensive about the risks. Will they have enough money? Will they be healthy? Will they still have friends? Will they have enough mental stimulation and entertainment? Is the danger real or imagined? But fears can cripple you; sometimes clinging to security is the worst approach.

As a major life event, my departure was perfectly timed. I no longer had anything to contribute. My morale and well-being had reached bottom and there was no gain possible in staying there, for me or anyone else. My values were not valued and I had little respect for the values that replaced them. I had set myself up financially, in my terms, ensuring enough income to pay the bills without too much worry. Ignoring any other minor fears was easy. Anything would be better than staying at that grim workplace. My family agreed, tired also of my constant fuming.

Outside of the university, in my life in ceramics, I had actually done extremely well from my move to Gippsland, having many exhibitions, doing talks at conferences, travelling overseas frequently and making friendly contact with international colleagues especially in the USA. The Gippsland campus was widely known as a centre for woodfiring; but it's a mistake to think that was my only interest in ceramics. The postgraduates had an extremely wide range of interests, something I encouraged. They chose what they wanted to work on, my role was to support them.

The publicity emphasising woodfire at Gippsland, though, meant that the anagama kiln had been something of a symbol of the school. Julie Adams, the head of school, suggested preserving the anagama as a kind of monument, but I decided to let the kiln go, feeling that before too long it would just become an enigmatic and meaningless pile of bricks. The subsequent history of the school has confirmed the wisdom of that decision.

That little old banana-shaped kiln is still associated by many people with many stories and much emotion. I still have mental images of people working all hours, firing through the night, dedicated to the task. Of people with blackened faces and dirty overalls, their faces lit up by flame as they stoked the kiln, filling the valley with smoke. Vapours of unknown composition emerged from the salt-glazing kilns and hung around on damp midwinter nights. And I can still hear the story told and repeated many times by the night watchman/caretaker who loved fishing, about the time he caught the whale. We never believed it but we always enjoyed it.

The Dean and the campus management at Gippsland could not wait for me to leave. The university had other plans for the site of the ceramics studio. Anyone coming in fresh and looking at the building would see why. The studio was a big old farm shed that was beginning to deteriorate. But the building had been irrelevant; what was important and valuable was what happened in it. It had been a home—of learning. It had been visited by some of the best people in ceramics in Australia, and other countries. It had housed some excellent postgraduates.

My last memory of the old tin shed studio that had been the centre of many years of my life is of a near empty shell containing only a few mismatched office chairs that we had scrounged, some sitting randomly, some tipped on their sides. I made an offer to buy the equipment and materials and rescued everything possible, working hard over a couple of weeks to beat the demolition—bricks, kiln shelves, cones, wheels, vibratory sieve, and many materials. All would just have been bulldozed otherwise.

The bulldozer did its work one weekend. When I came in on Monday there was nothing but a large heap of bent sheet metal, steel framing and bricks all mixed in a gross tangle. The anagama had disappeared altogether into the rubble. Nothing was recognisable. Not long after that, a man with a machine with two large steel fingers picked it all up amazingly delicately and sorted in to different piles: metal, bricks, concrete and wood. Everything was taken away in trucks. After leaving altogether, I went back one weekend to see what was there. Only a flat patch of dirt remained.

I left at the end of 2003 and life began again. People have asked me how long it took to adjust to retirement and my answer always is: 'About fifteen seconds'. I believed then it would be, and I know now it was, the most satisfying career move of my entire life. I left thinking of that quote from Nelson Mandela: 'As I walked out the door toward the gate that would lead to my freedom, I knew if I didn't leave my bitterness and hatred behind, I'd still be in prison'. I did leave it behind—until writing this—and have been wonderfully free ever since. What we don't forgive can haunt us.

Leaving was the perfect change. Before there had been perpetual anxiety or anger or frustration, a tangle of unpleasant emotions, and little control over my professional life. After leaving I morphed into a man with a face free of wrinkles. The deep furrows in my forehead became traces, and the deep cuts in my psyche healed over. I began to understand what happy meant. As someone said, everything turned out the way I would have hoped had I known what I was hoping for.

17
GETTING OUT THERE

You never know the results of all that you do ...

— John Williams in *Stoner*

The most satisfaction I ever had working at Monash University resulted from a 2001 Australian Research Council grant, to travel to the US and visit woodfire potters, researching a book comparing Australian and US woodfirers.

John Redmond, faculty head, prioritised applications before they went to the university research committee. He placed mine last in the pile without, I assume, even glancing at the contents. The research committee went through applications from each faculty and allocated grants, according to faculty priorities, until the funds for that faculty were exhausted. As the last on the list I missed out.

But, in their wisdom, the committee had set aside funds for applications they considered worthy, but wrongly low-graded by the faculties. Someone had read all the applications, selected mine, and argued its worth to the committee. They gave me $10,000, enough for an extensive trip around the USA. I wish I had seen the Dean's face when he heard. The result was six weeks travel, visiting around 30 woodfirers, and establishing personal connections. Everyone was hospitable and welcoming. In return I try to be as welcoming to visitors from the USA.

Reading a list of the names of potters I visited would be like reading a phone book. Some stood out, each for a different reason. Hiroshi Ogawa's anagama kiln in Oregon was eerily similar in design to mine, considering we had never met. Each has a long initial tunnel and a second chamber. We both had difficulty firing the second chamber, a problem that took me many years to resolve. My solution was to simply blow air into the base of the chamber, thus burning unburned fuel coming through from the tunnel. It was then perfect for firing glazed pots.

In Wisconsin, Randy Johnstone took me to the Stillwater studio of Warren Mackenzie, one of the most revered men in American ceramics, a man without ego, respected and loved by all. For comparison in Australia, Peter Rushforth had similar status. I was deeply impressed by the sheer simplicity of Mackenzie's setup. He worked in an ordinary but large old shed. Outside, a small crudely constructed tin shed, open on one side, had a shelf running around each of the three closed sides. Here he placed pots for sale to visitors. A sign read *'To buy, please put money in the tin'*. The tin was an old baked bean can. There were no pots; they all sold immediately whenever he put them out. It would have been easy to talk with him much more than the one afternoon, hearing about his experiences of people and places.

Gerry Williams, before his 2014 death, was one of the most widely known people in American ceramics, the editor and owner of *Studio Potter* magazine which he started in 1972. Over a week, we travelled around, visiting potters in New Hampshire, as well as some fine local attractions including Mt Washington in the north of the state, near the Canadian border. Another day we drove up the Maine Coast where Gerry had lived before moving to New Hampshire. There is nothing like fresh lobster for lunch, on the calm edge of the wild Atlantic.

The planned book never eventuated but in 2011 Janet Mansfield published my book on woodfire in Australia; and Amadeo Salamoni's book *Wood-Fired Ceramics* refers to the work of a hundred potters, mainly American.[10]

* * *

Overall, it was a miniature grand tour, confirming the importance of getting out there and meeting people, of establishing personal and working relationships. Almost all my travel in other countries has been work-related; taking up fellowships, studying traditional potters at work, participating in conferences, giving workshops or simply visiting people involved in my kind of work.

Australians in all forms of the arts have traditionally gone overseas to seek their fame and fortune, homing in on fashionable international centres. When airfares were beyond all but the wealthy, only seriously dedicated artists made their overseas pilgrimage, usually undertaking long stays in one place. Now it's feasible to make many short visits, and every hobby potter from everywhere has been to other countries. I was fortunate to begin travelling internationally just when it became easier and cheaper.

Air travel has become so ubiquitous as to be regarded by many who live at popular destinations as a pestilence. Cost is a factor. A 1977 Sydney-to-London airfare was $1496. In 2019, when it took $4.25 to buy what cost one dollar in 1977, a discount fare could still be had for $1500, effectively a quarter the price. Online access means that organising air travel now is not much more difficult than preparing breakfast, and takes about as long.

Eric Linklater said it beautifully: '*We are the first of mankind to see the great continents of the air, its enormous prairies and fantastic archipelagos, in sunlight from above—pleated canopies of clean-combed wool and vaporous high curtains—ten thousand little flocculent clouds like lettuces*', (in *Figures in a Landscape*, 1952). I think he meant cauliflowers rather than lettuces.

America has been my second home. Memory fails to recall how many times I have been to the USA. My stays have been as long as eighteen months and as short as a week, and I have been in thirty-eight of the fifty states. From outside it's easy to believe that America is a nation of mad people, fanatical about religion, fanatical about guns, fanatical about ideas of individual freedom. But most of the Americans I know are generous and harmless. It's a nation of extreme contrasts and I have generally experienced only the best of it. Pleasant, courteous behaviour is common and mostly real. The boy behind the counter wishes us pleasure, '*y'all have a nice day now*', an empty salutation we have adopted in Australia. Drivers of cars entering a freeway will courteously meld like a zipper, one from here and one from there in an unbroken sequence. New neighbours will be welcomed with gifts, sometimes simply left on the front step, often personally, delivered with a smile and an invitation to join in with whatever that neighbour joins in. Neighbours will all meet for a street party and everyone is involved in any street parade, either parading or cheering them on.

* * *

My reasons for visiting the USA changed considerably from about 1980 onwards. The decade before had seen me there because of my involvement in anthropology and archaeology. But after 1980 my interest in woodfiring developed; that became the reason for visits from then on. Now I go there to see friends, scattered around most parts of the country. A side benefit has been seeing some of the beautiful parts of America: the Cascades and the Rockies, or in the Southwest, Utah, Arizona and New Mexico, especially American Indian culture sites. Visiting some of the world's best museums and art galleries has always been a priority. But beyond all that I like to wander the streets anywhere, seeing the different sense of design, the different feel to Australia. I love the quirky eating places, the displays and lighting, the endless varieties of goods, the drug stores, the hardware stores and farm supply sheds; the ordinary stuff.

* * *

It's a good lesson for beginners—if you want to be known internationally then travel where you want to be known and get to know the people face to face. It's so much easier to get in contact with someone after you have talked to them in person and it's always enlightening to meet someone you have only known through media. Knowing where someone lives, knowing their family and friends, and their character provides far more pleasure than simply seeing their work pictured in a magazine. Networking is not just a pragmatic, clinical process; from it comes enduring friendships.

Conferences provide one of the best venues for networking; not just going to them, but giving talks or demonstrations. That puts you in front of people and helps you to contribute; in the end you are known by your contributions rather than some self-promoted opinion of yourself. And it is easy to become involved; conferences and workshops about ceramics are so frequent it is almost possible to travel the world attending one event after another without a break.

My first American conference was in Iowa City in 1999, at the woodfire event organised by Chuck Hindes. My role was chairing a panel on international woodfire. Chester Nealie, Tony Nankervis and I had been giving workshops. Dan Anderson had offered to drive us from Edwardsville, Illinois (near St Louis) up to Iowa City for the conference. As the trip went on a state of panic developed. The drive seemed excessively leisurely and I was scheduled first up on stage at the event, at midday. We finally got to the conference auditorium at ten minutes to midday. I had to rush from the car, find out where to go, get up on the stage and be introduced by Chuck and immediately begin speaking.

After several stints at smaller events in America, NCECA beckoned. This is the major annual US ceramics conference, attracting four to five thousand delegates. My first was in Portland, Oregon in 2006 and the next in Seattle in 2012. NCECA is the perfect venue to get together with friends who are rarely all in one place together. The most pleasing single event at the Seattle NCECA was seeing presentation of teacher of the year awards to two good mates, Chuck Hindes and Jack Troy. Both well deserved. I had a quiet wish that my mother could have been there to see it; she told me that you should always be selective about the company you keep. Americans are much more aware of contributions made by people and honour contributors in a way not seen in Australia. Organisers of our main events could learn something from the Americans but seem reluctant to do so.

My first experience of the International Academy of Ceramics (IAC) was the 1993 meeting and conference in Edinburgh. I had applied for membership. The good part was meeting people I had only read about, like Bill Hunt, editor of *Ceramics Monthly* at the time. The bad part was not being accepted into membership. Consoling voices, mostly American, were rather angry that anyone making their work on a potter's wheel was unlikely to get in. Only work made with a more European feel was more likely to succeed. The chair of the IAC at the time, Rudolf Schneider, ran the organisation with a Euro-centric focus. Side benefits were seeing the Glasgow School of Art with its Rennie Macintosh design, and some fine museums including the Yorkshire Sculpture Park with many Henry Moore sculptures. It was also my first introduction to the work of Andy Goldsworthy, which I have admired since.

After Markus Bohm from Germany was involved in the woodfire conference Paul Davis organised at Sturt in 2008, I suggested that Markus could organise such an event himself. He did in 2010, in Brollin, in the former East Germany about 15 kilometres from the Polish border in the top northeast corner of Germany. The conference was held in what had been a grand old farm. The residence and associated buildings had been converted into an arts centre. The local story was that the farm had been abandoned in the past. A Jewish star on the gable of one building suggested why it had been abandoned.

It was obvious that the people of former East Germany had not been wealthy. The train from Berlin was not the latest design and broke down half way. Towns had a general run-down appearance. A new shopping mall in Pasewalk, near Brollin stood in stark contrast to the shabby surroundings. I ran a workshop where we built and fired a small train kiln with a step grate firebox, based on one we had used at Fuping in China. We were supplied with new insulating bricks so the firing process mainly consisted of trying to slow it down and not overfire.

Janet Mansfield and I were both heading to Paris after the event, to take part in the 2010 IAC conference. We had independently asked organisers of the German event to book a sleeper in the overnight train from Berlin to Paris. We did not know till we got on the train that they had booked us both into the same sleeper. It consisted of two very narrow bunks one above the other, and a passage about 50 centimetres wide. We seemed to manage somehow and slept across Holland and Belgium, waking up not long before reaching Gare du Nord in Paris.

The IAC is affiliated with UNESCO. The meeting was held in the grand conference room in their headquarters building, replete with translators. Janet, as president of the IAC chaired the meeting. We were not to know it would be one of her last grand appearances; not long after that she became ill with cancer.

* * *

Along the way we constantly learn, sometimes from experience, sometimes because other people are willing to help. Workshops are arts events specifically designed to pass on knowledge, and I have felt obliged to do them as a thank you for help I have received from others. My first woodfiring workshop in the USA was in 1991 at Arrowmont School of Arts and Crafts in Gatlinburg, Tennessee. Arrowmont is one of the main workshop schools in the United States, offering a range of workshops: painting, drawing, papermaking, textiles and many more. A few hundred people were involved in the lively atmosphere.

My plan for the two-week workshop was to make enough work to fill a large (that is LARGE) anagama kiln, stack the kiln, fire it, allow it to cool and take out the work and discuss it. Before the event this appeared next to impossible; but an all-expenses-paid trip to the US looked attractive so I lived with the anxiety. On location, Gatlinburg was welcoming and relaxing. As a 'gateway' to the Smoky Mountains national park, Gatlinburg is set up as a tourist trap, with many weird attractions. Dollywood, Dolly Parton's fun park, is just down the road.

The anagama kiln was regarded by the Arrowmont management as a kind of national shrine, but Jack Troy had told me nobody had ever managed to get a comprehensively good firing from the kiln; usually the back section was cold. It was designed and built by Shiro Otani from Shigaraki. Arrowmont considered Otani close to sanctity. I suspect that at Arrowmont his knowledge and experience of these kilns had not been as fully developed as it was later in his career. Perhaps Otani was learning on the job, like the rest of us. I decided the problem of uneven temperatures could be solved by adding additional sidestoke holes; there was only one pair. The maintenance man supplied a jackhammer and we proceeded to punch some holes in the shrine, a sacrilegious act for which I have probably never been forgiven. But the back of the kiln did get hot.

The workshop went well. They usually do with a congenial group of people. Gradually fitting in, the fears I had beforehand eased and it felt like a normal teaching assignment. The work emerging from the kiln when it was opened was acceptable. The participants were happy with the whole experience. I definitely was. Running this workshop involved going to a country where I had never done a workshop before, with a group of people I had never met who were inexperienced in the anagama process, in a place where I had no knowledge of how anything worked, using unfamiliar clays and materials and firing in a kiln that was totally different to anything I had ever used before. And making enough work to fill the kiln, fire it and see the results in two weeks. As they say, no pressure then.

Working with all those unknowns and getting a satisfactory result gave me considerable confidence to do workshops again. In the arts, you gain by doing the hard things, the ones that seem too difficult, or impossible. You lose something each time you do the easy things, the familiar and practised; you lose courage; and the work become slick and clever, losing the raw edge that defines any kind of real art.

*   *   *

Some people thrive on workshops. Jack Troy has done over 250, more than anyone I know. Some people, like my friend Chester, become animated and alive in front of an audience; but for me they involve a kind of acting, working to hold the audience. Actors on stage only have to hold the audience for a few hours; a one-day workshop is much more intense.

The basic idea is that the presenter does their normal work in front of an audience. Again, it's difficult for me. In my studio, working alone makes it easy to get into a vacant frame of mind, allowing the looseness of hand that is so important. Too much consciousness gets in the way, too much thinking about it impedes the hands, producing tight forms. In front of an audience there is no way to achieve the right mental state so my work seems to me clumsy and lacking life.

Longer workshops, involving kiln building and firing, have been the most satisfying. It's possible to just stand back and watch sometimes, without needing to be the centre of attention the whole time, and it's possible to get to know each person. They participate, so a cooperative group of people work together towards a common end. That is rewarding. Among the most memorable of these for me were one at Montsalvat in Melbourne in 2013, and the Brollin workshop in Germany in 2010. Working closely with other people creates new friendships that continue long after the workshop is forgotten.

One memorable workshop was in 1997, at Utah State University in Logan, a one-week session. It involved moving from mid-winter at home, with frosts and cold, to mid-summer in Logan, with temperatures each day well over 38° (100°F). Despite the physical shock I got some work made and we had a successful firing in the train kiln, aided by some sage advice from Dan Murphy.

The biggest audience at a workshop was around two hundred people at the 2006 North Carolina Potters Conference, an event organised by Dwight Holland. Each year three people are invited to demonstrate; our three was Janet Mansfield, Chester Nealie and me. Each of us sat in front of a large screen that showed every tiny detail of what we were doing. Alone that would have been intimidating but working with two good friends meant we could pass the job over to one of the others when we ran out of things to say.

The most memorable moment at any workshop was at Mt Hood Community College in Portland, Oregon, in one of my *Little and Large* events demonstrating 5 cm miniatures and 75 cm jars. I had a large pot well under way and accidentally trod on the control pedal of the electronic Brent wheel. The wheel head went from idle to full speed instantly, and sent the pot flying across the room to smash against a wall; luckily, not against someone's head. Everyone in the audience was open mouthed, some with horror, some with fright as it whizzed past. I laughed out loud. It was the funniest thing I had seen for some time.

Another workshop firing at Cooroy, in Queensland in 1999, with a most pleasant group of people, was more useful to me than most others. The Cooroy kiln, now demolished, was designed and built by a Mr Ichino from Tamba in Japan. It became the main inspiration for the anagama I soon after built at my place in Boolarra South, with a series of closely spaced sidestoke openings along its length.

When all my other workshops are forgotten, the one that I will remember is firing the anagama at Sturt Workshops in Mittagong, NSW in 2003. These kilns often create clouds of black ugly smoke, a major reason that my lungs are now not in good condition. The end result at Sturt was a dose of pneumonia, at a most unfortunate time. Straight after Sturt I was to attend an exhibition of work (*The Rye Crop*) in Sydney by most of my former postgraduate students, a thank you from them celebrating my imminent retirement from Monash. At the opening I was feeling seriously ill, with a high temperature and alternate bouts of feeling extremely hot or shivering cold. The end result was two weeks in hospital, seriously ill. At the emergency department, the doctor did his check-up and sent me off to the wards immediately. As I walked out the door he said '*It's good that you came in today; if not you would have been dead tomorrow*'.

I don't do workshops now. Entertaining people sometimes for days on end was never my forté. Some people love being the centre of attention but for me it's a balancing act, between liking the attention but having to work hard to get it. My biggest difficulty has always been the inability to sleep well in the weeks preceding a large workshop. Why do fears create imaginary situations that become easier to manage in reality? The answer to these questions is simple—no more workshops. Perhaps some minor ones at home where the preparation is minimal and the setting is comfortable.

The main way of going public for artists is exhibitions. Group exhibitions, at home or in other countries can be quite simple. Sending a few pieces just requires some effective packing. The only international solo exhibitions I have done have been in the USA and I made the work there so that was also simple. The costs involved in doing solo exhibitions overseas from Australia would be unlikely to be retrieved even if the exchange rate was favourable, unless transport costs were covered by the gallery or organisation.

I have attended some exhibitions that included my work, in other countries. An IAC exhibition in Paris, a group woodfire exhibition in Korea and others. A significant one was the Australian ceramics exhibition *Delinquent Angel*, first held in in 1995 in the Ceramics Museum (*Museo Internazionale delle Ceramiche*) in Faenza in Italy. It travelled through several other countries afterwards. The now defunct organisation Craft Australia selected the work of twelve Australian potters for this exhibition, from entries around Australia, helped by Janet Mansfield as advisor. I did not waste time entering because woodfired work was not accepted by the ceramics glitterati at the time. Janet met the committee to review their selection, and asked *'And where is Owen's work?'* Told that I had not even entered for selection she said *'It doesn't matter, he is in'*. I was in. Apart from any other reason she ensured that at least the work of one woodfirer was included. They sent work from thirteen potters instead of twelve.

Craft Australia had originally indicated they would support artists to attend with airfares; but closer to the time they let everyone know, via bureaucratic language, that the funding was not available for artists to travel. Study leave from the Gippsland Institute paid my fares so I made it there, the only artist represented in the exhibition to do so.

I arrived in Faenza with no suitcase (it came two days later) and no worthwhile Italian language. The people at the museum gave me a warm and friendly welcome, and supplied me with some vouchers from the local city administration (Comune di Faenza) for free meals in local restaurants. They apologised that most of the vouchers had already been used by the 'Australian Delegation'. An enquiry revealed that this had been composed of bureaucrats from Craft Australia, who had used the available travel money to visit Faenza themselves rather than supporting the artists, and had lived well from the goodwill of the Faenza community.

In return for the hospitality the bureaucrats had offered nothing. In return for mine I did a talk at the Palazzo, a grand building owned by an eccentric Italian aristocrat. The talk was translated by a young female who obviously, by her hesitations, had no understanding of ceramics terminology. The audience laughed when I told a sad story and cried when I told my best jokes. Afterwards a Canadian who understood both languages told me that the translation mostly bore no relationship to anything I had said.

* * *

I was never inclined to do the Japan pilgrimage and have only visited Japan once. Becoming aware in the 1990s that insanely high prices were being paid for some ceramics in Japan, I decided quite naively that exhibiting there would make me extremely rich. How to go about exhibiting in Japan escaped me, until Janet Mansfield persuaded Mr Itoh to arrange an exhibition of Australian woodfired work in his Green Gallery in Tokyo. This was at the time one of the world's most salubrious places to exhibit.

So, in 1996 we put together the exhibition *Australian Woodfired Ceramics (Australia no magikama sakuhin)* at the Aoyama Green Gallery, 'we' consisting of Janet Mansfield, Bill Samuels, Chester Nealie, Tony Nankervis and me. Group planning suggested that one of us at least should attend. Since everyone else had a convenient excuse to not go I was left holding the short straw.

The gallery was a small narrow rectangular room. The work was displayed on a 600 mm shelf that ran around the three inner walls in a ⊔-shape. The effect was simplicity and understatement, unpretentious but powerful. It felt like being surrounded and embraced by the pots. At the end of each day every piece was laid on its side so as to not fall off the shelf if there was an earthquake.

Itoh kept a small apartment a few underground stops away from the Gallery, providing accommodation for visiting ceramicists. The interior was tiny but held two attractions. One was that it overlooked an entrance to the grounds of the Imperial Palace in Chiyoda, and it was possible to watch the regal comings and goings. Another was that anyone who stayed there paid for their stay by donating a piece to the collection in the apartment. For a week I lived with a fascinating collection of work from many international sources. One piece that stood out to me among the work of many famous potters was a cup (*yunomi*) by Tatsuzo Shimaoka.

Near the end of the trip Euan Craig, an Australian potter living in Mashiko, one of many foreigners who had studied with Shimaoka, offered to take me on a Mashiko tour including several anagama kilns, Hamada's workshop, and Shimaoka's studio. Shimaoka-san said he was busy selecting work for an exhibition; he could only spare a little time. Then he asked me that all-important Japanese question about pedigree. His demeanour changed after I said I had studied with Ivan McMeekin. He invited us in to see the work for his new exhibition and it turned into a two-hour discussion; my best two hours in Japan.

It's often said that there is a strong Japanese influence in Australian woodfiring. A prominent Japanese ceramic artist made the comment to me that our work seemed completely alien to him. A Japanese could see no Japanese influence. He also helpfully told me that my ambition to get rich by selling in Japan at phenomenal prices was naïve. It's necessary to have appropriate introductions by close connections, necessary to have experience of making work in Japan, and desirable to have lived there for some time. In contrast it's an easy matter to exhibit in England, Europe or America provided a galley there is interested in the work.

* * *

Art residencies involve living, working and travelling somewhere else than your normal studio. Sometimes they are fully funded, sometimes you pay. They are a good way to travel, see artworks, and meet other artists. At best they involve working in an entirely different way than normal, playing with new ideas, new materials, new discoveries. At worst you wish you were home again.

My longest was at Utah State University, over three months in 2007–2008, from November to February, with implications I had not considered—winter in the Rocky Mountains of Utah. Snow piled up beside the roads and sidewalks, requiring clearing each day. Going out meant ten minutes putting on clothes suitable for the outside environment, and then another ten removing them entering interiors that always seemed to be heated to an excessive temperature. On some mornings the walk from my apartment to the ceramics studio, past the Logan Cemetery, made me think if it got any colder, I might end up there.

University accommodation was a small but well-equipped ground floor apartment, conveniently located an easy walk from the art school. The first night, getting up to do what one does and turning a corner into the hallway, someone was moving towards me in the semi-dark. The adrenaline jolt softened and the terror moderated when I managed to find the light switch. There it was: a full-length mirror.

John Neely was in China during this time so I was asked to occasionally talk with the graduate students and help if possible. John, and Dan Murphy, run the best graduate school in ceramics in the United States. When I was there CJ Jilek, Sunshine Cobb and Denny Gerwin among others were students. Most MA graduates from USU have found teaching jobs in other art schools in the USA; they are a formidable influence in American ceramics. Talking with them as students never felt like work.

Logan is a little like Launceston, where I had a residency a few years earlier; too little to be a city, too big to be a town. It is a nicely manageable size, easy to navigate. My kind of town. The initial part of any residency I have been involved in, raised questions like: *'What the f... am I doing here? Why did I ever agree to this?'* The Logan solution was to begin by exploring the district; visiting local towns like Paradise (it wasn't), Honeyville and Deweyville—real names. John had introduced me years before to that fine commercial establishment Smithfield Implements, situated up north near the Idaho border. It supplied anything the average rancher might need and provided quality entertainment, studying its contents. All kinds of checked shirts and jackets, leather vests, anything to keep out the winter cold, cowboy boots and hats were compressed into the space along with anything that a farmer might need in the way of equipment. It would take a month to see everything.

The stay included a three-person workshop: Chuck Hindes, Ron Meyers and me. I love Ron's work and savour the contrast between the man himself, good humoured and mild in all things, loved by all, and the ferocious creatures he paints on his pots. Chuck is one of the most knowledgeable people in the USA about kilns for woodfiring and makes work that is uniquely his, in that crowded woodfire field. My main memory of the workshop is that the carefully organised images for my talk were rearranged from PC to Mac for the presentation and in the process the order was totally scrambled, leading to a profoundly embarrassing presentation. There's nothing worse than feeling like a mug in esteemed company.

What has puzzled me for some time is why so many ceramics courses have been dropped in Australia while so many flourish in the USA? Why are there so many galleries featuring ceramics there and so few here? Is the difference merely an issue of population numbers with thirteen times as many in the USA allowing much more diversity? Is it a cultural difference that Americans value art more highly that we do? I have no answer.

* * *

In 2012 Chuck Hindes organised for me to do a short residency at Gonzaga University, in Spokane, Washington, funded by their annual Kreielsheimer Visiting Artist Fellowship. As the recipient for 2012, this meant joining a long line of respectable former recipients including Don Reitz, Patti Warashina, Ruth Duckworth and Paul Soldner. Again, my mother would have been pleased about me keeping good company.

Chuck drove east from Seattle over the western mountains, then across plains extending monotonously across eastern Washington. We stayed in a fancy hotel beside the Spokane River. Big lumps of ice floated along in the water, something unknown in Australia. This atheist managed to present a workshop and lectures in the Catholic university without being struck down by godly lightning.

A side trip to Couer D'Alene in Idaho brought us to the superbly presented Art Spirit Gallery. How do the Americans conceive buildings and décor like that, places so distinctively theirs? Not just pots on plinths and paintings on walls, but large windows to see inside or outside, multiple types of lighting, signs, curved walls, everything arranged in staggered formations, complexity everywhere in a wonderfully structured visual onslaught. Entirely unlike austere Australian galleries.

We travelled back through the beautiful Cascades, on winding roads, past steep tree covered mountainsides, sometimes with snow on top, past stunning vistas of rivers and vertical-faced mountains where rock climbers tempt fate. Along the way we followed Chuck's hobby and stopped at every 'goodwill' store—the equivalent of Australian op-shops. In these Chuck selects and buys pots he hates and then fires them in an anagama to destroy them. That makes the world a prettier place, he says.

Chuck a few years later gave me the best gift I ever received. It's a book, originally Japanese—cunningly symbolic with Japanese text underlying his paintings and sketches of his kilns and pots. It's a beautiful thing that must have taken a long, long time to complete, a little each night.

* * *

In 2005 an invitation arrived to participate in a residency in the Korean Biennale, in the south of Korea. Our gig was the International Workshop on Woodfired Kilns, at Icheon. The organisers were generous, paying business class airfares and giving us accommodation in a luxury hotel for the event and meals in many classy restaurants. Woodfire artists included Americans, Europeans and Asians, including some old friends like Coll Minogue and Robert Sanderson from Ireland, and Chuck Hindes, Dan Murphy and Josh Deweese from the USA. It was inspirational to work with one of my heroes, Lee Kang Hyo, and other Koreans.

This Biennale was the best event I have attended anywhere in the world. Spread over three sites, it included many exhibitions of superb quality, parks full of sculptures, ancient and modern woodfired kilns, a shopping mall-sized ceramics market and many other attractions such as commercial galleries with top quality exhibitions. The basic rationale of the event was to highlight Korean culture, especially the role of ceramics.

Our workshop was open and free to the public and attracted many visitors. We made work to fire in a large new noborigama kiln. The intention then was to stack the kiln and participate in the firing, but the Korean potters involved wisely helped by doing the whole thing, so we could all see how they did what they did.

The front firebox of the enormous kiln was stoked continuously for eighteen hours with the whole front of the kiln open, achieving a fierce heat. I could not get any closer than about ten metres. Each chamber was then stoked in turn, the first for about four hours. By the time the fourth chamber was reached only about half an hour was needed to reach full temperature.

The two highlights I remember from this trip are my karaoke duet with Chuck Hindes in the hotel one night; and after the event having a few days in Seoul, staying in Insadong, a part of the city where every shop has something of interest and every gallery had a worthwhile exhibition.

* * *

The Chinese character *zhong* means centre or heart. It is the first character in the word China: *Zhong Guo*. In English this is often translated as *The Middle Kingdom* but really it means *The Land at the Centre of the World*. A 2007 residency at Fuping Pottery Village was my first (and only) visit to mainland China. Fuping is a privately owned centre, with a factory that produces roof tiles, finials and other decorative architectural elements. Residencies are organised with a group of potters representing one country, or one group of like countries all working together at one session. Ours included potters from Australia and New Zealand. The work produced during this session is then housed in a museum. There is a Scandinavian museum, a French museum and an increasing number of others, each devoted to a specific country or geographic area.

The Australasian museum was built while we were there, in roughly a month, an amazing accomplishment. Where else in the world is a museum built from bare ground to completion and fully stocked with new artwork in a month? The museum buildings all have arresting architectural interest. Fuping is a centre well worth a visit, and individuals can work there independently of the group arrangements. Nearby Xian, with the entombed warriors, is only an hour or so away.

Twenty people from Australia and New Zealand all working together made for a congenial and stimulating experience. I met many for the first time, including the New Zealanders John Parker, Richard Parker (unrelated), Chris Weaver, Cheryl Lucas and others; and was lucky to share a studio with Steve Williams and see how his wildly creative mind functioned. Most of our work was fired in a tunnel kiln. In addition, we made work for a newly built woodfire kiln, a variation on the train kiln with a step grate instead of a Bourry Box.

My approach was to ignore anything I had ever done before and make work based on what could be found around the large factory. My main piece, displayed in a widow of the museum, is a group of flowers made from coloured glass. I'm told by recent visitors that the petals are falling from the stems to which they were glued—the message being use good quality glue. It's not a disaster—real flowers lose their petals.

* * *

In 2004, Vince McGrath asked if I would like to do a residency in Launceston, at the Academy of the Arts, after finishing up at Monash. When I asked Vince what other people had done during a residency there, he said: *'Mostly not much, they just go off and travel around Tasmania'*. That seemed like a good idea so I did. But my first day there in 2005 found me sitting in a room in the art school wondering why I was there, and why I had agreed in the first place. As time went on, the residency allowed me to experiment with earthenware, fired in electric kilns, developing various glazes including some that looked like gold or bronze. I am going back to playing with that now, to see where it leads.

Another welcome residency in Australia in 2009 was at Strathnairn, formerly a farm outside of Canberra and now an arts centre with many workshops, a gallery, shop and accommodation for residencies. I was planning to build a gas kiln at home and needed to use the Strathnairn gas kilns to develop glaze and clay combinations for the new kiln. My anagama kiln, and woodfire bisque kiln limited to a top temperature around 1000°C, were not useful for that purpose. Having in the past lived in Canberra for ten years, I knew my way around and had friends and acquaintances to visit. The residency had a different feel to others, a little bit like a homecoming. And Strathnairn is a wonderful place to settle in and get some work done in pleasant surroundings, with congenial company.

* * *

I am not really interested in residencies now. Earlier, when teaching at Monash University, any excuse to be somewhere else was welcome. Now, everything necessary for my work is in my studio. In terms of materials and equipment there is no need to work somewhere else. I prefer to work alone; it's difficult to concentrate when there are other people around. The main virtue of residencies is that working in unfamiliar circumstances can generate new ideas for personal development, but I have more things to work on than I will ever get to. An important attraction of residencies is the travel; if funded they provide an opportunity that may be otherwise unaffordable. I am astonished that the Australia Council, which has no interest in ceramics, still funds some residencies for ceramicists.

* * *

A side benefit of travel for workshops or conferences is travel for pure amusement; and to accompany every trip anywhere I have done just that. I have travelled widely in America, usually stopping over in San Francisco for a few days to acclimatise and overcome any jet lag, before going on to work. That is my excuse anyway, it's a fine city to visit. The De Young Museum, with its strong selection of American crafts, and the Museum of Modern Art are always on the visiting list.

I was surprised on a trip from Tennessee, through the Smoky Mountains National Park to North Carolina, when I stopped in a 'pioneer village' in the park. A list of names of the early white settlers in the area read almost name for name with a list of early white settlers in Berridale, my home town in NSW: Oliver, Wallace, Caldwell, Burns (Byrnes) and others whose names can now be found on early tombstones in the Berridale cemetery. Obviously when there was migration from Scotland and Ireland in the late 1700s and early 1800s, some members of families had gone to the Appalachians in the USA and some to the Snowy Mountains in Australia.

To follow another conference, in Flagstaff, Arizona, I organised a side-trip with a local travel company. Coll Minogue and Robert Sanderson, Chester and Jan and I went off to the Grand Canyon, and then Monument Valley in Navaho territory, near the Arizona/Utah border. The Grand Canyon had definitely earned its adjective. Monument Valley, long on my wish-to-see list, would be familiar to anyone who had seen American movies, especially old westerns with John Wayne.

A brief look at the Arizona desert raised many thoughts. Their hot arid character made me wonder why anyone would live there. Chris Jones, in *Too Far From Home*: '*The desert draws out the peculiars, mostly because it takes a special breed to live in a place that doesn't want the company*'. Remote places invite poetic mythologies, one strong connection between Australia and the United States. America has the art and literature of the West, Australia of the Outback. The big skies and endlessly straight roads of Arizona connected seamlessly with roads I had travelled in Australia.

In France I booked into a ten-day tour focusing on ceramics, preceding the IAC meeting in Paris. The Limoges porcelain factory, and La Borne, well known for its woodfiring history, were among many stops. The delightful charms of rural France were finally revealed to me. One stop that I can recommend to anyone was Jean Linard's Sculpture Garden and house in Neuvy-Deux-Clochers, the result of many years of work by the eccentric Linard. It rates up there with the sculptures of Nek Chand in Chandigarh and other outsider artists around the world.

La Borne reminded me a little of Seagrove in North Carolina. In both, the tradition of woodfired pots (salt glazed in Seagrove) had been largely discontinued. New potters had come in recently, lured by the romance of the area, and perhaps the clay deposits. The Limoges factory makes traditional French porcelain, using amazingly skilled people at each stage of the process. Our fee for the tour included all meals, at many restaurants. Given the reputation of French cooking I was not as impressed as the French would expect. I was highly impressed though with the universality of the Gallic shrug, learning that it can cover all contingencies and answer all questions.

I met Torbjorn Kvasbo when he was a demonstrator at Claysculpt '95, one of the Gulgong events, and asked if I could visit him in Norway. He said he had been working hard at teaching and needed a holiday; so maybe we could spend a couple of weeks travelling around Norway and staying with his friends. After my time in Faenza, in Italy in 1995 I met up with Torbjorn in Oslo. Generous fees from talks I did in art schools in Oslo and Bergen covered all the expenses of what became a three-week trip. What a beautiful country, one of the most scenic and attractive of any I have visited; and Norway is politically one of the world's most sensible countries. Bergen is an attractive city, in terms of its appearance—if not its endlessly wet weather.

My only trip to Japan was confined mainly to Tokyo, where it was immediately obvious that we are far behind in terms of urban and city development, and public facilities. Despite the complex urban high-rise reality of Tokyo central, there are occasional small areas of nature in parks, with a whiff of forest and a hint of wind and rain and sun on things that slowly decay, interspersed with well-chosen rocks and tall grasses. It's easy to get around on the subway and visit some of the department store galleries. One, on the top floor of a six-store building, had an exhibition of ceramics for tea. At one end they displayed five-dollar teacups; I bought several. At the other end, thirty metres away, were a couple of five-million-dollar tea bowls.

18
GAME CHANGERS

… the shards of reality one person will cherish as a biography can seem to someone else who, say, happened to have eaten some ten thousand dinners at the very same kitchen table, to be a willful excursion into mythomania.

– Philip Roth in *American Pastoral*

We make friends through our working life, enriching both our professional and personal life. Friends have helped me through difficult times and shared good times. Most of my friends are people who work with clay, making things from it, or selling the things made from it, or writing about it. It has been a privilege to know some of the best in the business well.

The best in the world are not necessarily the best known. Some among us are desperate for recognition and affirmation; some have no need for any of that, making strong work that does not receive any great publicity. Don Court, Geoff Thomas and Denis Monks are prime Australian examples. Denis has thrown better sculptures down the hillside than most other people will ever make, just to find space to create new work. Don gives his work away if someone likes it. They were not thinking about publicity and fame and fancy galleries but of materials and shapes and results of firings. Geoff combines sheep farming with woodfiring, doing both extremely well.

The opposite are the the self-mythologising ones who yearn for fame, who seek adulation, the ones to whom ego is all. I do not like them much, generally. Some style themselves as internationally renowned, or some self-evaluation to that effect. I know a few of these and as an experiment have asked about them in other countries, to check on their renown. Almost universally the response has been *'no sorry, never heard of them'*. Picasso, as example, was internationally renowned, but there is not a single person involved in ceramics from any period of history except maybe Wedgewood, whose name is familiar to the average person in the street.

* * *

Ivan McMeekin was the first major influence in my life in ceramics. He was wiry, solidly built, neither tall or short. You might by his build guess he had been something like an ex-boxer; but his rather refined English-tinged accent and his interest in porcelains, the most delicate of ceramics gave a different impression altogether. His contributions are summarised in my article about him in the *Australian Dictionary of Biography*.

In the Industrial Arts department at the University of NSW in the early 1960s, Ivan was endlessly generous with his time, discussing, teaching me so much that most of it is just in my cells somewhere unseen, helping silently. But I do remember some aspects of his teaching clearly. He was never satisfied. Work was never finished, it just kept on progressing. He was like a professional sportsman, who thinks the important game is the next one, the last merely a guide to the next. For Ivan unloading a kiln was not a process of looking at successes and failures as much as a process of evaluating what to do next, the focus always on what you will do, not on what you have done. Taking up a pot of mine still warm from the kiln he would study it—he studied pots, he did not just look at them. Then he would say *'Now if you just ...'* That way you made progress.

Another lesson never forgotten, applying not just to working with clay but also to life in general, is to be observant. Ivan taught this by example, particularly when we went on field trips to source clay and other materials. Travelling in a car before meeting Ivan, I would just see countryside flashing past. But Ivan explained and discussed whatever we could see; what species of tree, or what types of rock and soil we were passing, and what use they might have, both in ceramics and otherwise. He was aware of both the aesthetics and the utility of whatever we passed. Despite being brought up in the bush and having walked many miles through it in younger days, I began to see all that I had dismissed as mere background to what I was doing. Fighter pilots have an expression for it that I like: situational awareness. He taught me to look, and to see; the world became more complex and more interesting.

Ivan had such a dominant personality (*'there are two ways of doing this: my way, and the wrong way'*) and had such a strong influence, it seemed essential to break away from it somehow or otherwise become a clone. I sat down once, some years after finishing as a student, and quite consciously went through every aspect of the process from beginning to end, writing it down in three columns. The first listed all the steps in making a pot. The second, Ivan's way of doing it. The third suggested the total opposite to what Ivan would do at each step. That third column became my way of working. It was the only way I could break free. Silly as it sounds to me now, and with many modifications along the way, that analysis was an essential step in finding a personal identity in ceramics.

Despite all that I still value and use some parts of Ivan's approach. One is the need to understand how materials behave and how they contribute to the final result. In the general world of ceramics out there that understanding seems sadly lacking. The idea now that many ceramicists have, as I understand it, is that the concept (the artist statement) is important and the materials—clay, slips, glazes—have no value other than as a means to an end. They can be bought from a shop, and there is no need to understand them.

But I have never placed much value on ignorance. Everything you know helps. Musicians must be conscious of sounds, painters must be conscious of colours, writers must be conscious of words and ceramicists must be conscious of materials. These are fundamental tools in each trade, without which nothing can be communicated.

Ivan's notion was that the search for theoretical knowledge is most valuable when fitted together with practical experience. This has particularly helped me to understand some of the behaviour of woodfired kilns. Having some idea of the chemistry contributes to trying out different approaches. For example, understanding the water gas reaction helps in achieving reduction cooling. Translated into plain English that means that some basic theoretical knowledge helps develop colours and surface qualities that enliven the finished pots or sculptures. Knowledge gained through practical experience, from doing it, then helps understand the theory. It's a circle of understanding.

I started as a student with Ivan in 1961. Since then there have been dramatic changes in ceramics as an individual art form. We did glaze calculations using a slide rule. Glaze recipes beyond count are freely available online now. We threw pots on a Leach kick wheel; now they can be made by CNC computer-controlled milling machines or digital printing. Brushwork has morphed into laser printing, and decoration restricted then to copper, cobalt and iron pigments, can now be achieved with an endless range of colours.

What was then the core of the potter's art, making things to use, such as cups, bowls, plates and vases, has now often given way to producing exotic sculptures, complex installations, virtual ceramics and architectural features on a grand scale. The few ceramics courses in the 1960s became many in the 1970s and 1980s and now have gone back again to few. And the small number of people describing themselves as potters has become the many calling themselves ceramics artists or ceramicists or a term I have not yet warmed to, creatives. I am not convinced that these new forms of artperson are doing anything more profound or moving than some of the old potters were doing, even though the end result looks different. The theory, sometimes termed 'philosophy', of the work has also changed. A Japanese/Chinese inspired aesthetic was followed by modernism, postmodernism, deconstructionism and whatever is the current *ism*; I have lost track.

* * *

Ivan developed an interest in Sung Dynasty ceramics while working on ships on the China coast, and decided after World War 2 to go to England and learn to make pottery. There he worked with Michael Cardew. He learned about firing kilns with wood. With efficiency in mind he developed the now well-known Bourry Box kiln design. The highly refined version published in *Pottery in Australia* 9/1 1970 was the model for many built later in Australia and around the world.

His Australian experience in ceramics began when he established the Sturt Pottery Workshop in Mittagong, with Les Blakebrough and Col Levy as assistants. Their relationship was not always harmonious. In fact, Ivan was involved in many disputes. He was extremely helpful and generous with his time to me when I was a student; but whatever he believed, he believed strongly. I think it's fair to say he was obsessive; he said so himself. In a taped interview with Lorna Grover in 1981 Ivan said: '*... what is needed at first is an obsession to the extent that you are willing to sacrifice other things in your life to it*'.

The last time I saw him was at one of Janet Mansfield's events at Morning View, near Gulgong in 1993. We had a long talk then; he was puzzled by anagama-fired ceramics and asked many questions. We talked about new directions in ceramics and I left him wishing that I had made more effort to keep in contact with him. It's a failing of mine, moving on and leaving people behind.

Ivan was so intent on experimenting with clay, glazes and firing that he only made minimal work. A few treasured pieces of his are in my home display cases, thanks to Janet Mansfield and Susie McMeekin. I had no pots he had made, but when he died Janet generously told me she had a small jug and a bowl in her gallery, that I could have for what she paid for them. She could have sold them for much higher prices. It's interesting to compare them with Ivan's daughter Susie's work. We did this once, placing Ivan's bowl and jug beside the equivalents made by Susie. The evolution of the family tradition is evident in her work but the styles are very different. His are strong and sturdy, hers are more sensitive. The glazes she uses are more developed, livelier and less sombre. This does not say one is better than the other; better to say they are quite different.

Having Susie as a friend is special in various ways, and anyone who knows her well knows about her generosity and her big smile. I value the family contact though, that it is possible to talk about the old days and talk about Ivan with someone who quite obviously knew him well. I am always pleased to get together with Susie and Don, her husband.

* * *

At the beginning of my research into porcelain bodies and glazes in 1967 Ivan suggested I should get in contact with Col Levy at Bowen Mountain, near Richmond. Col had been working with porcelain. I was not aware enough at the time to realise how kind Col had been in what was very much a one-way exchange, taking up most of his day asking questions, when he could have been working. He took me seriously, which was a considerable confidence boost to a student uncertain about where it was all leading.

Col had been salt glazing but was just beginning to experiment with woodfiring. Galleries and collectors had no interest in this new genre then, but Col's exhibitions at the David Jones Gallery in Sydney helped to make woodfiring more respectable. His reputation, well earned, for making high quality pots helped that impression. People began thinking that if he was doing it then that style of work might be acceptable.

More recent visits to Col's place have been fascinating. He has a very large shed full of pots of the highest quality, with a range of superb glazes. Why he does not exhibit some of the work is a mystery to those who have seen it; perhaps it's just his characteristic eccentricity at work. Anyone who does visit is put through a regime of tests of their knowledge. One of his standard tests is to bring out a few from his extensive Korean and Japanese tea bowl collection, and ask if you recognise who made them. It's a test that very few would pass. I can only speculate that he is probing to find out at what level he can talk to you about ceramics.

* * *

Janet Mansfield and Alan Peascod have been two of the most important people in my personal and professional life. I met both at exhibition openings at the Watson gallery of the Canberra Potter's Society, Alan in the mid-1970s and Janet in the early 1980s. In fact, Alan introduced me to Janet, completing a nice circle. The exhibitions themselves cannot have been memorable because I have no recollection of either; but I have retained a strong affection for the Watson Arts Centre as the source of two of my most valued friendships. Looking back now, both meetings were more than momentous occasions for me; life changing is more accurate.

* * *

Nobody goes through their professional life without help and support from others. Many people have helped me along the way and Janet Mansfield is near the top of this list. I valued her as a friend but she also acted as a patron. Her influence opened up many opportunities for me that might not have happened otherwise. Most people involved in ceramics in Australia could say they met Janet at an opening, or a conference, or some other event. Each would specify a different location for the meeting because one of her main activities was travellling, attending everything everywhere. In the process she got to know everyone; she knew more people than the census. Potters anywhere in the world would say *'Oh yes, how is Janet?'*

I had communicated with Janet before we met, sending her articles for the magazine *Pottery in Australia* which she edited at the time. Because of the serious and scientific nature of my early articles, she thought of me as a white-haired old man, and was surprised when we met to see I was young and healthy. She shared one thing with my mother, a dislike of my beard, which she often suggested I should shave off *'because it makes you look like you belong to the Hell's Angels'*. Neither woman succeeded. I am averse to removing body parts.

* * *

I can only describe Janet's travelling as relentless, in Australia and worldwide. It would be easier to name the countries she missed than the ones she went to. She was a member of many organisations, in most of which she became president, eventually becoming president of the International Academy of Ceramics for several years before her death.

During one exhibition I had at her gallery in William Street in Paddington she invited me to call around to her nearby home for breakfast the next morning. I knocked on the door and when she opened it she said *'Please be quiet, Colin (her husband) is asleep. I am going to Italy later this morning and he says I have been away too much so I don't want him to know that I am going.'* Colin did not enjoy her travelling as much as she did.

But her travel was not selfish; she created contacts, built networks, and brought Australia firmly into the international scene. She was Australia's ceramic ambassador. Her hospitable and friendly nature helped. A mutual American friend, Frank Boyden, phoned me when Janet died; he said: *'Everyone she met thought they were her best friend. There was something mysterious happening; she made you feel you were important to her.'*

After editing *Pottery in Australia*, she started one of her own magazines, *Ceramics Art and Perception*, in 1993. In a brave move she styled it *The International Ceramics Magazine*. She contacted people she knew well before the first issue, asking for a special favour, an article so it could get started. I sent her one on photography (which now seems antiquated in the new digital world). Later she started a companion magazine, *Ceramics Technical*. Both are still going, albeit combined into one, and are still international in scope. Janet also wrote six books and later, when her magazines had been sold, published several books by other writers, operating as Mansfield Press.

She worked harder than most people would know, promoting

and distributing the magazines, attending conferences everywhere, particularly the big ones like NCECA, running trade stalls. In this she was usually accompanied by Glenys Waller, her assistant. At other events she carried magazines around with her, doing the hard sell on one person at a time. I was astonished at an IAC meeting in Edinburgh when we had a meal and were walking together back to the hotel late at night. She looked a bit tired so I offered to carry her bag and discovered it weighed maybe fifteen kilos (about 30 pounds). It was full of magazines and books she was trying to distribute.

Glenys was central to Janet's business activities, the magazines and gallery. I admired as well as liked her. She was amazingly efficient. A phone call to her to renew a subscription, for example, would elicit from her no more than ten words and she would hang up and carry on. One of my greatest pleasures with Glenys was winning an argument with her about money, specifically about the GST tax. I had thought that accomplishment impossible. I was extremely sad when cancer took her away.

Several images of Janet stay in my mind. In one of her public roles, elegantly dressed, she is presiding, and I mean presiding, over a meeting of the International Academy of Ceramics in the UNESCO building in Paris, a gathering of several hundred of the best-known people in world ceramics. Janet made some radical changes to the IAC. The previous president, Rudolf Schnyder, a curator of the Swiss National Museum, ran the IAC in an autocratic manner. Under him it was Eurocentric, and members held rigid ideas about what aesthetic was acceptable, for example anyone who made vessels on the wheel was frowned upon. Janet opened it up enormously, recruiting members worldwide and accepting any expression in ceramics as valid.

In her public life Janet was skilled in the arts of diplomacy. She remembered everyone's name, and the names of family members. She could have been a capable politician had she been interested. From my point of view, she would have been on the wrong side of politics; that difference sometimes led to some short sharp exchanges between us.

Her enjoyment of the limelight was obvious to those who knew her well, but she admitted that she had to work at it. I asked her once how she survived the constant grind and she said she functioned best when her sleeping quarters were close by, because then she could disappear occasionally and have a short break from it all. She also said that she enjoyed the company of close friends more than public adulation. She was able to relax and have a red. Any red, she did not much discriminate. Sometimes after several reds she would totally discard the guarded approach and say the most outrageous things about people, things we all might say, that came as a surprise from such a diplomat; and would be an even greater surprise to the people she mentioned.

Another image is of her at home; hidden away from people, at the family farm Morning View, at her woodfired kiln deep into the dark hours of night, surrounded by flames and smoke. Her face is simultaneously blackened and reddened (she would be angry with me for using that image) and she is laughing at some story her fellow stokers had just told. To me the contrast in these images, in both of which she was equally comfortable, says more about her than anything else. She was always pleased to be making pots and her work is in collections all around the world.

She did not just make for exhibition and public display. She also made simple useful pots. She loved making them and she loved the company of people using them, understanding that there is deep value embedded in the simple cup or bowl that you hold in your hand each morning. Eating or drinking from something made by a friend retains intimacy with them through touching and holding that thing. This is poetry that potters understand, separating what they make from the two-dollar productions of the large factories. Their work has life and stories and personality, something distinctive and different from each different maker, telling us who and what they are; and telling us at the same time who we are.

* * *

Janet and I had a simple arrangement. If she asked me to do anything for her, I did it. In return she looked after me. In part this meant I was involved in each Gulgong event in some way, firing the anagama at one, organizing something that people could get involved in at others, such as building and firing small kilns. My suggestion, that I enjoyed most, was called Firelight. Participants formed groups and built structures incorporating fire; the light from the fire, not its heat, was the main point of the structure, and some of them were quite beautiful. The scene was inspiring at night with the flickering colours, using fire for no purpose but light, and delight.

I am pleased to be one of few people to have been at, and somehow involved in, every Gulgong event. As far as I know Geoff Thomas, Linda Ewin and Chester Nealie are the only others. Each of them has made major contributions to each event.

* * *

Janet had galleries focusing on ceramics. The first was at William Street, Paddington in Sydney. It most conveniently had a small flat upstairs where a visitor could stay. The gallery space was small and set up to look like a room in a house. Janet knew many collectors, helping to produce sales. Glenys Waller was the amazingly efficient business manager. The gallery later was moved to another more spacious location in Glenmore Road, still in Paddington. I had exhibitions in both, and was extremely pleased with the results. The connection between the galleries and the magazines was most useful. Janet could publish an article in the magazine before the exhibition, providing excellent publicity, and then print run-ons of the article (usually eight pages) that could be used as a separate catalogue.

I often asked Janet for advice about people or organisations, because she was as well informed as anyone. In 2005 I received an invitation to take part in a woodfire workshop in Korea as part of their ceramics Biennale. The invitation was so vague that I had no idea what they wanted me to do. I asked a Korean friend, Kwi Rak Choung, to read their literature but he could make no more sense of it than I could. So I phoned Janet to see if she knew anything about it. She said *'Are they paying your airfare?'* I said yes. She said *'Are they providing good accommodation?'* I said yes. She said *'So what's your problem? Go'*. I went.

* * *

Janet helped everyone involved in woodfiring in Australia in several ways. Australians who started woodfiring in the late 1970s and early 1980s were generally self-taught, learning by experience, compared with some of the Americans who had studied or apprenticed in Japan. She organised woodfire events in Gulgong starting in 1989, following on from my *Woodfire 86* conference in Gippsland. Over the years she brought in woodfirers from overseas, Jack Troy, Col Minogue and Robert Sanderson, John Neely, Fred Olsen, Torbjorn Kvasbo and many others. This set up contacts and helped us Australians become part of the international woodfire mainstream, making it much easier to travel to other countries and see developments there.

In the early 1980s woodfired ceramics had little value in the art community. Now there are many potters around experienced in the art, woodfire exhibitions are frequent and their work is accepted and valued by collectors. The fact that Janet was a woodfirer herself meant that she was sympathetic to articles in magazines she owned or edited, helping the growth of Australian woodfire. This can also be said of Gerry Williams and the US magazine *Studio Potter*, and Col Minogue and Robert Sanderson with *The Log Book*; all contributed to international exchanges of knowledge and ideas.

* * *

My friendship with Janet came close to ending terminally. My book on woodfiring, *The Art of Woodfire* published by Janet's Mansfield Press in 2010, was the end product of a long saga in preparation, and an unpleasant dispute between us.

I had been considering a book about woodfiring for at least fifteen years. My first plan was to compare woodfiring in the US and Australia. That book was never written although the background research was complete. My plan was to work on it after leaving Monash in 2004 but for a variety of reasons it was put aside—but not forgotten. Several people asked *'When are you going to do your woodfire book?'* Finally, Chester Nealie gave me a stern talking-to: *'You are talking about doing a woodfire book. Janet is talking about doing a woodfire book. Will you two please get together and work out who is doing what and then will whoever is doing it do it?'*

In 2007 we did. Janet was winding down somewhat having sold her magazines to Elaine Henry, and passed on the Ceramic Art Gallery in Paddington to John Freeland. She wanted to spend more time making pots and decided to move to Gulgong, to Morning View where she had her workshop and kilns, to live and work there full time.

She was not withdrawing from her professional life, but refocusing. She had always believed in the virtue of having several interests rather than just obsessively pursuing one. One new focus would be the IAC, where she had become president, in 2006. Another was to establish a publishing house, Mansfield Press, planning to publish a series of books on ceramics. The first was to be a book on Alan Peascod, who was near the end of his life when this was considered and who died before the book came out in 2010. It is a magnificent book, beautifully put together.

Janet and I met for breakfast at my favourite café in Errol Street, North Melbourne, to talk about the woodfire book, as Chester had insisted. The decisions we made were easy. Janet wanted to be a publisher and I planned to write a book, so the broad outcome was obvious to both of us. Had I known the dramas that were to emerge I might have abandoned the whole thing there and then.

I actually suggested doing three books. One was the autobiography you are reading here. The woodfire book was another. The third would be a book I would organise, of stories by ceramicists who had demonstrated that they were also good writers. She was dismissive of the collective book idea. She asked what would happen about royalties. I suggested giving the proceeds to charity. She raised an eyebrow. That book was later done as a contribution to the woodfire event Rowley Drysdale organised in Queensland in 2017, and published by Duck Books as *The Book of Mick,* a novel with chapters written by many potters from several countries. It has been said that the written word is mankind's greatest achievement. Whoever said that was not referring to The Book of Mick. A generous assessment might describe the book as not the greatest novel ever, but getting it together was a bit of fun for everyone. The profits went to help fund Rowley's event.

We agreed that I would write the woodfire book, and she would publish it and after that we would have another discussion about the autobiography. To me that looked unlikely with her as publisher. I was thinking of a book with words as this one is, and she was thinking of a book with pictures, all about the pots I had made, a typical 'book about the artist'.

We discussed who to include in the woodfire book and who to leave out. She insisted on including a couple of people I would have omitted and excluding a few I would have included. She insisted that the number of people included be restricted. I disagreed but was willing to compromise, on the basis that without a publisher there was no book. We agreed on a fee for writing the woodfire book rather than royalties. I had discussed this beforehand with a few people, including Milton Moon who had published several books. Royalties come in slowly and don't amount to much each year so a straight fee seemed to me a better idea.

Everything looked good. Janet had edited articles I did for the *Pottery in Australia* and later for *Ceramics Art and Perception*, and I agreed generally with her approach to editing. Some of her ideas seemed to me odd but I could live with them: don't say anything negative about anyone or anything; and use very conservative language. When she did her first book as publisher, about Peascod, she had left my chapter exactly as I had written it, not a comma changed, not a word queried. I had no worries about her editing.

Then it began. I had sent her a first draft to give her a rough idea about what I was getting down, with the caution that it was a first draft only and not a finished thing by any means, only meant to give a general idea of what I was considering. I remember sitting in her library at Morning View where I had gone to find at some background material and she handed me back the copy. I was immediately horrified. It had more words in her pencil writing than I had written. Almost every sentence was changed, mostly to say something I did not want to say. This was not editing; she had rewritten the whole thing and totally changed its content.

For me it created emotional turbulence. She was my friend, my 'patron', she had helped in so many ways, but here she was my opposition. I could not possibly agree with what she had done. What could I do? I soon discovered that politely disagreeing about the changes she wanted would achieve nothing. Soon we reached the point where our exchanges became mutually insulting. The emails emitted smoke and almost flames. When I pointed out that she had been really insulting she apologised, and said it was just like a family spat.

The German word *schlimmbesserung* seemed appropriate. It means 'an attempt at improvement that makes things worse'. I found a quote by Kinky Friedman: '*An editor is a person who takes something great and makes it good*'. Nothing said here implies that my writing was perfect. I was definitely open to editorial suggestions that improved the readability; but not to having anyone rewrite and entirely change the meaning. More openness to discussion on both sides may have lessened the angst.

What the hell was going on? Janet had never been like this before. She had over the years become a good editor. She had developed a good eye for written language and had been helpful with articles I sent to her. I had learned something too and later articles I sent her had been published essentially untouched by editorial hands. So why this deluge of changes?

It seemed obvious to me the problem was that she was intentionally or unconsciously converting my book into the one she had wanted to write, and her opinions and attitudes were quite different to mine. What I did not know at the time was that she was ill and not thinking as clearly as she normally had. She had cancer and it was having an effect on her mind as well as her body, as is true of everyone with this disease. She was not as sharp as she had been. This realisation only came to me later, partly from hearing her talk at the 2012 Adelaide conference where she was uncharacteristically hesitant and unsure. She was ill, more so than she realised and her confidence was ill also. Had I known that earlier I might have been more thoughtful and considerate.

Finally, we reached a shaky agreement. My contribution was that if she did not accept my writing, I would withdraw altogether and she could do the book. We ended up with a compromise, but I suppose most people who have read the book are unaware of any of this. The final book launch at Neil Hoffmann's woodfire conference in Deloraine, in Tasmania in 2011 was a friendly enough conclusion, and after that there was no point in continuing a dispute. Later I sent her a most conciliatory message pointing out that for me the many years of our friendship far outweighed any differences we might have had. She received it not long before she died.

I'm sad to say that we shall not see her like again. The grand scale of her achievements will not be, cannot be matched by anyone around now in Australia. She became a real centre of influence, able to create change in the most international of ceramics organisations, able to help many people along the way. It's been fascinating to observe the politics after she died, to watch others promoting themselves, circling and coalescing into little groups like cosmic dust forming small planets.

* * *

As with Janet, I first met Alan Peascod at the Watson Arts Centre in Canberra in 1977. He came up to me at an exhibition opening and introduced himself, suggesting quite correctly that we had a shared interest in Islamic ceramics, a subject of very little interest to almost everyone involved in ceramics in Australia then and now. Later when we were working together, that shared interest showed up in our individual ceramics: he was intrigued and influenced by reduced lustre and alkaline glazes. My interest was expressed in making techniques, and attitudes about glaze application, subtle influences possibly not obvious to most observers.

We shared an office in the Canberra School of Art from 1980 to 1984, and often talked about the world of Islam, not through any wish to become involved in the religion, but more about the amazing achievements. Our endless discussions ranged widely: what we most admired in the ceramics from Islamic countries, and how we might replicate some of their qualities, the politics of the Middle East, the plight of the Palestinians, and our experiences in Muslim countries.

In the early 1980s Alan was immersed in working with reduced lustre. He had built a woodfired kiln at the art school specifically to fire lustre work, believing that wood fuel gave better results than gas or oil. I loved watching him decorate the lustre pots. First the glaze was fired to a shiny blemish free, perfect surface. Then he applied the lustre brew with great precision. Too thin an application and the lustre would not develop. Too thick and it produced a dull scum on the surface. The difference to me appeared minute. His skill in getting just the right thickness was astounding. Once the layer he had painted on dried he would use a simple tool, usually a bamboo skewer, to scratch back through it and create drawings or patterns. When he got the whole process just right, which was nearly always, the finished fired surface displayed a range of iridescent 'oil on water' colours.

One of his pots from that time sits on the desk where I write. He fired twelve of them in one firing in 1983. We were looking at them arrayed on the floor in our office. He picked out three that he thought were suitable for an upcoming exhibition. I asked what he would do with the others and he said he would smash them. *'Not this one you won't, it's mine'* was my response and that's the one I am looking at here and now. Two of the ones he selected are pictured in the book Janet published about him. He was ruthless with any work that did not meet his standards and much more of his work was smashed than ever survived.

I like to use the Italian word *sprezzatura* to describe his approach to his work. It has been defined as meaning *'a certain nonchalance, so as to conceal all art and make whatever one does appear to be without effort and almost without any thought about it'* or in another: *'an easy facility in accomplishing difficult actions which hides the conscious effort that went into them'*. The Oxford English Dictionary defines it as *'studied carelessness'*. To me this nicely describes the looseness of any of his work, as opposed to tight perfectionistic form. He said once that his aim was to understand what constituted perfect proportions and then slightly distort them.

His work had nothing in common with anyone else's. He developed technologies that were entirely his own such as the saturated metallic surfaces. His lustre work was distinctive. He was secretive about his techniques, and angry about any imitators. I was not sure why because his work had strength that none of the others did. As Richard Schlesinger said, *'How mediocre is the prosaic imitator, when set beside his betters'* (in *Harpers*, October 2008). This was true for Alan's dry glazes, especially the vivid blue colour which came from copper. In the 1980s there were several imitators like Jo Szirer but Alan's work had strength that the others lacked. He did teach some students his techniques, later put to good use by Simone Fraser and Graham Oldroyd.

For some time when we first worked together, I was aware that he was keeping his secrets from me, but he gradually realised I was not going to go off and copy anything. My interest in what he did was motivated by curiosity rather than industrial espionage. In time he became open about what he was doing and I had the privilege of understanding just how simple some of his techniques were and how wrong the guesses were that some people made about them.

I began to realise how he worked. Sometimes his understanding of formal ceramic science was odd. He knew the words but misconstrued the conclusions. Strange to say, that distortion led him to try things others would say in advance would not work, and that was how some of his discoveries came about.

He could be difficult at times. For several years he was often angry. He went through a bad period after breaking up with Phillipa, harsh about everything, particularly his assessments of some people and their work. What he said was usually appropriate, but the intense passion was a bit wearing when it went on too long. When he finally got together with Ellen he calmed down a bit and became easier company.

It's interesting to watch how artists behave at their exhibition openings. Some love the attention they get and act out a dramatised interpretation of themselves, often quite different to their normal self. Some, more than you might imagine, wish they could disappear and hope it will all over as soon as possible. At his openings Alan did not change much, he was just a little more circumspect and polite in talking to people. Some have said that he was arrogant, and could not be bothered talking to them. We discussed that once and he said that he had no skills in small talk, and was actually quite shy in that environment, and that could easily be misinterpreted because people would not expect that to be part of his personality. He was much more comfortable when having serious discussions with friends or students, than he was idly chatting with strangers.

We lost contact, apart from the occasional letter when we both left the Canberra Art School at the end of 1984. I moved to Gippsland. He took a teaching job during 1985 and 1986 at the Glasgow School of Art and from 1986 to 1999 he taught at the Wollongong College of TAFE. The Glasgow experience exposed him to mean spirited and miserly art school administrators, and his satirical response was put to good use in sculptural figures made for his doctorate at Wollongong University, based on the Glasgow experience.

I called in for a visit sometime in the mid-1990s. His Wollongong house perched on a perilously steep hillside near the Bulli Pass. From then on, we stayed in contact more regularly. One good outcome for me from his time in Wollongong was that he introduced me to Don Court and Don has become a good mate. He is another man with interesting life experience and a thoughtful mind, who also makes good work from clay and fire. It's easy to see why he and Alan were mates.

When Chester Nealie and Jan moved to Gulgong, Barbara and I began to make an annual trip, arriving soon after Christmas and staying on for a few weeks. This broadened out a little when on a few occasions

Tony Nankervis turned up as well. It was a welcome time to sit and have a drink and talk about nothing in particular. Alan and Ellen joined in when he was about to end his time in Wollongong in the late 1990s. It became something of a ritual that we would all gather at Morning View on New Year's Day for a pleasant afternoon of eating and drinking with the Mansfields.

Alan became interested in moving to Gulgong. He felt that Chester and Janet would be good neighbours. He bought a property on Spring Ridge Road and began a process of building first a house and then a studio, both unusual in character. The studio was basically a large concrete water tank with windows and doors cut into it and an iron roof.

He travelled to Italy in 1999 and 2002 to participate in residencies in Gubbio, working with Giampietro Rampini. Giampietro came to Gulgong in 2004, for the Clay Modern ceramics event and Alan invited me to see a lustre firing in the new kiln he had built. Giampietro had also made some work for the joint firing. The ideal temperature for the lustres used in that firing was around 640^0C (1185^0F). At that temperature the air inlet was minimal, not enough air to burn the pine fuel properly. These are the perfect conditions for lustre firing, but the smoke was noxious grey-green oily stuff that would make anyone choke. A large amount came out through gaps in the brickwork. Alan put the kiln through a number of cycles, each time surrounded by that smoke.

His acute perception of different grades of smoke was impressive. He used it to assess the temperature like an Eskimo would assess different grades of snow. What frightened me was the fact that his lungs had been seriously damaged earlier, at the Canberra Art School. He was susceptible to lung infections. I was not sure whether firing lustre in that condition was dedication and passion, or madness. I think loyalty to his mate Giampietro motivated him; he was intensely loyal to the few people he counted as his real friends. Whatever the motivation a few years later he was dead.

His lungs had never been healthy. I remember him saying that having rheumatic fever as a child had damaged them. They were made seriously worse by some experiments we were doing in Canberra. We were both intrigued by the results of hundreds or even thousands of years of weathering on glazes, most particularly the lead and alkaline glazes of the Middle East. These types of glaze were shiny when just fired; but after long periods of burial their surfaces changed to a particularly beautiful and varied matte quality.

We wondered about and talked about how we might reproduce that weathering. Alan fired some alkaline glazes and I tried soaking them in a variety of increasingly toxic and dangerous chemicals. Sodium hydroxide was effective but its action was slow. Alan had used hydrofluoric acid to etch gold lustre on some of his pots and decided to try that, and in the process breathed in some of the vicious fumes. Up until then his lungs had not been strong, but from that day the nature of his eventual death was destined. He died in 2007 from complications of a lung infection that no antibiotics could treat.

* * *

After he moved to Gulgong we were in constant contact by phone and email. I phoned him one night and he, hesitantly, said that I was interrupting his favourite television program and maybe we should try emails. For years we did, and I have kept all of them. Some people have suggested publishing them but my answer to that is that most of the people we talked about are still alive. Maybe one day when they are dead and cannot sue me for libel. It would make lively reading.

I was devastated when he died. We had enjoyed talking about all kinds of things but it ran deeper than that. The shared interest in Islamic culture and history and the present-day politics of Islam was an obvious connection but there were many others. I was fascinated by his inventiveness and the sheer power of his work. He had struggled with writing and was intrigued by mine. As someone said, writing is not about selecting words, but about how you arrange them.

It was valuable to both of us to be able to talk totally openly about other people in the ceramics world and discuss their work, in a way that we could not with anyone else. Added to that was being able to talk about our own work. In public his approach was to explain his work in a most positive way. In private he could talk to me about any doubts or uncertainties he might have, and I could do the same with him. I deeply valued his advice, consulted him frequently and acted on his suggestions. He was the guardian of my reputation and saved me from my own stupidity often. When he was gone, so was all of that caring. Years later I have still not really recovered from that sense of floating around in the dark, wondering what is out there and what it might do to me, the doubts that he helped alleviate, frightening as the monsters of childhood.

* * *

I met Chester Nealie at the first Australian woodfire conference in Gippsland. He had asked if I could send him a formal invitation so he could raise some grant money to help his travel expenses.

I did some background checking at the conference. Alan Peascod had met Chester during a trip he made to New Zealand earlier, so I asked Alan about Chester and he said he was ok. Chester had also checked up on me, coincidentally by asking Alan and getting the go response. The end result of all this homework was that Chester invited me to come over to New Zealand and work with him sometime. He only needed to ask once.

In 1989 I had a month at Chester's place on the North Island, an hour's drive north of Auckland. Many places have been described as like paradise. I've never been to the original and not likely to make it there, but it seems possible to me that some corner of the real paradise is modelled on that place. The house stood on a rise looking out over the flats towards the Kaipara Harbor, some three or four hundred metres away, one of the world's largest inland harbours. The setting took away the need for a dictionary to define sublime. It was not just a scenic paradise but a source of the finest foods. Fresh fish could be netted in the tidal creek running near Chester's house and smoked in his smoker that looked like a tin dunny. Oysters in endless abundance were available among the mangroves around the harbour edge.

Chester introduced me to the fine art of flounder-spearing in the harbour. Despite my natural fear of water, or being in it at least, I followed him wading out through the shallows after dark. Half a kilometre out the water was still only up to my thighs. Using a flashlight to find flounder, I fully expected the whole time that a great white shark would come along and consume my legs. Chester had gone off in a different direction and we eventually lost contact but he had told me that to find my way back to shore all I had to do was head towards a couple of lights on a nearby headland. Otherwise everything looked the same all around and I had no sense of direction. Then the people in the houses went to bed and turned off the lights. The process of getting back to land was so traumatic I cannot even think about it.

Apart from a predilection to offer his mates to the sharks, as a host Chester could not have been more generous or friendly. I felt like a member of the family and joined in with their everyday life. He loaned me a vehicle to travel around in when I wanted to go exploring. In the workshop there were no secrets, everything was discussed in detail, both ways. We both wanted to learn more, considering that in woodfiring terms we were both really self-taught and managing these big kilns took some experience. It was the beginning of a lifelong friendship.

I watched Chester working on the wheel, building up pots in sections in a way that reminded me of the Palestinian techniques although his methods were different. The Palestinians joined already thrown pieces together, or used the 'upside down method' which was to throw the base of a pot, closing over the foot, leaving the rest thick. When the base had dried enough it was placed right way up in a chuck and the body of the vessel thrown from the thick portion. Other parts—the top, handles and spouts were made separately and joined.

Chester's method was to throw the body of a pot and then for the neck and top just join on a coil or ball and throw the top from that. It was beautifully simple and had the advantage of helping produce a somewhat erratic character of form. I use that technique with bottle and vase forms, and large jars, for the same reason.

Steve Bishopric and Beth, his wife at the time were visiting also. We built a small anagama kiln, working mostly in torrential rain, and fired it with reasonable results considering it was the first firing. I did all the filming for a half hour video movie titled *Kaipara Kapers*, shown at Woodfire '89, a woodfire event at Janet Mansfield's farm later in the year. It was billed as the world premiere. It was the only public showing ever of this amateurish comedy.

Barbara and I both went on the next trip in 1991. Chester met us at the airport and took us to the top of one of the old extinct volcanos in the middle of Auckland and gave us champagne and strawberries as a welcome. That set the scene for a month of learning interspersed with much fooling around. Tony Nankervis was also there. Each of us was keen to learn whatever we could from the others. We started off pots and handed them on to the next person to finish. We copied each other's styles to see who could do it well enough to deceive the others. We fired the small anagama kiln again, with better results.

The three of us had fired together in Australia. We had each stood back wanting to see how the others went about it. That was not a very useful learning exercise. For the Kaipara firing we decided that each of us would take turns in charge of the kiln. I had brought a Fireman badge and whoever was wearing it was in charge. We learned that Tony's work needed a different firing to get the best results from his materials, but Chester and I could interchange our work in the kiln because the firing method suited both our stacking methods and the kind of results were wanted. We could fire together anytime, and subsequently did, many times.

The final proof of that for me was a firing of Chester's many years later at Goanna Ridge in Gulgong. I was there to help out. He was extremely tired and trying to pack the kiln quickly so I told him to go and have a sleep and packed his work in the kiln for him with the end result that there was no real difference after firing.

After the first firing in that small Kaipara anagama we had a fishing trip to the Kaipara harbour entrance. That's where I caught my biggest fish ever, a snapper around 15 kilos; Chester hurt his back lifting it out of the water. Finally, I believed Chester had some local fishing knowledge. He had told me many times about all the fish that Don Reitz had caught around there. That had been deeply annoying because I had caught nothing on the many previous attempts.

The three of us worked together off and on after that. In January 1992 we fired Tony's kiln at the Southern Cross campus. It was an act of insanity in one respect. The humidity was around 100 percent, the temperature in the high 30s and the kiln had walls of double dense firebrick that radiated heat ferociously. I have never been involved in another firing so physically painful but we took out some excellent pots. Many of them were shown in a joint exhibition by the three of us at Janet's Ceramic Art Gallery in William Street in Paddington. Alan Peascod wrote a review in *Ceramics Art and Perception* (12/1993). He described my work as having: '... *a broad interest in fusion as an aesthetic principle ... with the imagery of clinkered or welded surfaces, with textures either silky or "crunchy", or pyroplastically adjusted proportions of form, thanks to the hellish environment of saturated heat'.*

He concluded: *'The exhibition was one of the most satisfying I have seen—a visual delight and a renewal of faith. Situated as we are in the midst of the distortions and misunderstandings of the principles of post-modernism, it is always welcome to be confronted by an artistic stance which is as uncompromising and undiluted as it is sure-footed. The exhibition is not pastiche; it is the result of mature artistic belief. It reinforces in my mind the need to challenge current mainstream attitudes and practice; to respect artistic sanctity and endorse the principles of insularity as a means to foster a genuine artistic identity.'*

* * *

Chester moved to Australia mid-year in 1991. His marriage with Hilary was at an end and he had become involved with Jan Irvine. For me, thinking selfishly, his move meant losing access to his place in New Zealand, no longer being able to visit him at that paradise. The gain was that it was easier to get together.

Soon after he arrived, I set him up as a visiting artist at the Gippsland Institute art school. Money was fairly freely available in the art school then, and such things were simple to arrange. Later that year we had a three-way exhibition at the art school with our ceramics and Jan's textiles. Chester went on to offer workshops around Australia, helping build his profile here. He was previously not well known in Australia, as he had been in New Zealand.

In 1993 he was in Gippsland again, shivering in my workshop at Boolarra South, in mid-winter. The workshop was difficult to heat because of its high ceilings, and offered nothing to make life comfortable and easy. The water supply was a tap on an outside tank. Clearly it was time for Chester to settle down. That became possible when Janet offered a rental house in Gulgong. The decision to move there was made easier by the promise of high-quality clays in the district, something that had earlier appealed to Ivan McMeekin and later to Janet. Having them as neighbours was a definite attraction for Chester. Later Alan Peascod moved to the area for similar reasons—the clay and the company. Alas,

Chester is now the only one left in Gulgong. Ivan, Alan and Janet are no longer with us.

For me Gulgong was an attractive place to visit, and Chester's move there made it more so. I have been there many times since, sometimes for events, mostly to visit my mates. I know the area well now and always love being there, and feel at home. Henry Lawson lived around there and described it well in several of his short stories about dry, harsh country and hard living. It's unbearably hot in summer; the heat is like a pain that hurts no matter which way you move, inescapable. It's said that you dislike your enemies because of their faults and like your friends despite them and for me Gulgong fits that scenario. I like it despite the weather.

Chester and I have had many adventures together, too many to talk about. We have met up at events in New Zealand, the USA and Europe and many times in Australia. We have often worked together, as in *Fire-Up Gulgong* in 1993 where we led the anagama firing, as in the *North Carolina Potter's Conference* where with Janet Mansfield we were the demonstrators. We have fired many kilns together: his, mine and other people's. We have had endless conversations about myriads of subjects, and continue to do so.

One trip stays in my mind. David Stuchbery, from Bendigo, suggested that we could visit his father Allen, at his opal mine at White Cliffs in northern NSW. David and Ruth, his then partner, Chester and Jan, and Barbara and I along with my young sons Tom and Mike made the long trek up through Broken Hill. At White Cliffs, in Allen's opal mine, sleeping underground was easy at a constant cool 18°C, well away from the heat above ground. By day we explored the seemingly post-apocalyptic surroundings, an ideal setting for the many movies that have been made there.

Later we camped in Tibooburra. From there I drove up to Cameron's Corner and on into Sturt's Stony Desert, which ranks with some of the extreme places I have seen. Out there it all seems simple visually, just a thin line of red and a vast upside-down blue bowl of sky. At first it all seems the same until you look closely. Then you see differences; the shapes of the stones polished by wind and dust to produce desert varnish, occasional pieces of petrified wood, an amazing diversity. It seemed almost like an Islamic vision, a complex pattern in a simple whole. It was easy to see how artists had become infatuated with the landscape and tried to capture the harsh character in their artwork. It did not have that effect on me—the anagama kiln creates its own environment and cannot be manipulated to represent another.

Chester and I have occasionally disagreed, in the mildest possible way. Early in his Australian life Chester was opposed to teaching, believing that making pots full time and deriving an income from that was preferable. I believed that teaching brought in an income that allowed me to experiment much more with my work, and more easily accept failures with no financial worries. It also allowed me to spend time writing, articles for publication and talks for conferences, activities approved of in universities. Those teaching jobs, especially under Monash rule, were sometimes unpleasant but now I receive the ultimate benefit from them, superannuation built up over many years. That gives me freedom from financial worries, to go on experimenting without concerns about having to constantly sell work.

Another difference between us was about having a house to live in. Barbara and I found a location that suited us and bought the land. We settled for a fairly standard type of house, put up by builders in a relatively short time. We both worked at our respective teaching jobs, helping to pay for it. Chester did not want a job, wishing to concentrate solely on his ceramics. For a house he and Jan wanted a unique design and took many years to build a house themselves, with occasional help from a builder friend. Our professional careers have run closely parallel despite those differences of approach. Chester and I have been involved in roughly the same number of exhibitions, in similar galleries and locations. We have both achieved a similar level of recognition albeit by slightly different means.

Chester to me is two different people according to his surroundings. In public he loves being the centre of attention and usually reverts to comedy, joking it up. In private when you get him alone, he is interested in many things. His grandfather Sigvard Jacob Dannefaerd collected artefacts around Polynesia for museums and had an antiquities business in Auckland. He was the original influence on Chester's interest in aboriginal sites, fossils and unusual minerals and his curiosity about the history of the area where he lives. He studies the natural world, and knows a lot about birds and animals both from reading and from observation.

Chester loves the ancient and weathered. The roofs of his sheds are rusted corrugated iron, partly because of finances, but more importantly because he likes the appearance. It fits well with old farm buildings that can be seen around the Gulgong district. He likes what anyone else would see as old junk, the patina of age, and the form of things made by hand rather than machine. He collects the Australian version of *wabi-sabi*; rusted metal, and old cast iron that tempts me to larceny every time I see it.

I see subtle differences between his early work in New Zealand and his later work in Gulgong. Slower cooling in the large New Zealand kiln produced matt or frosty or opaque surfaces. I like to believe that these surfaces reference long term weathering as seen in archaeological material, which gives these pots a feeling of antiquity. The smaller kiln at Goanna Ridge cools much more quickly and produces brighter surfaces, sometimes quite shiny when he has used glazes.

* * *

Tony Nankervis was one of the original Lismore potters. He and Kerry Selwood both moved into the area in the 1970s, when it was becoming Australia's main destination for the hippie movement. It was good timing. Pots were easy to sell then and the quality of their work was high. Denis and Malina Monks were other notable North Coast potters using woodfired kilns, partly because they were cheap to build and fire and partly because of the aesthetics. This fitted in well with the back to the earth ethos of the time. Many of the early potters are still active and there are now many more woodfirers in that region.

Tony, Chester and I worked together on many occasions. Tony and I had comparable jobs, teaching ceramics in a regional setting and a common interest in woodfiring so it was easy to cooperate. I visited Lismore many times, sometimes as an examiner, sometimes to participate in the art school's external advisor committee, and sometimes to go fishing with Tony. That worked in reverse also; he helped me build parts of my 'studio village' and worked in Gippsland a few times.

Tony was a generous, even-tempered man but exceptionally strong minded about what he liked and what he did not. He would open a kiln and on the spot smash most of what came out of it. I thought he was far too hasty. He liked clean flashed and coloured surfaces and hated dribbly ash from wood firings. Those ash laden surfaces on his work often consigned them to rubble. My interest in surfaces produced by ash landing on pots meant that firing together was not really feasible, although we did that several times. He was a valued friend but unfortunately, after each of us retired from teaching we somehow lost contact.

* * *

By the early 2000s I had been involved in group or solo exhibitions around Australia, tending though to focus on Sydney where the arrangement with Janet Mansfield's gallery worked well for me. Sales were always good and Janet helped a lot with publicity. But I needed to find somewhere in Melbourne. At the Christine Abrahams gallery in Richmond, I saw exhibitions by Milton Moon and Pru Venables and I liked the feel of the place and the attitudes of the people who worked there. I decided to approach Guy Abraham and Milton offered to put in a good word—just as the gallery closed down. Then I liked the look of Haecceity Art Gallery, and the young man who ran it seemed interesting. Gail Nichols had an exhibition there and spoke well of the place and an approach seemed promising—but then it also closed down.

In part I was searching for a gallery that had a good reputation, and could sell well. It was important also to find gallery owners or managers that I liked as people, after experiencing what it was like to work in the past with a few gallery owners that I did not like. It is easier to work out arrangements about such things as prices, how work is to be displayed and to discuss problems, differences and doubts.

I went to Skepsi gallery on Swanston Street in Melbourne, almost by accident, after seeing an exhibition in the Ian Potter Museum over the road. At first, I was not very impressed with Skepsi. It was a small space that looked more like a shop than a gallery, where I would expect to find a large austere space or a small intimate one. But first impressions are sometimes overrated, and can be totally wrong. It's a general principle in life for me that it's not the building that matters; it's the people in it. And I warmed to Anna Maas as a person. My Irish ancestors had intervened and dubbed me with their good luck stick. Working with Anna fits perfectly with my ground rule that I only do my art business with people I like.

My first involvement in a group exhibition at Skepsi went well. We then discussed and agreed to a solo show. That was an easy and pleasant experience. Anna has an exceptionally smart approach to running a gallery. That is, find the serious collectors and look after them well, educate them and be aware of what they are looking for. She knows many of them, not just in a distant way, but personally. She knows what interests them in life in general, not just in collecting. This is the simple secret of her success, just dealing with people as people.

One result of working with a good gallery person is that the prices of your work become well established and increase gradually at a sensible rate. Another is that the collectors are well informed about your work. Having serious collectors take an interest in my work has changed the process of getting the work out there. Anna's mode of operation is a large step up from the least effective gallery processes where work is displayed and the gallery staff sit and wait in the hope that someone might come in off the street and buy it.

Meeting serious collectors intrigues me. Finding out what they think about and how they see the work is enlightening. As far as I am aware that has no direct effect on how I make work but intellectually it can be interesting. The best comment anyone ever made about my work came from Ken Lawrence, whose collection was vast. I asked him why he bought one of my pots and he replied *'I could not live a day longer without it'*.

Anna has looked after me extremely well and I value her friendship; the other stuff follows on easily. My attitudes about my work involve never being satisfied, always wanting something better, stronger, more persuasive. Anna has a knack for convincing me that existing work is suitable for exhibition. I am constantly pleased about wandering into that Swanston Street shop many years ago—it became a moment of significant transition for me.

In the 1990s and early 2000s my main focus had been in Sydney, exhibiting at the two Janet Mansfield galleries; then with John Freeland when she passed her Glenmore Road Gallery on to him. That focus has now shifted to Skepsi and Melbourne. In each case the value has been the connections with collectors of the respective galleries. Outside of that in recent times my solo exhibitions have been in public rather than commercial galleries.

* * *

Other gallery people have been supportive. When Joe Pascoe was the director of Craft Victoria, he took an interest in my work and showed it several times. The main one was to mark the 40th anniversary of the founding of Craft Victoria. Joe named that exhibition *Golden Ashes*. Dealing with Craft Victoria also meant working with Debbie Pryor, who was professional in her work and likable as a bonus. And recently Simon Gregg of the Gippsland Gallery Sale has become someone I admire for his professionalism and his style of managing the gallery. His book on art and artists in Gippsland gives a deep insight into developments in this part of Australia.

I am no longer interested in having frequent exhibitions, satisfied to wait until there is enough work to exhibit, working at a casual pace, not feeling any great need to prove anything, tending to be selective about where the work goes. The invitations to exhibit and my ability to provide the work seem to have reached a happy equilibrium.

* * *

I feel a special kinship with other people who make ceramics but also write. Jack Troy and Milton Moon are two such. I met Milton while attending a national ceramics conference in Adelaide in 1993. The editor of *Object* magazine had asked me to review an exhibition by Milton and his former students. I arranged to meet Milton at his Summertown home to talk about the exhibition and for some reason he decided the review was going to be negative; possibly because when he asked me what I was going to say my answer was that I had no idea. That would emerge when the writing started. The final review was a quite positive comment about his teaching and from then on we were on good terms, talking frequently via email. I followed both parts of his work, words and clay, with interest until his death in 2019. I have some of his work here, both pots and books, and value both highly.

Jack I count as one of my best mates. There is a particular category of friend I value most; those whose work I admire, and I especially admire his writing and his enthusiasm for woodfired ceramics. The feeling that you have a friend who is doing something out of the ordinary adds value to any friendship. We met back in 1989 at Janet's first Gulgong event and have been mutually involved in many events since then including several Gulgong events.

There are many other Americans I consider friends: John Neely, Chuck Hindes, Jeff Shapiro, Dan Anderson and a long list of others. Sometimes it's difficult to have friends who are far away and not easily accessible. I would love to have more time with them.

I have left out many people here that have enriched my life one way or another. My policy is to only deal with people professionally that I like personally and I have managed that with a few exceptions. Now, from that time away back in 1962 when I started in ceramics as a raw student, most of the early ones are dead and my memory holds a procession of people I liked and whose company I enjoyed occasionally. Doug Alexander, the quiet sensible man from Cuppacumbalong in the 1970s. Big booming Frederick Chepaux, a man so overwhelmingly out there I could only handle him for five minutes before I needed a five-minute break. So many others. So many ghosts now.

19
MY WORK

The clouds flow slowly across the sky, the idea
Slowly takes shape, and slowly passes, and changes
Its shape in passing.

— Conrad Aiken in *Preludes*

My work involves making ceramics, and writing. Everything else that other people might call work has been a distraction—sometimes a rewarding or a pleasant distraction, but a distraction nonetheless; although learning about other kinds of work early in life has guided some of my approaches to work now. Those early jobs I had in Berridale taught me to concentrate on the pleasure, rather than the labour. Work and pleasure still intertwine now; there is no distinction when you are involved in the right kind of work. The designer Carl Neilsen expressed it well when he said: '*I am being paid to do what I would happily do for nothing.*'

Teaching and learning has been a constant part of my life. The three main teachers were my father, Ivan McMeekin, and experience. My father taught me that physical work needs spacing and pacing, finding a rhythm that can continue, not rushing in and becoming too tired too soon. Later it became obvious that the same applies to prolonged writing projects. He taught me about how to handle wood fuel, which helped feeling at ease about firing kilns with wood. McMeekin taught me about ceramics. Experience taught me that there is always more to learn. The more you learn the more you realise how little you know.

* * *

Someone, perhaps someone who had been mowing grass in November in Gippsland, once said: '*The way to a long life is to have a project that never ends*'. The complexity of working with ceramics ensures there is always another question, always somewhere else to go. I have continued with ceramics for a lifetime, seeking something just ahead somewhere. Mostly I don't know what I am looking for but I will recognise it when I find it.

Side trips into sculpture and other media provide some light relief at times. Sometimes what I consider my best work does not go public. My studio is full of one-off sculptures with no theme, unrelated works that have so little in common they cannot be assembled into an exhibition. I am more rewarded sometimes by this work than some of the ceramic work that ends up in exhibitions.

Regardless of the medium my best work is done when I am not sure what I am doing, sometimes wondering if it's even worth doing. That is the exploratory phase, aiming for the unknown, inventing or creating or developing or groping around in the dark trying to find something; maybe a different form, or a new glaze, or a sculpture that initially is not coming together, or in writing seeking the words to clarify a concept that is not clear. Seeking, always seeking is the key. Scientists and artists are equally involved in a process of discovery; for both the grandest discoveries often arise incidentally, by accident, but in a context of seeking. Those who do not seek do not find; those who already know everything discover nothing.

I relish the search. Attempting entirely new work is both exciting and problematic for the venturer. The first time you go somewhere it is an intense experience that seems to take a long time—compared to the brevity of later trips when familiarity has come along. Familiarity breeds designed work, aiming for a totally specific pre-determined result. To me that feels like sleeping with the lights on. '*Understanding makes the mind lazy*' according to the character Mr Brundage, in *The Bookshop*.[11]

So why do you do it, you may ask me, why this ceramics thing? It's a simple question but it's difficult to find a simple answer. I don't do it for the money although I am happy when something is sold. Any intelligent person has a healthy measure of curiosity and that is one of my main motivations, to answer the ever-recurring question '*I wonder what would happen if …?*' Another powerful motivation is the pleasure of seeing something beautiful, or puzzling, or distressing, or different and new for the first time.

My involvement in the art of ceramics cannot be described as passion. The way I work is too quiet and casual for that. It's not an addiction, a narcotic that causes you to need larger and larger doses and makes withdrawal too difficult. It's more like a gentle opiate, like opium itself perhaps, that in small doses causes pleasant dreaming in a relaxed state. This state is where the best pots are made, just a little detached from reality, far from any worries and concerns. Being too worried about making good work is the best way to ensure the result is not good.

It's not always easy. Like almost everyone in the arts I have some degree of vulnerability, some level of self-doubt. Having to go public, being exposed to critics enhances that. But like anyone who has been around for some time I have also built up a level of confidence, based on past achievements and on learning. Vulnerability and confidence sit uneasily side by side, one dominating one day, the other the next, like water in a cistern; up and down, flushing to unease and filling to assurance.

* * *

There have been many changes in the ceramics arts since 1962 when I became involved. Then, potters were being described as artist potters; later, as ceramicists. Then conceptualists, object makers and designers came along. These identity changes represent changing aspirations, reflecting the need to communicate a newly developing image. Perhaps they also reflect a need to escape from the shackles of the previous generation and create a new identity. Or maybe they are just reflecting changes in the world around them. The best people may even contribute to those changes.

What we call ourselves depends on what we aim to achieve. There is a distinction between production ceramics and art ceramics. Production work involves working to a prescription, as in the currently popular production of tableware for restaurants where the customer/client defines the outcome, modified somewhat by the input of the maker during discussions. This has never held any interest for me. I prefer the skipping of a child to the marching of a uniformed regiment.

Commissions are not in my repertoire. Too complicated. The person who places the commission has something in mind—in my experience, usually something vague rather than a clear sharp image. When they try to communicate this, the potter/ceramicist forms an image which is different. It may be related but it is never quite the same, setting up the final scenario where both people end up somewhat disappointed. Why bother? Its far more satisfying both ways for someone to choose something that appeals to them, that you have already made. When the money is handed over, it's like the trade between Huckleberry Finn and Tom Sawyer: each person walks away thinking they have had the better of the other—the hallmark of any good trade.

* * *

I have never needed an excess of money. Having enough to pay the bills and continue working has been my greatest ambition. Had I wanted to be rich opportunities have been there. When I was in Washington DC, I met a man who travelled around the US setting up workshops to run pottery classes. He would buy or build a suitable building, fill it with potter's wheels, slab rollers, electric and gas kilns and all the other appurtenances of teaching the muddy art, and would employ someone experienced to manage it. When it was working well, he would move on to the next one. He was looking for a partner to expand the business. But I decided to spend my time making pots rather than doing all the monotonous work of getting rich. Setting up private workshops seemed like a novel idea in the early 1970s although in Australia now it's become common since so many institutional courses have closed.

* * *

Early on my work was concentrated on developing stoneware glazes. Later, for a long period, woodfiring took up most of my attention. Now my anagama kiln has become a cold monument. I have gone back almost full circle to concentrating on glazes and simple pot shapes. Part of my current work is usable; part is intended for display. I particularly like making *yunomi*, cups without handles, and I have an extensive collection of these made by other potters; and like making bowls of various sizes, because they are an ideal shape to display interesting glazes. As a bonus you can eat your noodles or your cereal from them. Making vases is another focus, it's a pleasure to see flowers in any house. My vases tend to be plain shapes and muted colours, allowing the flowers to show their beauty without any clashing colours and shapes, although sometimes I like the shapes to be a bit eccentric. Vases that are elaborate and colourful relegate the flowers to the background and miss the whole point.

The feel of small pots in the hand enhances their intimacy. Experimenting with new clay mixes by making small pots helps quicken learning about the character of clay. Not much is lost if a rice bowl goes wrong in the making. Another reason for making small pots is that they are useful for experiments with glazes, for reglazing and refiring experiments. The knowledge gained can then be transferred onto larger pots.

* * *

Some artists like to work in company, and I can understand that and see the value. In cities groups form and share a building, for security or stimulation, or simply to ease the financial burden of renting a work space. In that setting individuals can if they wish work alone, but enjoy the company of like-minded others during rest-breaks.

Working in a rural area is different. There is space to move around and spread out, peace and quiet with no interruptions and the freedom to concentrate solely on the work. The rural choice can be taken to the kind of extremes I have chosen, rarely having visitors and preferring to work alone, having no need for help or stimulation—another way of describing distraction. When anyone else is around it becomes too difficult to concentrate. Working alone, other people and other concerns become irrelevant. I go into a kind of trance, so that the work feeds itself without the need for any deep thought. This is why living anywhere but in the country is not possible for me; living somewhere isolated, enough that nobody calls in, enough that my friends live far enough away that they require a special trip to visit, enough that there is no interruption to break the productive mental state. I cannot see myself living anywhere else; my home has chosen me, as much as I have chosen it.

Even the hermit must emerge sometimes. Then it becomes necessary to deal with people. I can be gregarious at public events such as conferences. The sociable extrovert speaking at the conference inhabits the same body as the reclusive introvert not wishing to see anyone. Sometimes it's difficult to know which predominates. It becomes confusing at my exhibition openings when surrounded by people and feeling pleased to be there and at the same time wanting to be alone. What does that combination of extrovert and introvert make me? An ambivert? A transvert?

It's not desirable to be completely isolated from the artworld out there. Some external dialogue is essential, either with people or preferably with other artwork. The increasing availability of words and images on the internet has some value but can easily become an unproductive distraction. Seeing a small image of art has no relationship to experiencing its presence. Relying on stimulation from online art can be a distraction that leads to wanting to do everything rather than concentrating on what you do best.

I am aware of the history of ceramics, and aware to some extent of current developments. Ideas from elsewhere can spark off new work but my sources are mainly internal. I don't want my head screwed around or distracted by what others are doing. I imagine that the person who needs to be communal in order to function would see my isolated life as, in the words of John Updike: *'the desolation of the uneventful'*.[12] I see it as freedom from distractions.

Everyone knows that ideas arrive erratically. It's important to act when an idea comes—otherwise it goes, lost. Isolation gives that freedom. I am usually confronted by a mixture of commitments: writing deadlines, conference dates and exhibition dates that lock in what must be done. In the midst of these commitments, working on something entirely different and new provides relief and pleasure. Once asked if I had a business plan, my discomfited answer was that I had never considered such a thing. Playfulness is more important than logic and planning. My current five-year plan is to be alive five years from now, still waking up in the morning and wondering what the day will bring.

* * *

There is an old joke about the traveller asking the farmer how to get to the city and he replies *'If I was going there, I wouldn't start from here'*. How did I get to where I am now from where I started?

Starting in ceramics in the 1960s I was indirectly influenced by that old bible, *A Potter's Book*, the *magnum opus* of Bernard Leach. Indirectly, because it never seemed necessary to follow his specific recommendations about kilns, or glazes, or clay, or how to go about the whole thing. The main influence from Leach was the concept of stoneware, the high-fired ware of Asia, with its mellow and subtle shadings of glaze. In the 1960s this contrasted with earthenware, the ceramics of earlier times. Think of the well-known Australian pottery made by the Boyd family as a prime example, with its elaborate painted decorations on soft porous low-fired clay (to me the best of it was painted not by the Boyds but by Neil Douglas). This genre was seen by the new stoneware brigade as old fashioned and obsolete, relict from a time when visual excess was the norm.

The formality of the new stoneware was well matched to the Western art movement known as the new modernism. It's somewhat ironic that the stoneware idiom adopted in Australia came out of Asia. The result was a kind of East–West fusion. Japan was one source of inspiration and Peter Rushforth was one Australian who actually went there to learn. Through his life he followed Japanese principles of practice and aesthetics.

China was another source. Ivan McMeekin had no interest in Japan. His wartime experiences had led him to the conviction that they were, and I quote: 'Barbarians'. He may have been aware of Japanese ceramics but he felt no need to say so. He held the Sung Dynasty wares of China to be the high point of ceramic achievement. Ivan was also interested in early Chinese porcelain from later dynasties.

Ivan and Peter had one thing in common; their belief that wood was the best fuel for kilns, that some glazes and surfaces that resulted from woodfiring were unobtainable by any other means.

Another major influence on craft design in the 1960s was the Scandinavian style. Strong then in design magazines, it has now long gone from the general consciousness. This style was expressed widely in furniture, in chairs with rounded sweeping curved timbers, beautifully made, fixed with perfectly fitting joins and surfaced with soft matt finishes from 'Scandinavian oil', a concoction available then in every hardware shop in Australia. The Scandinavian influence was also much apparent in 1960s jewellery, metal wares and other crafts such as weaving and rug making. My teacher for introductory silversmithing was a genuine Dane, Helge Larsen, a man who I remember with great affection as a wonderful teacher, a whimsical critic—and a superb craftsman.

In ceramics the Scandinavian fashion was expressed in Arabia Ware, industrial tableware with muted browns and yellows and formal shapes, blending Asian-derived technology with modernist European design. This was not the first time Asia and Europe had cohabited in the field of design; export Chinese porcelains made specifically for Western tastes inspired the development of porcelain in Europe and influenced design, especially surface decoration.

* * *

My work in archaeology through the 1970s meant a break in making ceramics lasting five or six years while I was overseas. Later back in Canberra, while working at the ANU Prehistory Department I built a gas kiln with the financial help of a grant from the Australia Council, something unimaginable now. It was intended for firing at 1480°C (about 2700°F, Orton Cone 17) so I could experiment with high temperature porcelain. At that time stoneware and porcelain was never fired much higher that 1280°. My experiments with porcelain bodies and glazes were promising but I had no facilities for making up the porcelain bodies in larger batches. Recently I made some work with oxidised porcelain, fired in an electric kiln and hope to do more of this. The softer, minutely off-white whites appeal more than the harsher, bluish tinged whites that emerge from reduced firing.

In 1973 a friend in Washington gave me two ash-glazed *yunomi*, Japanese cups without handles, that he brought back from a trip to Japan. They are still prominent among the hundreds in my *yunomi* collection. These two small pots started me off developing ash glazes. Lack of information then meant entering a long period of failures. Each kiln firing produced useful information about what not to do, a series of what Enzo Ferrari once called 'a highly successful failure'. If you do what you should not do enough times eventually you will isolate what you should do. After this long process the glazes had enough of what I was looking for to use them on exhibition work.

During the later 1970s and early 1980s books about Japanese ceramics became available. Images of Japanese woodfired ceramics from places like Shigaraki and Bizen were featured. I was particularly attracted to the Iga genre, and to vessels from Tamba. The new awareness of these Japanese styles inspired a new approach to woodfiring, especially in the United States and Australia, and later in rest of the Western world. The starting point for us was building suitable kilns, large structures that would be fired over several days, unlike anything else we had used before. The most common type of such kiln was the *anagama* or tunnel kiln; sensibly enough named because it was like a tunnel.

Some Western potters, especially some Americans, went so far as to work in Japan in order to learn the new medium. I was never really inclined to do the Japan pilgrimage. I like to find out things for myself rather than have someone else tell me how to go about it, perhaps like the five-year-old who stamps their foot and says *'I want to do it myself'*. I am not Japanese so I felt no need to make work that expressed their national identity. Neither am I interested in the question that was around in ceramic circles some years ago: what defines our work as Australian? It's irrelevant whether mine is symbolically Australian or not. If that was important then I could just attach one of those little green stickers with a yellow Kangaroo on it. My work is just mine. What I did see in photos of Japanese anagama-fired ceramics was some connection to abstract expressionism, an earlier art movement that had intrigued me as a student in the 1960s. I had been to see every exhibition of abstract painting in Sydney through my student years. I loved that something that made no sense, made so much sense. The feel of that is what I aimed for.

More of this woodfire work was appearing in magazines in the early 1980s. Col Levy was promoting his work from the Bizen-style kiln he built. Rob Barron was building a large climbing kiln. The US magazine *Studio Potter* was promoting woodfiring. I was fortunate to get a part-time teaching job at the Canberra School of Art in 1980 and that gave me access to the Bizen kiln built earlier by Bill Samuels. Here was my chance to work in that genre.

Peter Thompson (Peter the Potter, from Kuranda in Queensland) said that we imported these kilns from Japan but they arrived without the instruction book, so we had to work out for ourselves how to use them. In that spirit, the protocol with the Canberra Bizen kiln was to start firing it and see what happens, to study the work after firing and follow the clues, the suggestions about where to go next. Put very simply, the work was about the evolution of itself rather than about some tradition from some other country. Some of the students, most notably Daniel Lafferty and Yuri Weidenhofer, had their woodfire origins at that kiln also. That's where each of us really got started on our life long commitments.

My experience and awareness of possibilities developed much more rapidly at the Gippsland Institute, after being employed there in 1984. A small anagama kiln had been built by Kyoshi Ino. I later modified it to make it larger. We fired it several times a year, allowing relatively rapid learning. An important part of that learning was to accept whatever resulted from a firing. Pots often emerged distorted, broken, or stuck together. These apparent disasters appeared among some wonderful successes. I began to think of this art form as the pursuit of excellence regardless of the consequences, to see the virtues of imperfection, to see success where others might just see ugliness. My belief that there is no failure, just learning, was confirmed.

* * *

As it became obvious that it was time to get out of Monash University, I began to think about building a large anagama kiln at home in Boolarra South. My woodfire kiln building career had started many years before, in the late 1960s, with some drama. Inspired by Ivan McMeekin's talk of woodfired kilns, and thinking that salt glazing might be easier than trying to formulate glazes, I decided to build a woodfired salt glaze kiln in Berridale, in my parent's backyard, starting with absolutely no knowledge of what to do. As a kiln it was an abject failure; but as a learning exercise it was valuable.

I found some old house-bricks and used them to build a rectangular box, with what was intended as a firebox underneath. With only a limited number of bricks it was necessary to set them on edge rather than flat, so the kiln wall was only about eight centimetres thick (three inches). I knew from housebuilding practice that you built an arch by sitting bricks over a curved formwork and filling in the triangular gaps with mortar, in this case a mix of wet clay and sand. There was no bracing to hold it all together. In the first firing I got it up to maybe 1100°C (around 1200°F). Then the two sides gracefully moved outwards at the top, and the arch fell in with a spectacular emission of sparks and larger glowing things. My regret at the time was that nobody else was there to see this glorious event.

The Boolarra South anagama kiln has been more successful. It was built over 1999 and 2000 while still working at Monash University. Tony Stewart, Gail Nichols, Erica Algie and many other students at the time were extremely helpful with the hard work of building sheds, moving bricks around and all the other jobs involved. The kiln design was modified from the character of an anagama in Cooroy, Queensland that had been built by Kadsuke Ichino from Tamba in Japan. The main thing I copied was that it had many sidestoke holes so that wood could be stoked in all along its length.

The first firing gave some good results. I was pleased to have my American friend John Neely involved. He had travelled down with me from Gulgong after taking part in one of Janet Mansfield's events, *Clayfeast*. Others involved were Mal Butterworth, who had fired the Cooroy kiln and a was fine storyteller; Chester Nealie, Graham King, Kwi Rak Choung and Michael Rye. It's possible to say this because I have always kept a record of each firing: when it happened, and who was involved, by burning the information onto a wooden post with a hot poker. The kiln shed itself acts as a memory stick.

In 2000 I changed from full-time to part-time employment at Monash for three years, anticipating leaving altogether at the beginning of 2004. That meant I could seriously start making work again. Half time at the art school meant two days a week, giving me five days a week at Boolarra South. The large kiln was from then on fired once a year. That may not sound like much but it took six months to make the work, load the kiln and fire it and then do all the work of cleaning up and finishing the pots that came out of the firing. Doing that once a year was enough.

An anagama kiln is like a wild beast that has come to trust you and allows you near enough to feed it. Mostly it sleeps a deep cold sleep, a long hibernation, oblivious to anyone or anything that passes by. While it is being stacked for a new firing it remains still but becomes alert, knowing somehow that life is coming to it again. Then when the fire starts it stirs and stretches, begins to move, begins to make subtle animal sounds, creaking, expanding, beginning to glow with life. As the fire builds to a peak it becomes adrenaline charged, ready for anything, unpredictable in its response—it is after all still more wild than tame. Its perverse, unrepeatable behaviour makes each firing a new challenge requiring constant creative approaches to new problems. And when its feeding stops it slowly settles back into its repose, gradually resuming its heavy sleep.

Firings once a year in the anagama continued until the last in 2016, the year Barbara died. Grief takes away all ambition and any ability to concentrate. Long-term projects are not practical while it is at the forefront.

Other factors confirmed my decision to not fire the big kiln again. One was the diagnosis of severe lung problems, no doubt exacerbated over the years by breathing in smoke from woodfired kilns. The common view that woodfiring is exciting and romantic pales somewhat when it becomes difficult to breathe. Another insight came when an American friend Frank Boyden phoned with condolences after Barbara died. In conversation I asked him if he had fired his anagama lately and his reply was: *'It has become too undignified for a man my age to be crawling in and out of one of those things'*. Considering Frank is not much older than me I decided he was right, and I would give up on that kiln and concentrate on kilns that I could fire alone in a reasonable time, during daylight hours.

I am extremely grateful to everyone who has helped with firing the big kiln. We used a crew of six each time, three eight-hour shifts each day with two people per shift, and each firing took around four days. Each firing required five other people. They included Barbara and Kirk Winter more times than anyone else, Chester Nealie, Su Hanna, Susie McMeekin, Kwi Rak Choung, Michael Rye, Perla Gerlic, Su Acheson, Yuri Weidenhofer, Daniel Lafferty, Peter Pilven and Bruce Pryor. Rob Barron helped out in various ways on some firings. All of these people now are family for me. Most of them have large kilns themselves and several work together in firing each other's kiln.

I warmly remember the early days of woodfiring, when a group of us just made it all up as we went along, taking great risks and considering failure as a form of learning. They were the days when enthusiasm was a current charging the vitals with jolts and surges. Now, seeing exhibitions of woodfire, everything reminds me of something I have seen somewhere before. The genre has become repetitive. Much woodfire work has taken on an overall pallor of similarity. I have seen several large exhibitions of woodfired work in the USA, one at the 2012 NCECA, one in the 2016 woodfire conference in Chicago; where forms were repeated and repeated. The same ash runs, the same shadings, the same colours. There seems little effort to search for a new aesthetic, for new insights. A few are doing original innovative exciting work but the masses are—the masses.

My practice now involves two kilns, one fired with gas, the other with wood. Firings are completed in a few hours, generally somewhere between five and eight hours. The small kiln can be filled with pots made in one day, and fired immediately so any new idea can be tried and finished and evaluated in a few days. Where that is leading, I do not know; and the condition of not knowing is for me highly desirable. It's a vast improvement on the work being almost predictable. As well as working on new ideas I can now try ideas put aside over the years, and see what happens. If they lead to exhibitions that is a good result and if not then I have still discovered something new.

A question that other woodfirers might ask is: given the richness, variability and uniqueness of each successful woodfired piece, is the transition away from the anagama worth losing the quality of the work? My answer to that is simply—that is the challenge now. That's the point. Come up with something that has its own character and strength. At this stage in my involvement in ceramics that is a wonderful thing—starting again from nowhere, or what sometimes feels like nowhere.

* * *

I feel fortunate to have started in ceramics in the early 1960s, when there were very few pottery supplies shops and very little in the way of tools or equipment available to buy. I learned to—as far as possible—make everything myself. This fitted well with my Berridale background which had provided an excellent training. Making something yourself was a necessary part of life when it was either unavailable or unaffordable. Instead of employing people to do the work people helped each other, much like firing an anagama. And scavenging was part of life. My father would drive his ute to the tip half loaded with rubbish and come back with it full. He saw it as useful stuff; although my mother could not always agree about its value.

That has been my way with ceramics; doing it myself wherever feasible; asking for help when that was needed. Need a shed? Build a shed. Need a kiln? Build a kiln. Rig up what you need from what you have. I have made most of my tools; this way they fit my hands, and their purpose, perfectly, in a way bought ones never do. Some tools have been scavenged, such as used dental tools. Throwing batts are made from form-ply rescued from building sites. In the 1960s spirit of do-it-yourself, I have even reverted lately to using some local clay, mixed in with commercial clay bodies, and using ash from the kiln or from the house heater in glazes. Of course, not everything is home-made, electric potter's wheels for example, or my Peter Pugger clay mixer or log splitter. Self-reliance does not have to equate with being a Luddite. Contradictions don't bother me.

The home-made ethos helps especially with big budget items like kilns. My small woodfired kiln cost about $300 for example. Most of the materials were second-hand and free. A commercial equivalent kiln could cost $10,000 or more; that's a lot of rice bowls. Over the years I have built many kilns, more than a hundred if you include those built with students. That now includes the three I use regularly, a woodfired top-hat bisque kiln that fires up to about 900°C, a gas kiln and a woodfired kiln. The small woodfired kiln uses air blowers in a kind of supercharged arrangement and I fire it to cone 7 in about five hours and cone 10 takes about six or seven hours.

The attitude about making everything myself is not just about costs. It's more about everything being precisely suited to my way of working and my personal needs. The tools suit the size of my hands and the way I move. The old chairs suit my posture. And apart from money and function, working in buildings I have built, using kilns I have built and tools I have made all makes a large contribution to the pleasure of my work.

* * *

As the movie director Baz Luhrman said, 'It never gets finished, it just gets taken away'. Most of my work goes public via exhibitions. Some is purchased at home by collectors, through studio visit days organised by Anna Maas. Some of it, usually smaller pieces, is sold at events such as the regular Gulgong events. Some is sold through regional gallery shops at Shepparton and Sale (Gippsland Art Gallery), and shops at Sturt and Craft Victoria.

What starts off personal and private, conducted in isolation, becomes public and susceptible to general judgement, requiring careful selection of work for exhibition, evaluating each kiln load piece by piece as it comes out. Some are easily rejected either because of damage, or because they don't meet some standard difficult to articulate in words.

By way of inconsistency my general attitude is that liking or disliking something is an ineffectual way of evaluating its worth. Something I don't like, made by someone else, may be worthy and valuable; or I might take a strong liking to something made by someone else that others judge worthless.

Evaluating my work is different. If it's really not up to standard, out it goes in small pieces, down the abandoned wombat hole. If I'm not sure I'll put it aside and check again later. Then it may be refired if it has potential. If something has immediate appeal it will go public. I am generally unwilling to take much notice of anyone else's opinion before the work goes public, except in a broad context. For example years ago there was a fashion for white objects. I listened when someone told me that, and made some white stuff to see what it was all about. I rarely have any interest in anyone's opinion of specific pieces although if someone buys a specific pot I am curious to know what they see in it. They have paid to express their opinion.

It's difficult to explain in words how I evaluate work because I examine it in another language not easily translated, a ceramics language, a sensory language. In part this involves looking at form, colour and other technical attributes and comparing with all others of its kind I have ever seen. They are all filed away in there somewhere. As well I take notice of my emotional reaction to it. In reality we all have the same approach, whether maker or collector if we are considering buying 'objects of virtue for contemplation'. If we love it (and if we can afford it) we buy it. Or my version of that as applied to other people's work is 'What work in this exhibition would I most like to steal?' Instead of stealing I buy it, if the price is affordable.

Useful things can be selected using different criteria. The simplest thing to select is a personal cup or bowl, because this can be done—is best done—with your eyes shut. In the long term we go on holding the thing, but tend to stop looking at it. But given that we are so visually oriented, and undervalue our senses of sound, touch and smell (the latter of which applies most strongly when dealing with very old pots), we can do our selection in stages. I select usable personal pots by first picking out the ones that look right. Then I shut my eyes and choose from them, the one that most feels right. If none feels right I walk away.

My work moves along. What is made this year is different to what was made last year. This was less so with work from the anagama where the

305

kiln dictated the appearance of work, but is a factor now that I work in shorter cycles and continually experiment. Collectors want typical work and so there always some pressure to continue making the same thing. When new work is presented there is a time lag. Collectors take a while to catch up and appreciate the new work and by then I have moved on again anyway. One answer to that problem I suppose would be to be like Col Levy and just stack it all up in a big shed and have no exhibitions.

The final stage of going public is the exhibition opening. After being in isolation for long periods it's an intense experience, being surrounded by people, most of whom would like a chat. It's a difficult adjustment to instantly change from one mode of being to another, especially when cornered by someone who wants to tell their story about their involvement in ceramics, usually at great length. Usually when a response to the exhibition is expressed face to face it is the *'I love your work'* kind of reaction. People who hate your work tend to not say so, although that would provoke a much more interesting discussion.

The best part about openings is seeing friends you rarely see otherwise. It's a grand feeling when friends are there to be supportive. The most pleasing of these came when Jeff Shapiro from New York, who was doing workshops in New Zealand, flew over for an opening of mine at the Freeland Gallery in Sydney. Jeff flew in for one night and went back to New Zealand the next day. Terry Davies, friend and former PhD student has a habit of turning up from Adelaide for my openings. I have also been pleased to see Col Levy at one of my Sydney openings; also Helge Larsen who was one of my favourite lecturers when I was a student came to another. Its wonderfully uplifting when someone you respect greatly comes along to see what you are doing.

* * *

Art schools over recent times have intellectualised art almost to the point where the analysis and writing about it comes to the forefront and the artwork or object recedes to become secondary or even almost irrelevant. This creates a dichotomy between those who value the statement and the critical response highly, and those who respond to artwork with their senses. Seeing the colour blue is an entirely different experience than seeing the word: blue. Touching an object is a different experience than reading about what it feels like.

A story has gone around about a composer who played his latest piano piece before an audience. A puzzled audience member asked him the meaning of the work; so he played it again. Leonard Bernstein said: *'Why do so many of us try to explain the beauty of music, thus depriving it of its mystery?'* And *'Music, of all the arts, stands in a special region, unlit by any star but its own, and utterly without meaning ... except its own'*. He also said: *'I have been all over the world and I have never seen a statue of a critic'*.

It's possible to stir up an acrimonious debate by suggesting that any worthwhile artwork is its own message. Any explanation will be just one of myriads of possible explanations. It's possible none of these will reflect the artist's intentions; about which the artist may have been quite unclear anyway. Rimbaud's mother asked him about the meaning of one of his works 'A Season in Hell' and he replied: *'It means what it says. Literally and in every other sense.'*

At exhibition openings I am sometimes asked to explain my work, followed by an anticipatory silence. I am never sure how to end that silence. My internal answer is that ceramic objects have their own language, which I have learned over fifty and more years. I use that pot language to evaluate each pot; but I have not yet learned how to translate pot language into English. The best I can do is to say it's a kind of sensory language in which the person needs to touch and see and hear the pot for themselves. I cannot explain why something attracts me because that attraction is mysterious, in the same way as love between people is mysterious, or our attraction to the smell of a rose is mysterious. Perhaps visible signs like colour, form, texture and proportion can be used but this is a like discussing the parts of an animal—the eye of the tiger, or its claw—and missing the grace and movement and context of the whole.

Explaining has become a contemporary disease known as the artist statement. I am usually deeply disinterested in the statement about what the artist intended, and more interested in the effect the work has on me. I am not sure if it matters whether they have some rationale for their work or not. It's often difficult, even impossible to relate the words to the object. Its easy sometimes to dismiss the statement as indecipherable blather.

My friend Euan Heng, the painter, used the expression *'sphere of influence'*. This is the ultimate judgement of the overall value of someone's work. How widely have they influenced others? Locally? Within the state? Nationally? Internationally? That is best evaluated through the opinions of others, not of the artists themselves.

It's not my job to tell critics how to do theirs, although I could point out that if their writing is unreadable, they are not achieving anything by publishing it. The quality of writing about ceramics is often abysmally dull, hard to read, and immersed in mindless trivialities. When a good writer has something fascinating to say about their reaction to the work it is such a relief and a pleasure.

Criticism affects the artist. Positive criticism is more dangerous than adverse. Adverse criticism merely generates anger which can be converted into energy and a will to succeed, but positive criticism can create a disincentive to change, along with the probability of an ego problem. In my case praise creates lassitude and inhibits risk-taking—briefly. The worst response is no response. Indifference can create self-doubt when it is absent, or make it worse when present. How dare you ignore me?

Seeing ceramics exhibitions by other artists makes me wonder about the processes they used in making the object. That can spark a new line of thinking which does not necessarily have any relationship whatever to the source. Work that sits comfortably within the latest fashions is often uninteresting, unlike work that is enigmatic and does not reveal itself instantly.

* * *

How it all changes. Emperors and kings, dukes and barons all aspired to own the ceramics of China, inspired by the glistening whiteness of the porcelain clay, the perfection of glaze and the richness of under and overglaze colours at a time when the castle was a grey colourless place and the only glow of colour in everyday lives existed in flowerbeds. The flow of ceramics from China still continues, into the cheapest of shops now, the two-dollar ones. Seeing them is depressing in the context of China's highest achievements. Visually most kitchen-shop ceramics have an unrelieved monotony of whiteness, and dull precise forms, seen in their entirety at a glance.

The China analogy is useful when thinking about collecting ceramics. Work which receives little recognition when new, can later become highly valued, and work which was over-hyped at the time can later become worthless, making the job of curators of public collections complicated. Their role is to create the history of our art, of all the arts. Curators can easily make the mistake of leaving out what later becomes important work, or of including trivia. This can happen especially if they are too much influenced by their personal tastes and are too little aware of their role as history makers. It can also happen if they become king makers, attempting to promote personal friends. Curators may also be susceptible to following fashion; if one says someone makes marvellous work they all jump in to promote that.

I have been concerned ever since I started teaching ceramics that the history of our art has not been taught in art schools. In the USA Gerry Williams, the past editor and owner of *Studio Potter* magazine was deeply concerned about preserving the history of US ceramics and set up an archive in New Hampshire for that purpose. In Australia we have no equivalent. We must rely on ceramics magazines for an overview of changes in ceramics over time. In Australia this means our history is recorded in *Pottery in Australia*, later *The Journal of Australian Ceramics*. The word *'pottery'* was apparently embarrassing, and the word *'ceramics'* was thought to be more sophisticated.

Public galleries tend to have much more restricted collections. As I write this the main galleries such as the Australian National Gallery (ANG), the National Gallery of Victoria (NGV) and the Powerhouse Museum in Sydney seem to have no interest in collecting ceramics; although I am told by those in the know that there are some understanding curators but a lack of funding for purchases. The curators who do take an active interest and who do collect ceramics are in regional galleries and many of them are building up substantial collections. I hope they are also documenting the work appropriately so that anyone who wants to write a history can do so.

But I do like to visit public art galleries. They have interesting bookshops and the cleanest toilets in town. Sometimes they even show ceramics, sometimes they have some interesting new art. I particularly look for sculpture. Otherwise they can be like mausoleums, where old art goes to die. To see current developments in ceramics it's better to visit exhibitions in commercial galleries.

Good intentions were realised many years ago by those crafts men and women who set up organisations with the aim of people helping each other and learning from each other. These organisations were run by crafts people for the benefit of all crafts people. The Australian Ceramics Association still tends to fit this ethos. Any comments about the Australia Council are not particularly relevant here because that organisation takes no interest in ceramics. Their grants are not accessible to anyone working in the ceramics field, apart from occasional awards of residencies in overseas studios. I can only guess that those pioneers who established arts organisations would be distressed to see the decline of the artist in arts administration and the rise of the artocrat, the highly paid administrator who sits in a plush office in a city somewhere deciding who to promote and who to ignore.

These winner-pickers are paid well and live well while most creators of artwork have low incomes. In 2000 the Australia Council reported the average crafts income as a little more than $20,000 a year (equivalent to around $30,000 in 2020). In an ABC 7.30 Report in 2010 David Throsby said that '*The average income for a fully professional artist is, from their creative work, less than $20,000 a year and in fact more than half of them earn less than $10,000 a year from their creative work*'.

I am a member of some organisations. The International Academy of Ceramics is the main one globally. It serves a useful role in connecting people internationally. I am also a member of Craft Victoria and have been involved in a major personal exhibition there and also in various group shows. This organisation is active in promoting a range of crafts, not just ceramics and does so effectively. I believe the most important role for any organisation is helping younger artists find their way into the labyrinthine artworld.

* * *

My writing is as important to me as my ceramics. My first publication was in the Monaro High school magazine. At school my misbehaviour meant frequent expulsion from the classroom to the library. What kind of weird mind conceived a library as a place of punishment? It was a place of pleasure, full of books. It was there I learned to type, acquiring the two-finger approach. It's slow but I get there eventually.

Having my writing published in ceramics magazines here and overseas and attending and speaking at many conferences, means my name has become known widely. Exhibiting work is not necessarily the best way to develop a reputation, unless reports of it are published. At most a few hundred people see an exhibition; thousands read magazines and social media online reaches more again. Exhibition reviews in magazines publicise both the artist and the writer; increasingly though magazine articles are not actually read except by a small minority. I am guilty of this, often looking at the pictures but not reading the writing. That follows the old maxim that if writing is unreadable then nobody will read it. I usually give it two paragraphs to decide.

Will magazines disappear as social media take over? Social media are now favoured as the way to reach a wide audience. Online forums contribute to the general disinterest in reading longer articles by favouring, and so promoting, brief comments. Deep analysis is disappearing. Additionally, writing has lost the simplicity and storytelling of the earlier days of ceramics magazines and has become tarnished by the critical writing brigades who use either artspeak or complex academic language, neither of which appeal to or are understood by the wider audience. Pablo Picasso said: '*When art critics get together, they talk about form and structure and meaning. When artists get together, they talk about where you can buy cheap turpentine.*'

I feel strong pressure to produce writing that is either enjoyable to read, or contentious so it annoys some people, in the hope that it will stir someone to actually read it. It's partly a matter of language. Having worked with scientists, from archaeologists to nuclear physicists, and also with artists, I understand their different approaches to language. Science writing uses words defined as narrowly as possible to avoid any misunderstanding. The poet produces the opposite, broadly suggestive, hinting rather than explaining and sometimes misleading, at best inciting imagination in the reader. Poets can fill small spaces with immensities.

Writing in ceramics magazines is a strange combination of both. What is said in articles about glazes or clay bodies or developments in firing needs to be clear and precise. Artist statements and critical writing often are opposite, just plain obscure. One sometimes wonders if the person who did the writing understood their meaning themselves. Was it Michael Cardew who once used the expression *'formless scrawls and aimless babble?'*

* * *

At the beginning of a career it seems important to be recognised, to build up a reputation, even to become famous. Excessive publicity might achieve that rapidly, if it is allied with strong interesting artwork. A name seen frequently in print and in social media, especially over a long time, becomes well recognised.

In the small world of people involved in ceramics (should that be the tiny world?) it's easy to achieve some kind of fame. This provides an identity, recognition that you belong to a large family. That is all fine and dandy but I imagine it pleases an extrovert more than it does anyone with a reclusive nature. Standing on the stage with the spotlight in your eyes is dangerous. It makes you visible to everyone, but means you cannot see anyone.

I suppose we all aspire to achieve some level of fame. It helps to attract the greatest crowd at the event, or to bring the biggest price when work is sold, or eventually to get the biggest retrospective in the public galleries. Who will get the invitations, the online praise, the article in the magazine, the mention in the book, the complete book just devoted to them? The trick is to understand the difference between publicity and reality. The ones who do that best retain some level of humility. These are the people whose company I enjoy most. In the words of Mike McClellan, the Song and Dance Man: *'fame is just a momentary curse'.*

Hiroe Swen said something to me once I have always remembered. I showed her my attempt at a teabowl, asking for her comment. Her enigmatic reply was that a teabowl should feel like an old well-worn slipper. If you are going to hold something every day then it should feel right. This applies not only to pots of course, but to tools, doorknobs, cutlery and sleeping partners.

She then asked me what I thought of it. My reply was '*Well, I am not satisfied with it*'. She said '*Good. If you are ever satisfied with your work you should give up and do something else.*' That fits well with Ivan McMeekin's way of evaluating work from the kiln: '*Now, if you just next time, try …*' Always the next time. And something Alan Peascod said: '*It doesn't matter what is happening in your life, the only thing that matters is that you keep working*'.

20
MAKING IT

… to all those who work come moments of beauty unseen by the rest of the world.

— Norman Maclean in his story *The Ranger, the Cook and the Hole in the Sky*

Most potters will agree that listening to music is an important adjunct to making. The character of the music relates in some way to the character of the work, perhaps even helps determine it. When Janet Mansfield took on an apprentice in the early days her firm rule was that she and she only would choose the music in the studio. My preference in music to accompany making is for old familiar blues, jazz and country music. Their familiarity helps establish a musing mind set, creating a light touch and allowing the forms I'm making to hum along. Improvised jazz helps some forms adopt a sightly erratic stance, like a one-legged man with hands on hips. Blues works well with changes in direction, and blending multi-part forms into a unity. Old country music—going back early in the 19th century—is background that helps with anything repetitive, like turning bowls, taking the mind away from the work and loosening the hand.

* * *

My approach generally involves making a 'family' of similar forms. Rarely are two things exactly alike, everything is a one-off. I am happy when each piece has an individual character—like little inert people's faccs.

My main forming technique is throwing, working with electric wheels. Most wheels are supplied with a foot pedal—which is perfect for driving a car if you want to constantly speed up and slow down. I remove the foot pedal, and use a lever that locks into the one position best suited to whatever is being made, working with one speed only. That speed is usually slow. Fast wheel speeds produce forms with no emotional expression, a way to just get it over and done with quickly; good for rapid production. A slow wheel speed allows much more expression in the form. As a student,

I asked Col Levy to define craftsmanship and he said: *'Craftsmanship is economy of movement'*. Hand and arm movement is critical; graceful movements produce graceful forms. Slightly erratic movements produce slightly erratic forms. The character of the clay contributes to the nature of form.

Early attempts at throwing caused me to feel sad. The kick wheel was the culprit. Electric wheels revolutionised my emotions. When first using them, I felt a macho pride, throwing large pots from a single lump of clay, drawing up the clay so quickly and masterfully—until I became aware that skill alone was not part of art. The feeling transferred to the work, that feeling derived from macho skills—was not worth portraying. The whole process of throwing became easier when Sandra Johnstone, a salt glazer from California, came to visit Gippsland for a residency. She threw big pots with ease and gifted them with character so I studied closely what she did and have used her throwing techniques ever since—the inner hand dominating, doing the lifting and shaping.

For larger forms I use two, three or four wheels so I can make a number of large pots in the same session, moving from one to the next so they grow together. Almost always I finish the outside of the form with a flat rib as I go to remove throwing marks (to emphasise the vertical rather than the horizontal), before drying with the burner and repeating the process. These larger pots are often modified during throwing, beating them into a squared shape at the shoulders, or beating vertical grooves into the shoulders. These processes are not as simple as it may appear in the finished thing.

Most of my work is made on the slow-revolving potter's wheel usually seeking a slightly erratic form, aiming for a casual feel. I use clay generally in a fairly soft state, and mostly don't weigh clay, even if forms are being 'repeated ', just estimating equivalent amounts. That helps with making each pot a little different. Why would anyone want them all the same? Some of my pots such as bowls and yunomi (the Japanese word for cups with no handle) are thrown and turned. Plates are made in one go with absolute minimal turning. Bottles are thrown in stages, the main body first. Then I add a coil of clay and from that throw the neck. The coil is roughly formed by hand, not very precisely so there is some of that desired irregularity in the final result.

For larger forms (anything over about 12 inches/30cm, up to about 3 feet/1metre) I throw and coil with coarse gritty clay. A large coil of clay is joined to the upper rim of a part completed form and thrown to increase the height and further define the form. Then, using a propane burner, each newly thrown section is dried enough to take the weight of the next coil. This technique is a combination of throwing methods I have seen in Pakistan, and those used by Palestinian potters in Hebron, combined with the burner technique developed by Alan Peascod.

I sometimes make a lot of smaller 'bottle' forms around 5cm (2") high. These miniatures are always distorted in some way after throwing; squared, faceted, grooved, squashed, beaten on a bench to lengthen them or bent so they stand askew; generally whatever appeals at the time.

Bowls are another staple, the size again ranging from small to large. After throwing they are lifted off the wheel and placed with the base on cement board. That dries the thicker bottom at the same rate as the rim, equalising the drying. The bowls are then turned very quickly while the clay is still relatively soft. For soup-sized bowls that is about one every 30 seconds. For turning (what the Americans term trimming) they are not fixed to the wheel head or to any device, but simply placed upside down on the wheelhead, tapped into centre and held with a finger on the centre of the base.

* * *

The character of thrown work derives from the character of the clay, the speed of the wheel and the degree of relaxation or tension of the thrower. I always try to bring out the character of clay—lumpy, coarse, fine, difficult to throw with or easy. This must be suitable for the surface qualities that will emerge after firing. A smooth surface for a glossy glaze, a broken surface for a broken glaze. Working on a sequence of similar forms is helped by getting into a trance-like state where the forms seem to make themselves, without too much interference from thinking.

Throwing by its nature involves abstraction. Whether it is intended for use or display, a vessel is an abstract object with no direct replica in nature. It's important to me that they have some natural, organic qualities and avoid the machine-made look. This implies consideration of qualities such as the character of curvatures in the form, the nature of markings on the surface, and the details of directional changes where different parts of the form meet. All of these must avoid any hints of a machine-made character. This seems odd, really, if you consider that the wheel, the basic tool used in forming, is a machine. It seems less odd when you realise that the basic forming is done by a person while the wheel just sits there and spins mindlessly. No clock ever understood how to tell the time.

If 50 different people make the same pot from the same clay each will be different. It will reflect their level of skill, their attitudes to form, their state of mind whether confident and relaxed, or nervous and uncertain. As well as the emotional content, each person inflicts their sense of rightness of form; the hasty, the casual, the slow and measured or the precise. If I was skilled enough to try making fifty pots the same, each would be slightly different anyway. Instead of trying to make them identical I like to explore the form, investigating and developing its character through little nuances of change so that the end result is a family of related forms. Within this family a few finally stand out as superior. I will probably keep these best ones for myself.

* * *

The colour of ceramic glazes depends on combinations of minerals and oxides used in the mixture. The same can be said for fireworks in which strontium gives red, copper blue, barium green, sodium yellow, calcium orange and iron gold; violet comes from potassium or rubidium and white from platinum. Strangely, the colour of these same elements in glazes is quite different than in fireworks. Perhaps someone can explain that. The colour of glazes also depends on the atmosphere in which they are fired, whether reducing or oxidising.

I rarely use decorative procedures as such. I sometimes—rarely—do some painting on bowls, painting colours over the glaze layer before it is fired. When I was firing in the anagama, painted decoration would have been obliterated by the ash deposits on the surface. The 'decoration' if any, for that anagama firing process consisted of incised lines, grooves and other types of texture worked into the clay. Sometimes I mixed stones and other crude materials into the clay before throwing to create a rough character.

Combining with glazes, on some work I use slips such as a terracotta, to colour thin edges of glaze. Many of the glazes I use now are based on wood ash and I have batches of ash from a variety of types of wood. The ash is sieved down to a fine size—usually 40 mesh, and I will sieve the mixed glaze later to remove the coarsest material. Preparing ash this way retains the soluble salts. During firing the salts flash over onto any exposed clay surface creating warm colours on the clay. Placing the pots on silicon carbide shelves in reduction firings helps this flashing.

I often do several firings of a pot, each time adding a new layer to achieve rich qualities in the glazes. Early layers are poured on rather than dipped, so that the edges will be uneven, in character with the general eccentricity of the forming. Dipping would make harsh straight lines. When applying a new glaze layer over an already fired glaze I may spray the new layer, allowing variations in thickness around the vessel, or use a variety of other application methods.

* * *

Getting ceramic materials is simple. Go to the pottery supplies shop, get what you want in 100-gram jars or one kilo packets or even in 25 kilo bags. For gas kilns you can get gas in convenient cylinders, or pumped into a large cylinder from a truck that comes when you phone them, or from your connection to the mains if you have the misfortune to live in a city. Light some burners to start it off, and now and then make a few adjustments while you basically do something else. For electric kilns its simple: play with some controls to set up the firing you want, flick a few switches and go away and do something else. Someone else digs the coal and burns it to make the electricity so all you have to do is flick the switch.

Firing with wood is different to firing with other fuels. It requires noisy work to prepare it, and space to store it and let it dry. The kiln emits smoke as it is fired. For these reasons woodfiring is almost always a rural activity. I take a more than average interest in burning wood. Wood is my main fuel. Two of the three kilns I use now, the bisque-firing kiln and the fast-fire kiln are heated with wood fuel, and my house is heated with a wood-burning heater.

Being involved in wood gathering allows me the feeling of being at least a fringe dweller in the rural world of practical wisdom. It's a more productive means of keeping fit than the city equivalent, running about,

318

or using machines in a gymnasium, with no product other than sweat. Hard work and getting dirty, smelling of petrol fumes and oil overlaid on clay-stained clothes are integral parts of the woodfire art. It's always good to go into town in this condition so everyone can see you are a proper rural man.

In the past firing my anagama meant obtaining large amounts of wood. One firing could use two truckloads so it was a major task to prepare the wood for even one firing, and I always had enough wood ready for two firings, keeping ahead so each time the wood was well seasoned and dry. Most of the wood came as offcuts from sawmills. My wood was delivered in a Mack, or a Louisville Ford. Big trucks. Not many people in the arts have their materials delivered in a Mack or Louisville.

Now, the small kilns that have replaced the anagama require much less wood. The bisque kiln uses about a large wheelbarrow-full and the high temperature kiln about double, sometimes triple that. Most of the wood is gathered from fallen trees or branches on my place. It is illegal in Victoria to pick up wood from the sides of roads but some roads around where I live are conveniently isolated with almost no traffic, and the locals don't care. In whichever small kiln I fire now, it does not matter much what kind of wood is burned. There is no significant ash deposit in these fast firings so the wood is simply a means of heating. I use pine, Californian cypress and various eucalypts and wattles; whatever is around. Cypress and eucalypts produce the best ash to use as glaze ingredients so I try to not mix other kinds with them in the one firing so I can rescue the ash when the kiln cools.

Splitting wood, whether the old-fashioned way with an axe or the modern equivalent with a log splitter driven by a petrol or diesel engine, is an art in itself. Pine needs to be split straight through the centre. Eucalypts need to be split following the concentric growth rings. Blackwood and cypress are indifferent—split any way you like, it's all the same to them.

Once split, the wood is stacked to let air circulate around it, drying it for the appropriate number of summers—at least one for *radiata* (Monterey) pine, two for Californian Cypress and preferably five or more for eucalypts. Over that time the moisture content will decrease so the wood will burn effectively. Even city folks know you can't burn wet green wood. You can however at times use it for serious reduction. I use it at the end of firing as a way of both firing down and introducing water via the green wood for extra reduction.

I am a connoisseur, admiring the well-considered wood stack, elegantly stable and beautifully proportioned in its balance of wood and circulating air. Like the man who buys an umbrella during a drought, I prepare wood for the future, stacking it and waiting for it to reach the perfect state. I watch each stack through the seasons, as the drying easterlies of spring alternate with the rewetting rains, and then the winter south westerlies and the summer north westerlies dry it quickly. The cycles of wetting and drying produce the best kiln fuel.

Risk is an ever-present accompaniment of kiln firing. A multitude of things can fail, go wrong, surprise you. What was looked on as something wonderful before firing can be fused, broken or simply turn out ugly. The level of risk is greatest in a large kiln like the anagama where it's easy to lose a whole kiln-full, ruined beyond redemption. Even in the best firings there will be some work lost. The nature of the beast is such that the only possible attitude about firings is acceptance. The result is the result. Take pleasure in the unexpectedly good ones, accept that some—or many—have been destroyed in the process. Hammers have other purposes than driving nails.

Compared with the risks inherent in firing an anagama kiln—the likelihood of losing a year's work through some disaster, or the possibility that nobody will appreciate the aesthetic, firing a small kiln is bliss. Even when everything is lost, not much is lost; and the opportunity to learn something has been presented.

* * *

Back when firing the anagama, I preferred to be on shift at night. Opening stokeholes, seeing the fire lighting up shadows with the darkness beyond. Stoking a piece of old dry hardwood into a hot firebox, hearing the instant crackle and hissing fizz of a million tiny explosions as resins and oils escape and air sacs explode, mixed with the slurping rush of air induction, sounding like a hundred kilometre an hour wind with the volume turned way down. The flame racing away through the kiln, starting off the low rumbling sound of the chimney. A whoof of grey smoke emerges, then, dying down slowly, it leaves a cone of flame reaching upwards, at night illuminating the surroundings. As the wood burns away and the kiln quietens, it's time to stoke again. Compared with any other form of heating ceramics, woodfiring engages all the senses.

My bisque kiln is a stainless-steel drum lined with one layer of fibre. The drum can be lifted with a chain and pulley for stacking the pots inside. The drum sits on top of a firebox where wood is burned and flame travels up through the drum and out a removable flue placed on top of the drum while firing. I place a gas burner with a low flame in the firebox around 11 at night and by the next morning the temperature is around 200°C (around 400°F). I start firing with wood then and take around two to two and a half hours to reach 900°C (about 1650°F). Even with large vessels I have had no problems with pots cracking, either in the heating or the fast cooling.

The high-firing wood burning kiln is unique. It has two layers of insulating brick for the chamber and one layer, set on edge, in the chimney. The small firebox is built from dense firebrick and has a stoking port on both sides, each with a movable steel frame door with a Pyrex glass window so I can see into the firebox. The windows were scavenged from a disused wood heater. Two small electric air blowers, one either side, supercharge the firebox and allow me to fire to cone 7 in about five hours and cone 10 in around 7 hours. This fast firing necessitated developing suitable new glazes for those conditions.

My gas kiln is my design and I tend to use it for higher firings, to cone 9 or 10. These take around eight hours. Most firings in either the wood kiln or the gas kiln contain glaze experiments. Opening the kilns, even after all these years involved in ceramics, still holds surprises. Some are delightful, some are depressing. As ever in ceramics confidence and self-delusion are close companions.

It may sound odd, but with woodfired kilns the most important part of the overall making process is usually done after the pots come out of the kiln. I like the pots to feel smooth, regardless of their visual appearance. That involves working on them with wet and dry paper or perhaps other tools, to achieve the right feel.

I often leave pots outside in the weather for periods up to several years so they acquire an aged character, with soft crackle in the glaze. Some of my best pots ever were seasoned in this way.

21
Barbara

The death of a beloved is an amputation.

— C.S. Lewis

The strongest relationship of my life began in the most ordinary of circumstances. It's a well-known story: doctors and nurses, or bosses and receptionists or, as it was for us, lecturers and students. Place two people together who are attracted and guess what? In the Gippsland art school ceramics studio with me as teacher and her as student (an adult student I should note, formally known as mature age) Barbara Heeley and I clearly had some mutual attraction. For some time we did not act on that attraction. I had nothing to offer, my home life was all-consuming.

In the end, or more accurately in our beginning, we had an assignation at the ceramics conference in Sydney in 1988. The details are none of your business but in general such events are not unusual. Free and away from home, placed close, many are tempted and some go through with it. We did. My previous marriage had ended in pain and hers had gone stale. We each had what the other needed.

This could have brought the dramas that can accompany such a relationship to the art school we both inhabited. I believe such involvement is now forbidden in some or maybe all Australian universities. Students shall not lay with lecturers. Good luck with enforcing that, I say. We were each committed, and our relationship was not a secret but quite open. All the other students in our proximity knew about it, and I had made it public in staff meetings particularly when the issue of bias in assessments came up. I asked to be replaced as the assessor for Barbara's work. The other staff decided that this was not necessary; they trusted me to be objective. My memory is not clear about whether or not I erred a little on the positive side.

The near thirty years that followed was remarked on by a friend recently. He said someone asked him about relations between students and lecturers in his day. He told me his answer was that he could only recall one case that was well known and his reply had been '*They stayed together until one of them died*'. That we did.

We moved in together in 1989 and lived in the village of Boolarra for some time. Then we bought a former schoolhouse and five-acre block at Boolarra South, in rural surroundings where the nearest visible neighbour is about ten kilometres away. We had a house built, and from 1994 we lived in this peaceful countryside. It was a perfect location for both of us. There was more than enough room to indulge Barbara's love of gardens, and neighbours did not intrude into my work time. The local council has not interfered in the process of building sheds and kilns. They have not burdened me with rules and regulations and I have not bothered them with details. We gradually learned to live independently; and now living in a town, with neighbours, would feel like extreme deprivation.

Eventually she made a decision to not work with clay any more. I disagreed with the decision. She said that it would work best if we concentrated on my work. I am still sad that she stopped. I did not see it as necessary in any way. Despite that, her interest in ceramics continued. She worked with me in many small ways. We made some pots together, my forms and her painting. We stacked wood together. We moved pots outside to dry or inside when it rained. When I did the annual anagama firing, a six-month process, she helped with all the preparations. My policy was that the only people who could come and help with the firing were ones she liked, because they would stay in our house. No matter who they were or how prestigious, if she did not like them, they were not invited (nor were they if I did not like them).

Barbara worked constantly during each firing, doing whatever was needed. She took over the evening shift when we were all having a meal, so she could have the kiln with nobody else around. She liked to watch the pyrometer, trying to gain temperature and taking great pleasure when it said so. And she was there when the kiln was opened, keenly interested in what came out and willing to get in and unload, not a pleasant process among the ash and rubble. Later, when I built a small woodfired kiln, she enjoyed taking a turn stoking that.

We both understood and loved the work that went into making pots. The shared interest made for an easy understanding on her part of what I was doing. Much more than that, she was a constant source

of encouragement and support. She helped me to survive Monash. She came along to exhibition openings, placing her hand on my shoulder and diverting me when she could see some conversation becoming a struggle. When I doubted that an expense travelling to some event was justified, she insisted that I go. When some equipment or materials seemed too expensive, she insisted I get them anyway. When I was away and she stayed home we both knew that she was uncomfortable, even at times frightened being alone in our isolated house, but she was willing to accept that.

We travelled well together. Usually we divided up the days, one planned by her, another by me, but there was no hardship either way, we both were interested in whatever the other had chosen. Mostly she chose gardens and I chose galleries. She was worried about going to America because so much television and movies from the USA involves shootings and murders; but over several trips she came away with new friends and pleasant memories of amiable and hospitable people.

At Richard Rowland's in Oregon to do a workshop, we stayed in their cosy little cabin in the woods, away from the main house. It protected us from the incessant Northwest rain but was not helpful when getting up in the middle of the night for a call of nature. The toilet was fifty metres away through what seemed like impenetrable jungle and who knew what was out there in the dark—grizzly bears?

I asked her once where in the world she would like to go, and she said she had always wanted to go to Istanbul; so we did. We had great pleasure there, remembering why we were together, something that can be forgotten in the daily grind of work and living.

Living together was easy because we liked the same food and liked being surrounded by the same temperatures, cool rather than hot, we had similar ideas about shopping and we had an easy agreement about money. Those simple things are important. She warmed to my family and I to hers; that is more than important, it is essential for harmony.

It may sound like the support was all a one-way process but it was not. I always helped her in whatever way I could. That came into full maturity when she was ill with cancer. She had developed breast cancer in 2004. I had left Monash, and could devote all my time to the hospital visits and whatever else was needed. The medical response made it go away until 2015 when the cancer metastasised. She was then increasingly ill. She was not, in the popular terminology, *'having a battle with cancer,'* an expression that is just plain wrong because there is no battle involved, it's a one-way overwhelming process. She described it as *'being eaten from the inside out'*. I endured her pain along with her. She died in May 2016.

I will never forget, after sitting with her for days before she died, and for some hours after, walking out the door of the hospital into the blinding sunlight. Nothing out there was real. Nobody seemed to know about the enormity that had just happened. Never have I known less about where to go or what to do. Other urgencies faded; no other considerations held any importance. Sometimes something lost can be compensated by something new gained, but not this loss. It is permanent, never to be reconciled.

She was my muse, in the sense that she inspired me to be myself, to follow whatever I wished regardless of how sensible or silly it might be. She was part of everything I did and I was part of all her life. There is no intimacy like the kind that comes from being with someone night and day for almost thirty years. There is so much history lost when the person who shared it is no longer there; the parts of it that are remembered lose their meaning.

There is no longer the touch on the shoulder as she walks past, the hug when all is not well—or when all is well; no clothes drying, hanging on the line jumbled together. Instead there is silence.

Working with clay has never had the same pleasure or meaning since she died. That applies to most other areas of life. What was easy is now hard. Art is only one part of life. The most important part of my life for many years has been family.

George Moore in *Home Sickness* (1914) wrote: '… *the desire to see Margaret again grew intense. But … she was dead … There is an unchanging, silent life in every man that none knows but himself, and his unchanging silent life was his memory of Margaret Dirkin … the things he saw most clearly were the green hillside … and behind it the blue line of wandering hills.'* [13]

22
AT HOME

I loved my fellow man the best, when he was scattered some.
— Don Edwards, in the song 'The Old Cow Man'

I live at a climatic clash point where grand weather movements meet. Boolarra South is not many kilometres north of the southern tip of the Australian continent, Wilson's Promontory. On this continental fringe warm north winds sometimes collide with the edges of the Roaring forties down below in Bass Strait. On a good day—good that is for climatic drama—the whole sky stirs with discontent as conflicting wind movements cause giant clouds to swirl and stagger, feather and stream. When the gales come on the edges of the roaring forties, it feels like the earth has shifted up a gear and is revolving faster, and Tasmania might have been blown a little closer to the mainland than it was yesterday.

In the twenty-five years I have been here the view out over the hills and sky has never been the same twice. Today, midwinter, there was a morning frost, then a sun-bright day. This afternoon, near the horizon the sky was the palest blue, so nearly grey. Now, at day's end, that has become a soft iridescent blue, grading up into the most wondrous pink with a tinge of the palest purple. The sky is part of my life here. I watch it constantly.

Looking out over the Strzelecki Ranges, named after the Polish explorer, my small block of five acres surrounds what used to be a one-teacher school. The old schoolhouse, from the 1920s, is my workshop. Large trees, many started a hundred years ago, give it a park-like feel. Originally the block was cut from the surrounding farm. The farmer donated an adjoining block to the Uniting Church but nothing was ever built on it. We later bought it and named it the Holey Ground because it was covered with holes caused by horses squelching into the muddy surface; and for the other obvious reason.

When we first lived here the neighbouring farmer was Mr Hindes. I never knew his first name. He was elderly and such a dignified gentleman

that nothing but Mr Hindes would do as a form of address. There are many men like him in country areas; quietly spoken, polite (never a swear word), thoughtful, caring for the land and the animals. I remember him in the heights of a drought on extreme hot days, out on the bare dusty hillside that used to be covered in lush grass. Or there in the depths of winter, with gales spraying wild sleet everywhere, limping on his frail leg, in both extremes feeding hay to his sheep and cattle. Not a day went by when he did not check to see they were OK. We talked over the fence occasionally, sometimes jointly mending some damage caused by his cattle. On one occasion during the drought, I said *'It hasn't been a very good year, has it?'* and he replied *'There aren't good years and bad years; there are years when you put hay in the shed and years when you take it out'*.

It was a bad day for us when he left and the farm was bought by a plantation company that surrounded us by trees, changing the grand view from twenty kilometres to about 100 metres. No more seeing who was travelling on the local roads or watching the weather developing on the distant hills. The transition from living with a likeable next-door neighbour to neighbouring a company has been difficult. It's easy to talk to a neighbour about mutual issues. How do you talk to a company? What do you talk about?

Fences are one topic of discussion. Over the years, cattle have bent the droppers, the smaller posts, at a wrong angle. Tree limbs have fallen on the fence, big ones sometimes. Lambs could infiltrate though loose wires. The fence has many layers of patching. One section is now new but the other retains the history. Mostly the history of the land is not found in books.

When next door was a farm, I welcomed seeing the sheep and cattle, especially when the new-born were charging up and down and chasing each other around in circles. Now a strip around my place has friendly horses wandering about; we say hello over the fence. It's a fine part of the country life to be able to check on the condition of the land and the grass and the animals without having any responsibility for them. If you are considering moving to the country, take my advice and buy a small block surrounded by a big one belonging to someone else. And hope that that someone else is a good neighbour and if they leave that they will be replaced by another good neighbour.

* * *

Day to day, I am just doing what I am doing. If I am stacking wood, I am just stacking wood. I have no need to think about anything else. My mind is not troubled by the demands of others, or their opinions. They are far away, and here there is just me and the birds and the kangaroos, and they are untroubled also. A Punjabi once told me that the average Punjabi farmer cared not at all who was in power in Islamabad, because his life was no different to his ancestors in the 14th century. I understand what he meant.

I am always aware of my roommates, the wombats and koalas and kangaroos that share this residential address. The wombat down his deep burrow through the day considers where he will dig the next trench under my fence and place a small pile of his dung to indicate his rights over that particular bit of territory. When he abandons the beginnings of a new house, I use that as a convenient hole to get rid of sherds from smashed reject pots. I would like to discuss his digging habits with him and suggest he digs somewhere else. A wise man once told me it's always better to negotiate first before entering into litigation. The difficulty is that I've not yet figured out how to negotiate with a wombat.

The koalas come and go seemingly randomly, although if I understood them better I might see a pattern. Sometimes they are away. Sometimes they are here, sitting sleepily in the fork where a branch meets the main tree-trunk. They look at me once, registering my presence, blink, and go back to meditating, if that's what koalas do. Perhaps they are just sleeping. I meet them sometimes on the ground, where they stop and look at me with some curiosity, slowly considering what they might do next. Usually they climb a tree to about my eye height and allow me to come in close for a good look before they climb higher, and rest. Several times now I have watched a mother carry her young one on her back and wonder how she survives those sharp claws that cling to her.

The kangaroos are more circumspect and keep a distance. They were in the past inclined to run (or should I say hop) when they saw a person but now some, especially one mother and growing son, are unmoved by me being around. Each time I see them I quietly say that they have nothing to fear from me, hoping they will hear.

The possums live in several places. One is a metal cylinder on its side in the roof of the kiln shed. They come out when the gas kiln is fired because it gets too hot up there. Once a mother emerged with a baby clinging to its back. They also live in vents in the roof of my studio. I intend one day to block the vent off but have not got to that yet. They never bother me at the house.

The birds are many and varied. I am guilty of having favourites such as the willy wagtail, for his terrier-like aggression towards birds four times his size. The grey bird for the most beautiful song, followed closely in the song-world by the magpie and butcherbird. The wattle bird for its contortions to get at the nectar on some flowers. The kookaburra for a reminder that this could only be Australia and nowhere else in the world. The black cockatoo for the ability to crush a new pine cone. The eagle for supreme mastery of the air currents, and disdain for the attacking magpies; and the magpie who flies like no other, like a Spitfire, changing direction instantly with a deep whoosh of air. The galah for its hanging-upside-down silliness. The corella for its pure whiteness, and creaky door call as he passes overhead. The blue wren for its fidgety nervousness and its flash of blue colour. The king parrot for its stunningly beautiful green and red, and lack of fear. The tiny twittery wrens. I could go on. They are all wonderful. I love living with them. I like them all; I think each in its own way is my favourite. My real favourite is the one I am with at the time.

One young magpie would come and peck at the window or the back-door glass in a Pavlovian response which, in the absence of Pavlov, she had invented for herself. It was a request for feeding, a reminder it's time. I feed them at random times, so they do not become dependent, and these birds are calm. The magpies do not swoop when they are nesting. They know me as I know them. They recognise people just as I recognise individual birds. That is made easier because each bird is as different as each person we know. Some are timid and avoid me. Others almost ignore me. One magpie known as The Boss would sit resolutely as I walked toward him, not moving even as I stepped over him. Another was abandoned by its parents and adopted people as substitutes. It followed people around hoping, often successfully, to be fed. It sat and watched as I worked outside. Like a child raised by foster parents and now grown up, it left when the time came to leave.

Yellow-tailed black cockatoos come to eat the pine cones, or the nuts off some of the native bushes. Their creaking squark as they sit high in the pine trees sounds like an old door that is being opened for the first time in many years. Chomping apart pine cones and eating them, they represent a threat to any life underneath when they drop a half kilo pine cone from the heights. They are the Bleriots of the bird world with their wings set forward and their slow, erratic and ungainly staggering flight.

The grey birds, as I know them, sing songs finer than any heard in La Scala. The man—I assume it was a man—who named them grey shrike-thrush should be ashamed. Such a songbird should have the most poetic name of all instead of such a harsh tag, sounding like some disease. They follow me around as I walk through the grass. Whether that is merely being companionable or instead waiting for me to stir up insects is not clear to me; either way their company is delightful.

Kookaburras daily follow the same track, perching at the same time of day on the same branch, studying the same familiar patch of ground for anything edible. Before dusk they laugh in a choir of three, four or five rather than individually like most other birds. I wish the kookaburras could be introduced into parliament and sing each time a politician tells lies or makes promises they know are false, or especially when politicians shout at each other. That might introduce a sense of reality to proceedings.

When we first lived here, I sometimes thought, with a fright, at night someone was knocking on the windows but whenever I looked nobody was there. In time I realised that tawny frogmouth owls were taking bogong moths in season, and other moths at other times, from the windows where they were attracted by the light, accompanied by a gentle thump of the owl's body on the glass. Through daytime the owls sit together on a high tree branch and look at you stolidly, heads slightly canted as if pondering the vagaries of existence, sometimes opening just one eye in an unstated question.

The gang-gangs come down from the hills when the cooler weather arrives, around May, or June if May has been a little warmer than normal. You know they are there when you hear the creaky noise high in the trees, or in the bushes with hard seeds. They creak and crunch, spitting out unwanted bits of seed. If I had my own country, as an impossibly wealthy magnate or perhaps a king, I would base my national colours on those

of the gang-gang, a particularly distinctive reddish pink and a rich deep mottled grey. A deep and mysterious colour allied with one vibrant and exciting.

I have had the experience enough times now to know that wild birds and animals have a deep understanding of human intentions towards them. I have rescued a koala caught in blackberries by carefully cutting away and removing the spiky stems, knowing that the patient koala, sitting unmoving, understood that my motivation was purely to help it. I have several other times helped koalas cross roads, out of danger, also with their obvious understanding. And once a small bird, a honeyeater, became trapped inside my studio, unable to find a way to fly out even though the door was open. The windows are high and difficult to open. It perched on a curtain rod and when I held my hand up close to it, it hopped on to my finger and clung as I slowly walked outside. I held the bird up close to a tree branch and after a long pause it hopped off my hand onto the branch, and just sat there, looking at me. It clearly was fully aware of my intentions. That calm and trusting awareness is usual in tame birds and animals but truly exciting in wild ones.

* * *

People have tracks they follow. Every place where someone lives has personal tracks. In an apartment or a house these are minimal, familiar and easily navigated in the dark. Larger areas of land have more complex tracks, each with a reason for existence. Personal tracks are characterised by knowing where to turn, where to duck, and where to look first before reversing. One of my tracks involves picking up sticks that have fallen from the trees, to cut to length and use in my woodfired kilns. This converts going for a leisurely walk into a useful job, much as gathering shells at the beach can be justified by later using them in the kiln to separate pots. What a life I have, when a day at an isolated beach picking up shells can be considered work, especially a winter day when there is nobody else around and the waves are crashing.

I always feel better after a walk around my tracks. I can stop to check on the clouds and see what might be developing for tomorrow. Weather is important to me. If it's too cold and wet to be wandering around hillsides then it's a good day for writing and if it's one of those most glorious of days, a sunny autumn wonder then I can easily find something urgently needing to be done outside; preferably one of those brief and mildly strenuous jobs that leaves plenty of time afterwards for sitting and recovering from my exertions, under a shady tree looking out over the hills.

A wander about allows time to think. Every man who has achieved maturity knows that thinking about doing something can occupy enough time that insufficient is left to actually do something. Anyway, it's almost always so when living in the country that better weather will arrive tomorrow and make it a much better day to do that kind of work. What I most like about thinking while wandering is that it covers a range of mental territory from the profound to the insignificant, a useful balance.

Sometimes thinking leads to one of those profound insights that should be written down for use somewhere in future writing. Usually by the time I get to a piece of paper and a pen I have been distracted by thinking about something else I should be doing or should do tomorrow and there's no need to write that down so I forget the original thought that I meant to write down and end up not writing anything down. Anyone who writes will tell you that is how their most brilliant thoughts have been lost forever.

* * *

Living in some rural parts of Australia means living with fire. Sometimes it means confronting the real thing, sometimes just the threat. For those who have not experienced it, wild fire may merit only a shrug and a passing thought. For those who have, it means deep trauma, the kind that comes only to those who have been in battle. The bushfire sun, a dull sulky red, hanging in the sky surrounded by a murky haze that renders breathing difficult, is never forgotten. It signifies danger of the worst kind: unpredictable. In war the soldier knows the enemy is like him, another human. In the war with fire the combatant knows that the enemy is entirely alien and has no thought, no plan, no intent, just overwhelming malice. It can pass by with no effect or at a whim move sideways on a passing breeze and consume the work of a lifetime.

Those with no experience fear they might lose their house and their photos but those who have experienced it know that it takes much more than that. Nothing is left: no history, no routines, no mental peace and none of the charms of living that filled their life before. They have experienced the agony of knowing that animals are burning—of hearing them scream. They understand the work and time involved in restoring life later.

* * *

Eric Linklater (in *Figures in a Landscape*, 1952) expressed it well: '*The distinguishing feature of civilization is that it makes far fewer demands on one than a simple life in communion with nature*'. To those who dream of bucolic bliss in open spaces I offer a caution. Living in the country necessitates owning and learning about machinery. Pumps, mowers, chainsaws, generators, quad bikes, all have idiosyncrasies that only become glaringly obvious when they break and you discover that you have lost the user's manual. Your next discovery when you pull the machine down is that the small part that has broken in half can no longer be purchased, is not amenable to repair and serves an unknown function anyway. The simplest approach is to place it on a shelf where it might be found again if it's absolutely essential, and then see how well the machine functions without it. Wisdom suggests that when any machine that is no longer usable is disassembled all the parts should be kept in case something new can be made up from combining or modifying old parts. This explains why farmers all keep such a large pile of rusting stuff under a gum tree somewhere.

The size of your land dictates the size of the machines. My five acres means I have relatively small machines, but all machinery large or small has its own rules. First, something goes wrong with it only when you go to use it, not conveniently at some other time when it does not matter. When something goes wrong you have choices. You can take time off to go into town and take it to one of the many machinery repairers. Their frequency is an indication in itself of the nature of machinery. That involves at least two half-day trips. Apart from charging an extortionate amount for repairs, dealers usually replace the oil and spark plugs, both of which you had just done yourself two days ago and forgot to mention.

Fixing it yourself and saving time, trouble and expense is the sensible choice. That involves knowledge. What type of oil and what quantity each uses, which sparkplug, questions like these involve hours of looking on the internet for the one manual that seems to be missing because that particular machine is too old to be supported any longer.

When taking machinery apart an important rule comes into play. Disassemble the machinery over concrete, because if you do it over grass a small vital non-magnetic part always falls in the grass and becomes irretrievably lost at which point it becomes necessary to go into town to one of the machinery dealers for a replacement. After a long period of research to find the part number, enabling an order to be placed, it becomes necessary to pay an extortionate amount to replace the part with a new one which is just out of stock. They will order one, and it's expected to arrive in about a week if the distributor has one in stock. He often does not and it must be imported from somewhere far away like Sweden in which case it will arrive in about a month. If they still have them.

Having disassembled the machine over concrete you end up with a large number of unfamiliar parts. When reassembled there will sometimes be enough parts left over to build something else. And you must remember to put Bandaids on your shopping list, to replace the ones you used on the skinned knuckles that resulted when your fingers would not fit between the gaps in the machine where you had to put your hand to hold the other end of the part that you were attempting to assemble with the aid of a spanner that was about five centimetres too long to turn in the space available for it. So that pretty well covers machinery.

Rural do-it-yourself has no resemblance to city style do-it-yourself where you build a patio in between frequent visits to Bunnings for materials and advice. Doing it yourself involves having a complete range of tools and machinery for doing it. Rules apply here also. The tool you want is always in the other shed so repairing machinery consists mainly of walking to and fro between sheds. The socket you need to undo a vital nut that holds the whole thing together is the one that your neighbour across the road borrowed last week just before he went away for three-week holiday. Or the one you cannot find because it fell in the long grass on the one day you made the mistake of fixing on the spot where you were working, rather than taking it to concrete so you could find whatever you dropped.

As for repairers, I have the local choice of one who is conveniently located and whose charges are very modest but who has very little idea of repairing machinery so usually when his work is done the machine has developed several new faults as well as retaining the original. Alternatively, the other can fix things a treat so that they not only work perfectly but have been cleaned for the first time since you bought them and gleam in the sun so it's tempting to just sit there and look at them rather than put them to their intended use. The downside is that he charges at a rate that causes you to believe he bathes each night in a mixture of imported mare's milk and Veuve Clicquot vintage champagne before he relaxes in a pashmina robe in front of his 300 cm television.

Using machinery, when it is working, has some inflexible rules. One is that the day you intend to cut up all that wood is either the hottest since 1864, or raining so heavily that the road to the nearest town is cut off by floods for three days and you keep slipping over in the mud. Another is that you should have as many limbs when you finish as when you started.

The log splitter offers one potential form of severe self-mutilation. I can vouch for that having tried it. Do not place your hand in the path of the wedge. The doctor in the emergency department told me that the finger I had trapped in this machine, which by some act of salvation had not been cleanly removed, had not been cut open, but due to the pressure involved had burst open like a stomped-on orange. She sewed it together so well it again functions like a normal finger. The strange thing about such injuries is that there is no pain when it happens, just surprise; the pain begins later.

Finally, since every country man drives a ute or a 4-wheel drive, he must understand ute culture. When he meets someone he knows, travelling in the opposite direction, he should execute a ritual understood only by the initiated. He will give a wave. The subtle nuances of the wave to a particular individual are a clear indication of his relationship to that individual. The smaller the wave the better you like them. The left hand is never used for signals. Nobody would understand them. Lifting the hand slightly from the steering wheel and quickly pointing with the right-hand index finger applies to any stranger in another vehicle, or working by the roadside. It's a simple friendly country greeting. Slightly raising just the right-hand index finger from the steering wheel is a greeting to someone familiar, someone you might expect to see almost every day, or someone you know well. Raising all five fingers from the steering wheel means thanks—it could apply to the flagman who stops and then lets you go at a work site, or to someone who shows a courtesy such as not driving out in front of you from a side road without looking. A wave out the back window is reserved for the man on the tractor who moved off to the side of the road to let you pass safely.

* * *

A few times a year, of necessity or on a whim, I go to the Melbourne on the train. Ten minutes there is enough to convince me that I should get back on the train and go home away from the crowds and the noise. The suburbs are worse. Just one species (and their tame pets) live crowded together.

The dacha, the hill station, the country property, and now the tree change, each fulfils a similar desire for the city dweller—to leave the metropolis and enjoy the tranquillity of rural life, temporarily or permanently. If temporary, scenery is important, preferably seen from the veranda just before dusk with a cheeky white or a mellow red at hand. If the stay is intended to be long term, it begins with visions of old-fashioned community and a simpler life among scenic beauty. The ones who survive the long-term best are the ones who need to be there to do what they do—gourmet farmers, or potters.

A city innocent choosing a change to a life of rural bliss will almost certainly not consider the disadvantages, most of which revolve around people, apart from fire, flood, gales, earthquakes and the usual range of natural disasters. The tree changer will not be aware at first that they may not be accepted as a member of the community until they have waited twenty years, and not necessarily then—unless they have been active members of the local fire brigade, or have joined every local women's organisation.

The tree changer dream will probably not take into account the redneck element. This consists of people who shoot, cut down, bulldoze, burn and generally bugger up the surroundings. They may be uneducated and unworldly, but usually have well developed skills in these activities. A single redneck neighbour can make life unpleasant daily.

Rednecks are not amenable to rational discussions and if their influence becomes too bad the only solution is to move elsewhere. It would have been better not to move there in the first place, so good advice to potential tree changers would be to consult the neighbours about the neighbours before they become neighbours. The neighbours will almost certainly feel that because you come from somewhere else, what goes on in their neighbourhood is none of your business. But if a single redneck is annoying enough, they might just mention them in passing as a pestilence. No matter how pretty the scenery or how desirable the community, that is a clear signal to keep well away.

Corporate versions of the redneck are even worse. They are away—in a city, and quite often that city is in another country far away. The owner or director of the coal seam gas company or the plantation company or the mining company is well hidden behind layers of protection, both physical and electronic. There is no hope of discussion, or getting your point across to those responsible. Do not be deceived by public consultation meetings before they begin to destroy your surroundings; anything you say will be completely ignored; and the politicians are on their side, not yours.

Dialogues with the company would achieve nothing anyway. Their interest is in making as much money as possible as quickly as possible and to hell with the consequences for land and people. The local representatives are spin doctors, trained liars who lack the necessary brain connections to understand any argument that involves you living peacefully in blissful communion with your surroundings and making art. *'How can you make a quid out of that?'* they might ask.

One consequence is that around the countryside are small groups of earnest and well-meaning people who hold rallies, sign petitions and hand out leaflets from their stalls at local markets. This allows them to form friends with like-minded people and have long discussions about their shared passions and their aims to change corporate behaviour. But in Australia their activities usually achieve precisely nothing. Corporate interests prevail.

If all that sounds a bit grim the fact of country life is that most people you meet are friendly enough, and polite. Most country people—here I am thinking about farmers and people on the land—are thoughtful about what they do and have a deep understanding of the vagaries of weather and markets. On these subjects they can sustain a prolonged discussion and a well-reasoned analysis. Move on to politics and the reasoning may harden and a few slogans suffice. It can be a challenge when you attempt a long conversation.

* * *

Living anywhere involves communication with those around you. This always involves learning a specialised vocabulary. The necessary rural vocabulary would make no sense whatever to the average sophisticated urbanite. In order to make conversation the weather is a relatively straightforward subject, but details of dairy farming or breeding sheep require some time to absorb. Reading the local farming newspaper helps slightly. You will be required to communicate with farm supplies stores as well as the local rural tradesmen. For poly pipe for example you need to know the distinction between sockets, elbows and nipples, none of which are related in any obvious way to the regular human versions.

The problem with learning this vocabulary is that there is no dictionary or guidebook, although online trade catalogues might be worth browsing; and farm supply stores are not like your average chain store where browsing is perfectly normal. Here it's not. When the bloke behind the counter asks if he can help you, he expects you to ask for what you want using the proper technical terms and measurements like: *Can I get five litres of 32 hydraulic oil?* Simple and easy. If it's something small you can show him one and ask if he has one like it. A useful tip difficult to put into practice is to find a store with a female employee because they are often far more tolerant of ignorance and far more willing to educate the naïve about the proper language.

Rural tradesmen are usually male. Some are trained and competent, such as plumbers and electricians. They invariably have a longer waiting list than a Victorian hospital. One kept me waiting three years to replace some gutters, although once when I phoned him and told him our water heater had gone to Valhalla, he was there in half an hour with a new one and it was ready to use an hour later. Generally, they arrive sooner if you corner them in the street. Phoning provides a distance that allows them to make promises they have no intention of keeping.

I believe you can usually recognise people who have been raised in the country by a certain directness and honesty of expression, a straightforwardness of thinking, and a practical nature of understanding how to fix things or make things. Then there are the others, such as Bluey, who put up some post and rail fencing for us. The posts rotted away in the ground in just a few years so the whole thing is held up only by the vines growing on it. Bluey's method of working involved forgetting to bring any tools and borrowing mine to get the job done, followed by standing back and telling me how to do most of the job for him, because his back was a bit irksome that day.

There are many rural men like Bluey. The work they do is dodgy at best and they eke out a poor living doing it because they charge very little for the work. There is no point in becoming frustrated with them. It's better to consider that rather than providing useful infrastructure they are providing a half day's entertainment, or if you supply them with the lunch they forgot to bring, a full day. It's our social obligation to see that people like Bluey live a reasonable life. It would be grossly negligent of us to have them go cold or hungry.

Our prime example of the entertainer is Eddy. He never learned to read as a child and so some of his pronunciation of words requires experience to interpret. Some words he uses seem to be derived from an obscure foreign language because interpretation proves impossible. He gained my admiration and respect (I already liked him) a few years ago by going to school with kids who were slow learners, and learning to read. That must have taken considerable courage and resolve so that when I see him all I see is a brave man.

Eddy does a bit of anything you can do with a tractor. This includes breaking things, knocking things over, and rendering previously smooth ground impassable by churning it into mud. Among other jobs he does fencing. He invariably arrives late in the morning because he first has to fix something that has broken on his worn-out old tractor. He then digs a few crooked postholes which instead of going vertically into the ground tend to incline at around 45 degrees. Then the tractor breaks down again. When he goes away to find some parts to fix it his truck breaks down and that requires a trip to the city to obtain parts from a wrecker. A short length of fencing can take anything up to a week to complete and since he keeps careful and honest mental track of his working time, and charges only ten dollars an hour, his weekly income can amount to something like fifty dollars.

What Eddy and Bluey and others like them do is easy to understand. What I do is not necessarily easy for them to understand. Making pottery? Writing? It leaves most of my neighbours a little bemused about why anyone would do it and what purpose it serves, because for county people work must serve a useful and practical purpose. Artwork does not fit. Despite that, in a general spirit of accommodation they accept that I do what I do without understanding it. It's a country trait that even if you disagree totally with someone else you are better off just saying nothing and getting on with your work.

* * *

I see how the years have passed and what they have brought me. Like a mirage shimmering in the distance, much is forgotten, gone where all goes in the end. Some is remembered from seeing old photographs and video. In some of these I look young but now it would take some persuading for me to believe I was, once.

I do notice the passing of people. Older people do this. It helps with fitting into a grander perspective than the here and now. Reflection can fix a time when you first met that person or can take you back to music you heard in someone's company all those years ago. Reflection raises memories that have no meaning to most people around you. Like a lovable entertainer on stage, some evoke memories that give smiles of pleasure. Some, like a cruel murderer carving a corpse into disposable pieces, shred into fragments our inner being, leaving only fragments of those who have been close to us. I can no longer consult Peascod for advice about clay and life. I can no longer meet Janet in some foreign country and see a friendly smile in all the strangeness. I can no longer hug Barbara.

Getting older is a little like being a soldier in a war. Some of the most important people in your life die and a complex part of you dies with them. With each goes a part of your personal history. The friends who are left take on increasing importance. I have not been conscientious in maintaining friendships when moving from one state to another or from one country to another. Good friends, lifetime friends; where are they now? The laughter, so loud and heartfelt has faded away. although a genuine few are left and cultivated in whatever way possible.

Ageing brings health issues. I have now had various parts of me probed and carved, removed and remodelled. One particular hospital episode is still clear in my memory, the time in 2003 after a Sturt workshop I ended up with pneumonia and almost died. I was aware at one point that I had a choice to make, one that I have never needed to confront before or since, either to die and make it go away, or to live and resist. There is no better way to become aware of mortality than taking a good straight look at it right there in front of you.

These sessions of illness fade away in time. I am left with poor lungs. The lung testing man asked me if I wanted the results of his tests in medical terms or in layman's language and when I asked for plain English he said *'Your lungs are fucked'*. I assume this is the result of smoking earlier in life, and inhaling many and exotic forms of dust as well as large quantities of wood smoke. Wind direction, and having fans running, are now significant when firing my small woodfired kiln.

Sometimes I wonder why I have survived and others have not. I have had near misses in cars, some exceptionally near, and have emerged from danger situations in other countries unscathed. The simple conclusion to such wondering is to just accept what is and keep working.

A variety of terms could describe my life at home: out of it, life in the slow lane, at the end of the road, in the middle of nowhere, gone bush, gone missing, buggered off, hermit. All of which allow me to keep working with no unwelcome distractions. Of course, there are welcome distractions. Mostly none of them involve people. One that I enjoy is going for a drive along a lonely local road to see where it leads. Or walking on a back road where there will at most be one passing car a day.

I have experienced the range from tragedy to comedy. But I envy nobody and I would change nothing. The worst of it gave me strength and the best of it made life worthwhile. In art I am restless but in life I am content with what I have seen and not concerned with what I have not. Too much concern with experiencing everything offers the prospect of madness. There is too much of everything anyway.

Today is one of those
warm
perfect autumn days
sunshine highlights, everywhere.
I cruise in my sporty car
the top down,
smells of the countryside,
songs of the birds
no hurry to get anywhere.
Yellow leaves
dance and flutter in my wake.

References

1 Wulff, Hans, *The traditional crafts of Persia*, Boston: MIT Press, 1966.

2 Kalter, Johannes, *The Arts And Crafts Of The Swat Valley*, London: Thames and Hudson, 1991.

3 Rye, Owen, 'A pottery kiln in Old Cairo', *Pottery in Australia*, 1974 ,13/1.

4 Saint-Exupéry, Antoine. *Wind, sand and stars*, London: Picador, 1939.

5 Murchie, Guy, *Song of the Sky*, Pickle Partners Publishing, 2016.

6 Lamie, Katherine, 'Archaeology in Palestine: The Life and Death of Albert Glock', *Nebraska Anthropologist*, 2007, vol. 22.

7 Baumgarten, Helga, 'The Three Faces/Phases of Palestinian Nationalism, 1948–2005', *Journal of Palestine Studies*, 2005, 34/4.

8 Landgraf J. and Rye O., *Palestinian Traditional Pottery*, Belgium: Cahiers de Revue Bibliques Peeters Leuven, 2021.

9 Fox, Edward, *Palestine Twilight*, Glasgow: Harper Collins, 2001.

10 Salamoni, Amadeo, *Wood-Fired Ceramics*, Pennsylvania: Schiffer, 2013.

11 Fitzgerald, Penelope, *The bookshop*, London: Gerald Duckworth, 1978.

12 Updike, John, *Marry Me*, New York: Alfred A Knopf, 1976.

13 Moore, George, 'Home Sickness', *The Untilled Field*, Sydney: Wentworth Press, 2016.

INDEX

www.ingramcontent.com/pod-product-compliance
Lightning Source LLC
Chambersburg PA
CBHW021109270326
41929CB00009B/801